U.S.-SOVIET COOPERATION

U.S.-SOVIET COOPERATION

A New Future

Edited by
NISH JAMGOTCH, JR.

PRAEGER

New York
Westport, Connecticut
London

Library of Congress Cataloging-in-Publication Data

U.S.-Soviet cooperation : a new future / edited by Nish Jamgotch, Jr.
  p. cm.
  Includes bibliographies and index.
  ISBN 0–275–93082–3 (alk. paper)
  1. United States—Foreign relations—Soviet Union. 2. Soviet
Union—Foreign relations—United States. 3. United States—Foreign
relations—1981– 4. Soviet Union—Foreign relations—1975–
5. International cooperation. I. Jamgotch, Nish. II. Title: US-
Soviet cooperation. III. Title: United States-Soviet cooperation.
E183.8.S65U7 1989
327.73047—dc19   88–27504

Library of Congress Catalog Card Number: 88–27504
ISBN: 0–275–93082–3

First published in 1989

Praeger Publishers, One Madison Avenue, New York, NY 10010
A division of Greenwood Press, Inc.

Printed in the United States of America

The paper used in this book complies with the Permanent
Paper Standard issued by the National Information Standards
Organization (Z39.48–1984).

10 9 8 7 6 5 4 3 2 1

CONTENTS

ACKNOWLEDGMENTS

Like its major topics, the origins of this book illustrate the importance of cooperation. Collectively authored works are uncommonly dependent upon mutual respect, compatible approaches to a discipline, acceptance of a common purpose, uniformly careful scholarship, and scrupulousness about deadlines. In these respects, this editor and author could not have worked with a more outstanding and dedicated group of scholar-specialists. Let me acknowledge my respect and admiration to them first and foremost.

Many of the ideas for this study arose and matured over the years in annual and regional conferences of the International Studies Association (ISA), most notably in activities sponsored by its American-Soviet Relations Section. Conferences stressing global values, conflict moderation and resolution, and joint problem solving in East-West relations supplied creative environments for panel papers and round-table sessions from which chapter themes and major subsections of this volume resulted. The value of these professional academic settings where ideas are advanced, exchanged, challenged, and defended must never be underestimated. It should not be surprising that, when they are purposefully integrated, kindred academic interests and diverse specializations, however widely scattered geographically, can spring to life and impart creative vitality and dynamism to a subject.

For more than half a dozen years, annual ISA conventions have been attended by delegations of scholars from the Soviet Union's most prestigious research institutes. Their participation as panelists and discussants have afforded us firsthand experience with Soviet thinking on both superpower relations and the state of the world. The delegation of eight that attended the twenty-ninth ISA convention at St. Louis in April 1988, provided an especially poignant experience. This was true because of strikingly frank and open assessments conveyed in a specially arranged evening plenary session that included even heartfelt disagreements among themselves—unprecedented in open professional forums—over the optimum scope and pace of Gorbachev's programs and about their prospects. (Imagine the reaction when some of them ventured that Gorbachev's economic reforms cannot succeed without political reforms!) All of us who have developed excellent relationships with our Soviet counterparts have surely benefited from these joint professional gatherings.

Gratitude is expressed for research funds from the United States Institute of Peace, inaugurated by the Congress in 1984; the Physicians for Social Responsibility (Mecklenburg-Metrolina Chapter of North Carolina); the Blumenthal Foundation of the Carolinas; and the UNC-Charlotte Foundation and Faculty Grants Committee. Their support was most vital and timely in an era when financial assistance for peace research is in such woefully short supply. Their generosity, however, in no way implies responsibility for the ideas and conclusions of this volume.

Appreciation is expressed to individuals who supplied important expertise, insights, and information, much of it unpublished, thus facilitating a better product. Of these, the most important include Jack Segal and Sandy Vershbow, Office of Soviet Union Affairs, U.S. Department of State; Jon Gundersen, Arms Control and Disarmament Agency; Lana Andreeva and Dennis Pepe, National Oceanic and Atmospheric Administration, U.S. Department of Commerce; Steve Zaidman, Federal Aviation Administration, U.S. Department of Transportation; Ned Hodgman, Federation of American Scientists; and Terrel Rhodes, Department of Political Science, and Frada Mozenter, Atkins Library, University of North Carolina at Charlotte. Special thanks are due to Cheryl Almond of Charlotte for typing large portions of a complex manuscript.

From the beginning, the objective of this volume, culminating a two-year project, has been to make peace research more readily available and useful, and to educate students, the general public, and government officials about the values of U.S.-Soviet cooperative agreements, especially at a time of more active summit and middle-level diplomacy since the end of the first Reagan administration and the beginning of the second.

U.S.-Soviet cooperative measures to solve problems, build confidence, and reduce tensions, quite apart from their intrinsic merits, can also have the long-term value of moderating outmoded perceptions and threatening stereotypes in the interests of better public policy on both sides. There is no guarantee, of course. But the more promising future we all seek must begin, at a minimum, with a systematic and comprehensive analysis of what the superpowers have devised jointly in order to manage their natural but very dangerous rivalry. Only then can we fully appreciate what has already been achieved and what has yet to be achieved.

U.S.-SOVIET
COOPERATION

1

INTRODUCTION: A NEW FUTURE?

Nish Jamgotch, Jr.

Why cooperate? These two words—the leitmotif of this book—explain that in contemporary international politics, even avowed enemies have mutual interests.

Despite some seven decades of troubled and conflictual U.S.-Soviet relations, there is an impressive untold story of accord that warrants better understanding and more complete assimilation into superpower images, at the levels of governments and of their respective publics. To impart clarity to the bewildering complexity of superpower cooperation, frequently thought to be a contradiction in terms, this volume presents a select inventory of U.S.-Soviet projects, some in the name of confidence building, all of them enterprises with wide-ranging intrinsic benefits. Instead of merely assuming an interest in a more peaceful future (what nation, after all, is not for peace?), what is undertaken here is an enumeration and analysis of specific joint ventures: their purposes, evolutions, utilities, outcomes, and futures.

The story of superpower cooperation is hardly popular against a backdrop of Cold War hostilities and years of exaggerated ideological and military one-upmanship that have generated the most costly and life-threatening arsenals since humanity began. At the same time, more and more thoughtful citizens of goodwill, hope, and vision are asking strikingly relevant questions: How could two such implacably hostile enemies have survived this long without some modicum of understanding and concerted strategies to escape catastrophe? How have they reached the end of the 1980s without actualizing some of the worst-case scenarios contrived by their modern military research and weapons deployments? How have they managed to elude the nuclear Armageddon that frenetic military activities on both sides appear to make possible, probable, or even inevitable? How can one explain that the two most vastly empowered allies and victors in World War II engaged each other in an unprecedented arms race during the postwar peace and simultaneously struggled to negotiate safeguards against the very war they were preparing for? And, finally, what can be done to strengthen and perpetuate their more cooperative tendencies, and to deflate and decelerate their self-destructive ones?

Beginning in 1981, a group of kindred scholars began to pose these very questions at professional meetings of the International Studies Association. What began as searching discussions and convention panels on the themes of conflict and cooperation in superpower relations evolved into a collectively authored work published in 1985 under the improbable title *Sectors of Mutual Benefit in U.S.- Soviet Relations.*[1] One of the book's objectives was to formalize a network of researchers who wished to make certain that superpower relations that are cooperative (as opposed to conflictual) are better monitored, better analyzed, better understood, better explained, better recorded, and better reported both in the academic community and to the public. Without minimizing the critical importance of arms control to wind down tensions, there was a pledge to establish a national academic resource for the study of cooperative relations. Authors focused on agreements in crisis communications, trade, science, agriculture, environmental protection, space, and medicine. Clues were sought for the following: Which areas of U.S.-Soviet relations have yielded the most significant mutual advantages and benefits? How can we explain successes and failures? To what extent are problem-solving projects a reflection of an interdependent world and a confirmation of the functionalist doctrine set forth by David Mitrany and popularized by integration-minded Europeanists after World War II? Where has U.S. policy gone wrong? Where was it correct? Can we expect that productive relations will continue and even serve to ameliorate political and military tensions?

Our work was not alone. Well-received books from academic think tanks and research institutes created a receptive atmosphere for probing once again the foreign-policy motivations of the United States and the Soviet Union, combing for fresh insights that might steer their relations onto a safer, more manageable, and mutually productive footing. This was without doubt a very tall order. A selection of just a few titles reveals the mood and range of inquiries: *The Nuclear Delusion: Soviet-American Relations in the Atomic Age; Managing U.S.-Soviet Rivalry: Problems of Crisis Prevention; Soviet International Behavior and U.S. Policy Options; Hawks, Doves, and Owls: An Agenda for Avoiding Nuclear War;* and *Reluctant Warriors: The United States, the Soviet Union, and Arms Control.*[2]

The early Reagan years were hardly propitious for fresh approaches to superpower dilemmas. The old principles of détente and cooperative projects from the Nixon-Kissinger years, 1969–1974, had been resoundingly discredited because of their failure to prolong the superpower honeymoon much beyond the Nixon presidency. Soon after President Reagan settled into the White House, U.S.-Soviet relations were repeatedly jolted and chilled by official recriminations; several cooperative agreements were languishing or suspended; Washington's bent was retaliatory. Collaborative programs were curtailed, as they had been by the Carter administration, to chastise the Kremlin for errant behavior in domestic human rights and for opportunism and aggression abroad. Much contentious debate ensued over who was to blame for so short a superpower honeymoon, why there were such grandiose expectations from détente on both sides, and whether there was ever enough mutual interest to forge a bona fide marriage (or even to sustain the excitement of a honeymoon in the first place).

Much has happened since 1983 to justify a detailed reexamination of the tone and direction of bilateral agreements. Both sides, predisposed to tossing insults, have gotten on with the business of low-risk relations; and with survival in a nuclear world more and more precarious and dependent on prudent judgments, many of the old principles of détente are gaining fresh luster. Beginning in 1984, President Reagan, with impeccable anti-Communist credentials, started to pump life into superpower relations by reviving activity under 4 of the original 11 bilateral cooperative agreements dating back to 1972–1973: environmental protection; medical science and public health (including artificial heart research and development); agriculture; and housing and other construction, especially to promote commercial arrangements aimed at opening Soviet markets to U.S. industries. In December 1984, the World Oceans Agreement was renewed for three years. In December 1985, the Atomic Energy Agreement was extended through June 1988. And in December 1986, it was announced that the Environmental Protection Agreement would extend through May 1992.

Against a background of earlier U.S. curtailments of all bilateral scientific agreements and the lapse of four (space, energy, transportation, and science and technology), a new Civil Space Cooperation Agreement was signed by Secretary of State Shultz and Foreign Minister Shevardnadze at Moscow in April 1987. At the 1985 Geneva summit, President Reagan and General Secretary Gorbachev advocated accelerated international collaboration for the development of thermonuclear fusion as a source of potentially inexhaustible energy for peaceful purposes. Under the auspices of the International Atomic Energy Agency, discussions were initiated for scientific research to include the Common Market and Japan in the design of a fusion test reactor. At the 1986 Reykjavik summit, both powers agreed to explore the possibility of renewed collaboration in the basic sciences and transportation. With marked boosts from the Geneva and Reykjavik summits, people-to-people contacts, public and private, were elevated, it seemed, to the level of U.S. national policy. The White House repeatedly encouraged the idea that communicating U.S. views and values to influential elements in Soviet society would enhance bilateral relations by dampening tensions and distrust, and that Americans and Soviets would get on much better if only they could manage to learn more about each other.

The prospects of a quantum jump in goodwill and understanding are doubtless commendable and salutary; yet a great deal more appeared to be at stake. The Reagan doctrine, a rationale for escalating U.S. military strength, was pressed to produce a more secure and stable relationship with the Soviet Union, in order to vindicate the president's leadership. Without significant breakthroughs in arms control and a build-down of arsenals, his massive military spending, with a budget twice that of his predecessor, stood to be branded as the most profligate and dangerous gamble in peacetime history without any commensurate achievement of security. Exceptionally popular, politically secure, certainly no equivocator when it came to the manifold weaknesses of Communism as a political and economic system, President Reagan also had a historic opportunity to strengthen cooperative enterprises that heighten mutual confidence and the values of the status quo, in order to render U.S.-Soviet conflict dysfunctional and unattractive.

The time was unusually favorable on the Soviet side as well. A decrepit and irresolute Kremlin leadership of the late 1970s and early 1980s gave way to one of vitality and convincing policies of *glasnost* (open disclosures of errors and incompetence) and *perestroika* (a restructuring and reform of the Soviet Union's economic and social order). Since March 1985, General Secretary Mikhail Gorbachev has exhibited rare political acumen in presiding over a consolidation of power.

As the Soviets sometimes say, in foreign policy, words must never be taken for deeds. Yet their commitment to change is unmistakable. There is no question that years of enormous military spending—12–15 percent of the Soviet Union's gross national product per year—have taken their toll. Unless Soviet Communism produces something of the elevated quality of life promised from official platforms since revolutionary days, it will fail its people and reach the turn of the century not the example that Lenin believed it could be. Instead, it will loom like a muscle-bound military colossus, a jabbing threat to its neighbors but embarrassingly underdeveloped, groaning under an archaic, cen-ter-heavy economic infrastructure and a deplorable standard of living. Its image will be pervaded by startling contradictions—breathtaking feats in space but plumbing and vacuum cleaners that refuse to work.

The time is favorable for a fresh study. Developments since 1984 justify a bold reexamination of the tone and direction of superpower relations. The dilemma persists that the world has changed signifi-cantly while many ideologically conditioned perceptions of U.S.-Soviet relations are enduring anachronisms. More than ever, two overarmed superpowers are suspiciously and cautiously eyeing each other, probing for assurances that a genuine modus vivendi can be worked out.

There are already books aplenty on their historic rivalry, ideological incompatibilities, the Cold War, competitive foreign policies, strategic arsenals, the perils of the nuclear age, and negotiations for arms con-trol. In making its appeal to officials and publics on both sides, this book seeks to fill a major void by offering readers a comprehensive analysis of prominent U.S.-Soviet problem-solving ventures. Because most scholarship on U.S.-Soviet relations tends to find more receptive audiences in the United States and Europe, it is hoped that special publication arrangements can be made to convey this message to cit-izens and academic specialists in the Soviet Union, at least more widely than is usually the case.

Let us be clear at the outset about what this book does not do. U.S.-Soviet collaborative projects were never intended to be panaceas or exercises in fundamentals—that is, radical transformations of conflict-ing national differences and value systems. The challenge-response, action-reaction syndrome, so much a part of time-honored international relations and the games nations play, cannot be suspended to accom-modate some utopian vision of a perfect world, one great happy family, superpowers and all. There is no argument in these pages that some awful catastrophe was avoided because of a cooperative enterprise, or that potential hostilities were subdued because of a successful agree-ment between Washington and Moscow. There may be evidence and excellent examples, but they are not the subject of this volume. Sim-ilarly, concerning quantifiable measures of superpower agreements or their precise influence on the ebb and flow of tensions, we can present no case. There is, in addition, no attempt to address in any systematic way U.S. and Soviet negotiating behaviors—motives, styles, eccen-tricities, similarities, and differences. It remains for another book to relate the full story of negotiations, their atmosphere, personalities, tactics, and compromises, based on firsthand observations and expe-riences of the participants. That is another untold story.

Instead, we have focused on the most valuable cooperative projects themselves: their need, evolution, outcomes, shortcomings, benefits, and futures. It was natural to dwell most carefully on those enterprises that have generated the greatest public interest, those on which, as this book shows, there is considerable historical information, as well as a number of scholar-specialists who have concentrated on portions of the puzzling mix of intense hostility and significant cooperation.

Chapter 2, by Yale Richmond, addresses the importance of academic and cultural exchanges. The motivations of the two governments, and events leading to the signature of the first U.S.-Soviet cultural agreement in 1958, reveal some of the earliest beginnings of bilateral cooperation. Distinct phases in the life of the agreement include the learning years (1958–1971), the détente years (1972–1979), the hiatus caused by the Soviet invasion of Afghanistan (1979), the forging of fresh approaches at the Reagan-Gorbachev summit of 1985, and President Reagan's many initiatives for accelerated citizen-to-citizen contacts. Academic programs have supported undergraduate students, graduate students, senior scholars, lecturers, teachers, and exchanges between universities. On the basis of extraordinary firsthand experience, the author provides illuminating reasons why numbers are still small after some 30 years of dedicated efforts. Cultural exchanges have stressed performing arts, exhibitions, motion pictures, radio, television, publications, public diplomacy, sports, and tourism. The chapter highlights a number of frustrating problems and concludes with a comprehensive assessment of results.

In Chapter 3, Christopher C. Joyner elaborates on his thesis that the 1959 Antarctic Treaty originated in Cold War rivalry but ever since has nurtured a genuinely cooperative diplomatic relationship between the superpowers. Underpinned by the twin principles of scientific cooperation and peaceful uses of the continent only, the treaty stands as the most successful disarmament agreement since World War II. It demilitarizes and denuclearizes the Antarctic area south of 60 degrees south latitude and provides for verification and unannounced on-site inspection, including aerial observation. Critical to success has been the willingness of the United States and the Soviet Union to cooperate, even on unforeseen issues. Agreements on the protection of flora and fauna, conservation of seals, marine resources, and the negotiation of an Antarctic minerals regime are products of the two nations' working together on regional problems. A total of 160 consensus recommendations have been adopted as governing policies. The treaty system shows that the national interests of both parties are much better served by diplomatic cooperation than by geostrategic competition in the southern circumpolar region.

Chapter 4, by Gary K. Bertsch, analyzes the purposes and dynamics of U.S.-Soviet trade, with special attention to historical background, the 1972 agreement, commodity credits, trade restrictions, and major domestic and international political forces that generated both inflated hopes and abrupt letdowns. The chapter seeks to illuminate one of the great enigmas of the modern era: Why are the world's two largest economies not more interactive? Comprehensive tables and government statistics provide answers to the most frequently posed questions regarding commercial relations: Who really benefits from U.S.-Soviet trade? What specific commodities are sold, and what are their monetary values to the respective economies of the parties? And what of the highly contentious issue of national security and unwitting transfers of high technology? Finally, what economic opportunities and challenges does the future hold?

In Chapter 5, Donald R. Kelley presents the case that U.S.-Soviet cooperation in environmental protection has proven to be one of the most scientifically productive and politically durable of the exchanges linking the two nations. Signed at the 1972 Nixon-Brezhnev summit in Moscow, the agreement bore both scientific and political significance. It signaled the recognition in both nations that environmental problems require effective governmental action and that there is a scientific basis for beneficial collaboration between Washington and Moscow. In politics, the agreement was one of several manifestations of détente and was intended to function as a bellwether of U.S.-Soviet ties. By the late 1970s, environmental exchange had become the most active cooperative agreement between the two nations; but the Soviet invasion of Afghanistan and the treatment of dissidents and minorities at home led to U.S. cutbacks designed to signal Washington's displeasure. Official Annual Joint Committee meetings were suspended from 1979 to 1985, and overall exchange levels dropped by 50 percent. In 1984 the Reagan administration reactivated the exchange as one of several signals that it was willing to better relations with the Soviet Union. Collaboration for global preservation is, of course, theoretically unlimited, since Americans and Soviets have no choice but to share the planet Earth as a common home.

In Chapter 6, David D. Finley recounts the saga of U.S.-Soviet rivalry in space, beginning in the late 1950s when Sputnik startled U.S. scientists and politicians into a crash program to regain technological leadership thought to have been lost. Military competition fired a race in which the U.S. side prevailed; but in the era of détente, space also provided a fascinating context for dramatic cooperation. The high point came with the spectacularly successful Apollo-Soyuz Test Project in July 1975, an event that commanded rapt public attention and seemed to promise more mutually valuable enterprises. With the collapse of détente by the end of the 1970s, this direction was reversed, demonstrating the fragility of joint projects confronted by sudden, powerful political necessities. Linkage politics and U.S. reprisals undercut space cooperation sharply in the early 1980s, followed in the mid–1980s by renewed interest in payoffs from a relationship that had been an arena of conflict and cooperation for 30 years. A generation of experience now allows both sides to make realistic estimates of potentials and limitations of space cooperation, quite phenomenal for the imagination when one considers a possible joint venture to Mars.

Chapter 7, by Harold Sandler, explains that medical exchange programs and interactions of U.S. and Soviet physicians challenge Cold War logic and rhetoric. (You cannot trust or work with the Soviets!) Such a mind-set is plainly unfounded and dangerous. U.S. and Soviet doctors have eradicated smallpox from the face of the planet; shared complex medical breakthroughs to improve the health and well-being of their patients; and were awarded the Nobel Peace Prize in 1985 for educational efforts alerting the world to the menace of nuclear war. Medical scientists on both sides also have worked harmoniously and productively to gain invaluable information that will allow for a permanent manned presence in space. Close cooperation will aid greatly in conquering cardiovascular disease and cancer; it also will be needed to end the nuclear arms race. The history of U.S.-Soviet projects in medicine verifies that this can be done and, although relatively unknown by the general public, there is dramatic evidence that the two nations can collaborate for mutual benefit and the good of mankind.

This author's Chapter 8 addresses the life-or-death issue of bilateral cooperation to minimize the risks of nuclear conflict through accident, miscalculation, or breakdowns in communications. In collaborating to protect themselves against each other, the superpowers have devised wide-ranging mechanisms for security communications to guard against destabilizing acts that might lead to the loss of lives or even unintentional war. Included are the 1963 hot line and its two extensive modernizations; the 1971 Accident Measures Agreement; the 1972 Incidents at Sea Agreement; the 1973 Agreement on the Prevention of Nuclear War; the 1980 Satellite-Aided Search and Rescue System; the 1985 agreement linking Anchorage, Tokyo, and Khabarovsk in a North Pacific communications system; the 1986 Stockholm Agreement; and the 1987 agreement for the establishment of Nuclear Risk Reduction Centers. The values that flow from these complex and detailed understandings confirm that in a profoundly interdependent world, nations—not just the poor but especially the rich and powerful—must cooperate to survive.

The concluding chapter, 9, by this author caps the volume with a sixfold typology of mutual benefits in perceptions, ecological management, functionalism, culture and education, commodity exchange, and security. Two themes predominate.

First, the study of international relations has traditionally stressed incompatible national interests, military competition, and conflict. Research on mutual benefits through cooperation has been generally neglected, and in the case of U.S.-Soviet relations, practically nonexistent. The authors of this volume have sought to change this partial picture by reinforcing the academic study of U.S.-Soviet joint projects in nonmilitary fields, and by compiling a reference work. What especially telling messages are conveyed by highlighting seven distinct fields? How can we best summarize their values and shortcomings?

Second, we believe there are significant public policy implications in our scholarship, including promising material for a new future in superpower relations. This volume's extensive and intensive analysis of the record indicates that modifications in perceptions and images are clearly warranted and that a bold, purposeful, new policy agenda is needed to enlighten and elevate the quality of U.S. foreign policy.

NOTES

1. Nish Jamgotch, Jr. (ed.), *Sectors of Mutual Benefit in U.S.-Soviet Relations* (Durham, N.C.: Duke University Press, 1985).

2. A fuller list would include the following: Lawrence T. Caldwell and William Diebold, Jr., *Soviet-American Relations in the 1980s* (New York: McGraw-Hill, 1981); George F. Kennan, *The Nuclear Delusion: Soviet-American Relations in the Atomic Age* (New York: Pantheon, 1982); Alexander L. George, *Managing U.S.-Soviet Rivalry: Problems of Crisis Prevention* (Boulder, Colo.: Westview Press, 1983); Erik P. Hoffman (ed.), *The Soviet Union in the 1980s* (New York: The Academy of Political Science, 1984); Joseph S. Nye, Jr. (ed.), *The Making of America's Soviet Policy* (New Haven: Yale University Press, 1984); Dan Caldwell (ed.), *Soviet International Behavior and U.S. Policy Options* (Lexington, Mass.: D. C. Heath, 1985); Graham T. Allison, Albert Carnesale, and Joseph S. Nye, Jr. (eds.), *Hawks, Doves, and Owls: An Agenda for Avoiding Nuclear War* (New York: W. W. Norton, 1985); Arnold L. Horelick (ed.), *U.S.-Soviet Relations: The Next Phase* (Ithaca, N.Y.: Cornell University Press, 1986); Stephen F. Cohen, *Sovieticus: American Perceptions and Soviet Realities* (New York: W. W. Norton, 1986); Marshall D. Shulman (ed.), *East-West Tensions in the Third World* (New York: W. W. Norton, 1986); Coit D. Blacker, *Reluctant Warriors: The United States, the Soviet Union, and Arms Control* (New York: W. H. Freeman, 1987); Michael Mandelbaum and Strobe Talbott, *Reagan and Gorbachev* (New York: Vintage, 1987).

2

ACADEMIC AND CULTURAL EXCHANGES

Yale Richmond

Academic and cultural exchanges usually come to mind when cooperation with the Soviet Union is mentioned. Students, professors, dancers, musicians, athletes, experts in a wide variety of professional fields, and ordinary people represent some of the fields in which the United States and the Soviet Union have cooperated since the 1950s. The oldest U.S.-Soviet cooperative activities in the post-World War II era, they involve large numbers of people from the two countries and thereby lend themselves more easily to historical review and assessment.

The focus is on people. Rather than seeking solutions to economic, political, or security problems, the major objective of academic and cultural cooperation is to increase mutual understanding. And with good reason, since mutual misunderstanding has been, and remains, one of the most pervasive problems in the U.S.-Soviet relationship.

This chapter discusses the origins of this cooperation, the objectives of the two governments, the various programs and how they developed over the years, some results, and suggestions for the future. To understand where we are, we must first know where we have been.

Despite misunderstandings, political and ideological differences, and diametrically opposed values of the two societies, the Soviet people bear no animosity toward Americans; in fact, they admire and like us.

In a country whose thousand-year history records war after war and immense human suffering, Soviet citizens know that they have never had a war with the United States. They recall their alliance with us against Germany in two wars. Many remember the U.S. aid they received in the famine of the early 1920s, the industrialization of the 1920s and 1930s, and the lend-lease of the 1940s, during the darkest days of their life-and-death struggle against Nazi Germany.

Both countries are multiethnic continental powers. Both tamed a wilderness, the Russians expanding east across Siberia and the Americans west across the Great Plains until they reached the shores of the Pacific.

Soviets and Americans share common traits. Both are energetic, enterprising, inventive, and possessed of a "can do" spirit. Both have a love affair with machinery and technology. The Soviets' fascination with the United States is legendary, and there is no country they wish to visit more. In the 1920s they saw the United States as a model to emulate, and in the 1980s many Soviets see it as a model for the standard of living they hope to achieve.

For the privileged few Soviets who visit the United States, much of what they see confuses them—the free choices Americans have, the seeming lack of order and central planning, the emphasis on the individual as opposed to the collective, and the concern for human rights. Nevertheless, Soviets feel a common identity with Americans, both being citizens of big countries, each with a messianic mission to bring its own form of enlightenment to others who are less fortunate. Political and ideological differences, mutual suspicions, and distance separate us. Exchanges bring us together.

While both governments agree today that academic and cultural exchanges are useful and should be expanded, there were many obstacles to overcome when exchanges were under consideration in the mid–1950s. In the years before the first U.S.-Soviet cultural agreement, it was not possible for a student from one country to study in the other. There were only rare exchanges of performing artists, no competitions between athletes, and almost no tourism. Each country was terra incognita to the other. Within its borders, the Soviet government had a monopoly on information about the United States. Foreign radio broadcasts were jammed, and there was no way to challenge the distorted views presented by the Soviet media. In the United States there was similarly little objective information about the Soviet Union because few Americans could travel there. This was in sharp contrast with the 1920s.

Exchanges between the two countries were active in the 1920s and early 1930s.[1] After the end of the Russian civil war and the victory of the Bolsheviks, the country was economically devastated and starvation was rampant. In 1921, the nongovernmental American Relief Administration, headed by future president Herbert Hoover, fed millions of starving Soviets. When its work ended in 1923, it left behind a reservoir of goodwill toward the United States and a favorable atmosphere for the cooperation that followed. In the first U.S.-Soviet people-to-people exchange, thousands of U.S. tourists and scores of delegations visited the Soviet Union. U.S. industry brought technology and thousands of engineers and technicians to help build Soviet industry, thereby ensuring the success of the first Five-Year Plan. These exchanges and cooperative activities were encouraged by the Soviet government and the U.S. private sector. No objections were voiced by the U.S. government despite its lack of diplomatic recognition of the Soviet regime.

With diplomatic recognition in 1933, prospects for continued cooperation appeared bright. The early 1930s, however, saw the consolidation of Soviet power under Josef Stalin and increased controls on cultural and intellectual activity. Within a few years various obstacles had been erected by the Soviets, and the inflow of visitors greatly declined. Stalin's purges of 1934–1938 and his campaign against foreigners ended more than a decade of cooperation.

During World War II the U.S. government proposed a resumption of cultural and information exchanges to its Soviet ally. The Rockefeller Foundation in 1944 offered fellowships for study in the United States. And in 1945, with the war over, the State Department proposed to exchange performing artists, students, and exhibitions. These initiatives either were rebuffed or went unanswered. The Iron Curtain and the Cold War soon erected barriers to cooperation of any kind between the two former allies.

After Stalin's death in 1953, the Soviets showed interest in establishing a dialogue with the West that included exchanges of people. This led to the Geneva summit conference in the summer of 1955, attended by the heads of government of France, the Soviet Union, the United Kingdom, and the United States. The agenda included disarmament, German reunification, trade, and East-West contacts. At the Geneva foreign ministers' conference that October, the three Western powers proposed a 17-point program to remove barriers to normal exchanges in information media, culture, education, books and other publications, science, sports, and tourism. The Soviets rejected the proposals, charging the Western powers with interference in their internal affairs.[2]

They were interested, however, in some of the Western proposals and indicated they might agree to conclude agreements in some fields. Further developments had to await their twentieth Party Congress in 1956, at which Soviet Premier Nikita S. Khrushchev attacked Stalin and announced new policies of peaceful coexistence and increased contacts with the West.

After the Party Congress, the Soviets signed cultural agreements

with Belgium and Norway in 1956, and with France in 1957. Negotiations in Washington began on October 29, 1957, and the first U.S.-
Soviet cultural agreement was signed on January 27, 1958. The title
of that first two-year accord, Agreement on Exchanges in the Cultural,
Technical and Educational Fields, indicated the cooperation it encompassed.[3] To reflect Soviet priorities and to emphasize cooperation, the
title of the next agreement, in 1959, was amended to General Agreement for Cooperation in Exchanges in the Scientific, Technical, Education and Cultural Fields....[4] Also in 1959, the U.S. National
Academy of Sciences and the Soviet Academy of Sciences signed their
first agreement for scientific cooperation, which included exchanges of
scientists for research and lectures.

Commonly called the "cultural agreement," the General Agreement
encompassed many forms of cooperation intended to increase contacts.
It included, for example, exchanges of youth and women's groups, and
of specialists in agriculture, industry, and medicine, and a provision
for direct air transport between the two countries. In the following
years, the cultural agreement would serve as the crucible for testing
other forms of cooperation.

For both governments, signing the agreement represented a radical
policy change. The Soviets agreed to open their borders, albeit under
controlled conditions, to limited numbers of students, scientists, performing artists, exhibitions, motion pictures, athletes, and others in
such fields as culture, education, government, and youth from the
United States, its major ideological adversary and leader of the capitalist West. The United States agreed to receive similar visitors from
the Soviet Union at a time when it had legislation in force denying
entry to most Soviet citizens. Moreover, the agreement and its attempt
to broaden relations came only a few years after the hysterical anti-
Communist crusade of Senator Joseph McCarthy.

What motivated the two adversaries to reach out and cautiously
touch each other, despite major political and ideological differences,
and to initiate contacts and cooperation?

U.S. interest in exchanges should be seen in the context of major
international events during the first Eisenhower administration.
Dwight D. Eisenhower became president in January 1953. In March
of that year, Stalin died and a new Soviet leadership came to power.
An armistice in Korea was signed in July. In May 1954 there was a
settlement in Indochina ending the war between France and the Viet-
minh. The following year the Austrian State Treaty was signed in
May, and Soviet and Western forces were withdrawn from that country,
a move signaling the approach of détente. These events set the stage
for the Geneva summit in the summer of 1955 and the foreign ministers' meeting in the fall. In 1956 the new Soviet policy of peaceful

coexistence was announced. That year, however, also saw the Hungarian revolution, the Suez Canal crisis, and the Polish October revolution.

Thus, within four years there were signs that the Soviets were seeking an accommodation with the West, but there were also regional flash points that might have sparked a war.

Eisenhower, determined to avoid war, concluded that the United States should explore all possible peaceful means of settling differences with the Soviet Union. In response to the new Soviet overtures to the West, on June 29, 1956, he approved a National Security Council (NSC) statement of policy on East-West exchanges (NSC 5607).

The main objective of NSC 5607 was to moderate Soviet foreign and domestic behavior by removing barriers to a free flow of information and ideas. U.S. objectives, the NSC said, were to promote changes "toward a regime which will abandon predatory policies... and will increasingly rest upon the consent of the governed." To accomplish this, the United States should increase the knowledge that the Soviet people have about the rest of the world. And, in a preview of the human rights movement of the 1970s, the NSC stated that it was U.S. policy "to stimulate the demand of Soviet... citizens for greater personal security by bringing home to them the degree of personal security... afforded by our constitutional and legal systems."

A secondary objective was to learn about the Soviet Union, a desire shared by government and the private sector, and fanned by Soviet secrecy about foreign and domestic affairs. U.S. industry saw the Soviet Union as a vast potential market as well as a possible future competitor. The scholarly community saw it as an unknown area for study and research.

With these convergent interests, exchanges enjoyed broad support from the public and Congress that did not flag over the next 30 years. Support has been given by every U.S. president from Eisenhower to Reagan.

For the Soviet Union, the main motivation was, and remains, acquisition of Western technology and know-how. The new Moscow leaders, aware that their nation lagged far behind the West in economic dynamism and productivity, recognized that it is cheaper and faster to acquire technology from abroad than to develop it at home. Following Russian historical tradition, they turned to the West for scientific and technical know-how. In the same tradition they attempted to keep out the Western ideas that come with it.

Politics also played a role, as it does with every Soviet action. Exchanges were an element in the new policy of peaceful coexistence, contributing to the normalization of relations with the United States and creating an atmosphere of confidence and mutual understanding.

Bilateral agreements also implied legitimacy for the Soviet government and recognition as a coequal. And as Soviet confidence and experience in dealing with the West grew, Moscow became more skilled at using exchanges to influence Western public opinion.

Another Soviet objective was to show Americans the best of their culture, science, and technology, of which they are justly proud and which they see as achievements of a Communist society.

Moscow found it useful to vent the pent-up desire of its intelligentsia for foreign travel, employing the interest of its professionals in the arts, scholarship, science, and engineering to learn what is going on in their fields abroad. And for Soviet athletes, there was recognition that foreign competition was vital if they were to reach world-class levels of performance.

Earning foreign currency was also a priority. The Soviets need hard currency—dollars, in this case—to purchase essential imports, and they soon learned that they could command world-class prices for their world-class performing artists.

Although U.S. and Soviet objectives differed from the start, there has been a consensus that exchanges are in their mutual interest. Differing objectives, however, were to cause persistent problems in carrying out agreed programs.

Differences in how exchanges are conducted in each country would also cause friction. The Soviet government, highly centralized and obsessed with control, closely monitored all activities. On the U.S. side, in contrast, there was from the start a cooperative effort between government and private sector, with the Department of State exercising overall direction. Over the years, however, the private sector role has increased while the government role has decreased, as has its direction. What began in 1958 as a government program has evolved into a largely private-sector effort.

THE LEARNING YEARS, 1958–1971

The early years were a time of learning, when two vastly different societies attempted to work together. Watchwords on both sides were control, suspicion, and strict numerical reciprocity.

Before an exchange could occur, it has to be included in the next two-year cultural agreement and become part of lengthy and difficult negotiations. Conditions had to be agreed to: the number of people involved, whether interpreters were to be included in the agreed number, where they would go and what they would see, the length of their stay, and who would pay which costs. Negotiations were fractious and frustrating, but they served to establish, for better or worse, procedures that were to govern these and other U.S.-Soviet exchanges for the next

30 years. More important, in a wide variety of fields contacts were established between people and institutions of the two countries that were to develop into cooperation when relations between the two governments improved during détente.

THE DÉTENTE YEARS, 1972–1979

Détente brought many changes. The learning years were replaced by years of cooperation as the two sides sought to move beyond exchange tourism—look, see, and tell—to cooperative activities in which Americans and Soviets would work together to solve problems in fields of mutual interest.

Scientific and technical activities were spun off from the cultural agreement and placed under 11 cooperative agreements in science and technology, environmental protection, medical science and public health, space, agriculture, world ocean studies, transportation, atomic energy, artificial heart research and development, energy, and housing and other construction. For each agreement there was a joint commission, cochaired by cabinet-level officers, that met annually to review ongoing work and select new areas for joint research. Some 240 working groups of U.S. and Soviet scientists were created that conducted research in their own countries and met jointly, alternately in each country, to review results. Some 750 Americans and an equal number of Soviets were exchanged annually for one-to-two-week visits.

U.S. motivation was mainly political—to develop patterns of cooperation and interdependence leading to shared interests and, it was hoped, to Soviet restraint at home and abroad. Secondary objectives were to solve practical scientific problems and gain access to the Soviet science community. Soviet motivation, as in the past, was to acquire Western technological know-how.

Academic and cultural cooperation also benefited from détente. The American Council of Learned Societies (ACLS) and the Soviet Academy of Sciences established a Commission on the Humanities and Social Sciences for collaborative research. A Fulbright lecturer program enabled professors to lecture for a semester in each other's universities and colleges. The Soviets permitted their universities to have direct exchanges with U.S. universities. They also discovered the private sector, the major player in U.S. cultural life, and permitted Soviet institutions to deal directly with organizations such as the YMCA, the National 4-H Foundation, and the American Bar Association. In 1977, the number of Soviets coming to the United States on all exchanges, including the cooperative agreements, reached 4,615, four times the level of the 1960s.

The major Soviet change, however, was in attitude. Soviets became easier to work with. Younger, more professional people appeared in their delegations. Their earlier hesitation gone, they had fully recognized academic and cultural cooperation as a legitimate element in bilateral relations.

This came to a halt in December 1979. What had survived the war in Vietnam was dealt a major blow by the war in Afghanistan.

THE END OF DÉTENTE

In response to the Soviet invasion of Afghanistan, the Carter administration allowed the cultural agreement to lapse at the end of 1979. Many exchanges between the two governments were suspended, a policy continued by the Reagan administration and reinforced after the imposition of martial law in Poland in 1981.

Cultural exchanges were allowed to stagnate during the first Reagan administration. Without an agreement, there were no government-approved performing arts or art exhibition exchanges, and many cooperative programs that had been funded or encouraged by the government were suspended. Private organizations did not need Washington's approval, but many were reluctant to differ with their government. On the Soviet side there was reluctance to continue in fields such as performing arts and art exhibits without the sanction of the intergovernmental agreement.

Academic cooperation continued, although at a lower level, evidence of how much it is valued by both sides. To fill the gap created by withdrawal of the U.S. government, private organizations stepped in, including many peace organizations, reflecting their disagreement with administration policies and their desire for increased dialogue with the Soviet people.

In mid-1983 the Reagan administration began to seek an improvement in U.S.-Soviet relations. Negotiations for a new cultural agreement were to start in September, but when the Soviets shot down Korean Airlines flight 007 in that month, they also shot down efforts to improve relations and plans to revive the cultural agreement.

THE REAGAN-GORBACHEV GENEVA SUMMIT

It was not until August 1984, when efforts to improve relations had resumed, that cultural negotiations finally opened in Moscow. They were to continue for an unprecedented 15 months, the longest yet for a cultural agreement, before signature on November 21, 1985, at the Reagan-Gorbachev Geneva summit.

The new six-year agreement continued the previous format, with general language giving approval to a broad range of academic and cultural programs to be conducted, on the U.S. side, by the private sector and the U.S. government. A three-year program for 1986–1988, annexed to the agreement, listed cooperative activities between the two governments. It resumed and expanded previous activities, added a few new ones, and continued the slow but steady progress toward broadening contacts. All other programs were to be conducted by the private sector. One new initiative, long sought by U.S. negotiators, was a provision for appearances by representatives of each government on television in the other country.

REAGAN'S U.S.-SOVIET EXCHANGE INITIATIVE

The joint statement issued at the Geneva summit noted that President Reagan and General Secretary Gorbachev "... believe that there should be greater understanding among our peoples and that to this end they will encourage greater travel and people-to-people contact." Included were several academic and cultural activities that the two leaders agreed to carry out:

... cooperation in the development of educational exchanges and software for elementary and secondary school instruction; measures to promote Russian language studies in the United States and English language studies in the USSR; the annual exchange of professors to conduct special courses in history, culture and economics at the relevant departments of Soviet and American institutions of higher education; mutual allocation of scholarships for the best students in the natural sciences, technology, social sciences and humanities for the period of an academic year; holding regular meets in various sports and increased television coverage of sports events.[5]

To follow through, the Coordinator's Office for the President's U.S.-Soviet Exchange Initiative was established in the United States Information Agency (USIA). The administration made it clear, however, that the new initiative would be largely a private sector effort, with no government funding. The Coordinator's Office would act only as a broker between U.S. and Soviet partners in cooperation.

The Private Sector

The cultural agreement endorsed "contacts, exchanges and cooperation between organizations of the two countries ... in other related fields of mutual interest which are not being carried out under specialized agreements" between the governments. If an organization in one country seeks cooperation and has found a willing partner in the other, it can start after modalities have been agreed to. Soviet partners will need Moscow's approval, but Americans are free to proceed without Washington's approval. Washington's only function is to approve or deny U.S. visas for the Soviets.

ACADEMIC COOPERATION

Academic cooperation with the Soviet Union reflects the variety of U.S. education. Program participants range from undergraduates to university professors. Some programs are negotiated and funded by the U.S. government, and others by private organizations or the universities themselves.

Undergraduates

Presidents from Eisenhower to Reagan have wanted to exchange thousands of students with the Soviet Union. Eisenhower, in 1958, worked on a proposal to bring 10,000 Soviet undergraduates to the United States, all costs paid, while leaving it to the Soviets whether to invite U.S. students in return. He never made his proposal because the State Department at that time was trying, without success, to get Soviet agreement for 100 students. They finally agreed to only 20 for the first year.

It would appear natural for two countries with many mutual interests to encourage student exchange, but after 30 years opportunities are still limited, especially for undergraduates. The Soviets prefer study abroad by advanced graduate students in their late twenties or early thirties who have completed formal studies and are doing what the Soviets call scientific research. Their first undergraduate program with the United States, for ten students in a group, began in 1974. And in 1987, after almost 30 years of U.S.-Soviet exchanges, there were only 20 Soviet undergraduates studying in the United States.

U.S. undergraduates and beginning graduate students can study Russian in the Soviet Union under several programs. These are mostly one-way—Americans to the Soviet Union—with all costs paid in dollars. These programs, although small, have produced a growing pool of Americans with Russian-language capability.

The American Council of Teachers of Russian, in Bryn Mawr, Pennsylvania, sends some 250 students to the Soviet Union annually to study Russian in Moscow and Leningrad. The New York-based Council on International Educational Exchange sends another 200 each year to Leningrad. Ohio State and Purdue universities, and Middlebury College send 30 students each to Moscow for language study annually. The State University of New York has an exchange with Moscow's

Maurice Thorez Institute of Foreign Languages for 10 U.S. and 10 Soviet undergraduates each year.

President Reagan, in his 1985 address to the nation on the eve of the Geneva summit, called for an expansion of student programs. He asked why we should not exchange "thousands of undergraduates each year, and even younger students who would live with a host family and attend schools or summer camps?"

The Soviets appear to be moving in this direction, but slowly and cautiously. In April 1987, they signed an agreement with the Institute of International Education, in New York City, under which five U.S. students study for two semesters at Moscow State University and ten Soviets study for one semester in the United States.

This is a start toward Reagan's "thousands," although it is not a junior year abroad. The Americans, who apply as college seniors, have their bachelor's degrees by the time they go to Moscow. The Soviets are in the final year of their five-year undergraduate studies. In the fall of 1987, the Soviets were enrolled, at their request, in groups of five each at Yale University and the University of Maryland, studying chemistry and physics, respectively. U.S. students were at Moscow State University, studying the humanities, and natural and social sciences. Each group was accompanied by a leader; for the Americans, an advanced graduate student, for the Soviets, two instructors who also were studying chemistry and physics.

A university pairing program permits nonstudy visits of one or more weeks for undergraduates. The first pairing, between Yale and Moscow State, began in 1985. During the 1987–1988 academic year some 150 Soviet undergraduates were scheduled at 10 U.S. universities. An equal number of U.S. undergraduates visited Moscow State. This program is conducted by the Citizen Exchange Council, in New York City, and the USSR Committee on Youth Organizations.

A start with high school students has been made. In 1987, eight students from Phillips Academy, Andover, Massachusetts, studied for five weeks at the Physics-Mathematics School of Novosibirsk, and ten from Novosibirsk studied at Andover. A similar program was planned in 1988 by Choate Rosemary Hall, Wallingford, Connecticut, with a Moscow school. In 1989, 25 high schools in the United States expect to begin similar exchanges with Soviet Schools.

Graduate Students

The cultural agreement provides for the exchange each year of "at least 40 advanced researchers, instructors and professors for study and scholarly research in the humanities and the social, natural and applied sciences. . . . " The program is administered by the International

Research and Exchanges Board (IREX), Princeton, New Jersey, and the USSR State Committee for Public Education.

The Americans are mostly advanced graduate students or young instructors in the humanities and social sciences who have completed their course work for a doctoral degree and are researching dissertations. They are selected by a panel of scholars in an open competition without government screening, although costs of this program are funded by grants to IREX from government agencies—USIA, the Department of State, and the National Endowment for the Humanities—as well as private foundations. The Soviets, in their early thirties, are researchers in frontier areas of science and technology who have completed formal studies and have the near equivalent of the U.S. doctorate. They do not apply but are selected by their government on the basis of the importance of their work to the Soviet economy.

Due to limitations on exports of critical technology under the Export Administration Act, the United States each year is unable to accept a number of Soviet nominees. Because of reciprocity, the Soviets reject an equal number of Americans, usually in social sciences that deal with contemporary Soviet society. As a result, the number of participants each year is usually less than the 40 specified in the agreement.

The Soviets want to enlarge this program and have proposed several hundred "students" each year. This has not been feasible due to the U.S. government's unwillingness to accept a slate of Soviet nominees heavily skewed toward the physical sciences, as well as to the limited number of Americans qualified for this elite program. IREX, representing U.S. universities, believes that the quota, "at least forty," is about right.

Scholars Doing Short-term Research

There are several reciprocal programs for senior scholars—postdoctoral students and professors—to do short-term research. The IREX Senior Scholar Exchange with the State Committee for Public Education provides for "at least" ten persons for two to five months each. The academic profile is, for the U.S. side, humanities and social sciences; for the Soviets, science and technology. IREX also administers a program with the Soviet Academy of Sciences for scholars in the humanities and social sciences totaling 100 person-months a year on each side, including cooperative research under the ACLS-Soviet Academy Commission on the Humanities and Social Sciences. In 1987, ACLS signed three more agreements for cooperative research in archival administration, pedagogy, and music composition and musicology. Additional agreements on library science, cinema studies, fine arts, and theater and dance were expected in 1988.

Lecturers and Teachers

University lecturers have been exchanged under the Fulbright Program since 1973. The cultural agreement provides for "at least fifteen" persons on each side annually to lecture in all disciplines. The Council for International Exchange of Scholars, Washington, D.C., and the State Committee for Public Education administer the program.

Ten U.S. and ten Soviet language teachers are exchanged each year for two months by AFS International/Intercultural and the State Committee for Public Education. The Americans teach English in Soviet secondary schools and teachers colleges. The Soviets teach English in U.S. high schools and colleges. Efforts to increase the length of stay have been rebuffed by the Soviets.

Russian-Language Teachers

Americans and Soviets cooperate in improving the teaching of English and Russian. IREX sends 35 U.S. teachers of Russian, mostly at the college level, to Moscow for study each summer, and receives an equal number of Soviet college teachers of English. A similar program for high school teachers of Russian and English is conducted each summer by the American Council of Teachers of Russian (ACTR), with 25 teachers on each side. ACTR has also been cooperating with the Pushkin Institute in Moscow to prepare textbooks for U.S. college students of Russian. Two volumes have been published, and a third is in preparation. Volume I, for first-year students, is used in some 60 colleges and universities. An ACTR-Pushkin team is also working on a four-year series of texts for U.S. high school students of Russian. ACTR and Pushkin support 15 U.S., and an equal number of Soviet, foreign-language curriculum consultants who work in universities and high schools of the two countries.

Universities

The largest university pairing is between the State University of New York and Moscow State, dating from 1976. About ten graduate students and five professors participate annually from each university. Similar pairings, for faculty only, include the Mid-West University Consortium for International Activities, representing eight Big Ten universities, and the University of Missouri, both with Moscow State. The Soviets, in most cases, send scientists, while the Americans are in a variety of disciplines. The University of California in 1987 signed an agreement with Leningrad State University for a program to begin in the academic year 1988–1989 after the terms—numbers, length of stay, and other conditions—have been agreed to.

And Thousands of Students?

In 1986–1987, after 28 years of exchanges, there were about 650 U.S. students, scholars, lecturers and teachers in the Soviet Union (for periods longer than one month) and 385 Soviets in the United States. These figures should be contrasted with those for academics from other countries who studied in the United States in 1985–1986: India, 13,791; Japan, 11,467; United Kingdom, 5,097; West Germany, 4,060; and France, 3,161. And from the People's Republic of China (PRC), there were 12,000, about half PRC-sponsored and half privately supported.[6] (The actual figure for Chinese is believed to be more than 25,000.)

Why does the PRC, which began U.S. exchanges in 1978, send so many, while the Soviet Union, which began in 1958, sends so few? Security is the main reason—an obsession for control. The Soviet Union is unwilling to send large numbers of students abroad because it would be unable to adequately monitor their activities and prevent occasional defections.

James H. Billington, a scholar of Russian and Soviet culture who is now librarian of Congress, believes the United States should take a new initiative to reach the Soviet post-Stalinist generation. He recommends a dramatic increase in the number of Soviet students coming to the United States for study:

Massively increasing the numbers would remove the heavy control that the *nomenklatura* elite inevitably holds over a small program. Although it would pose problems for our security, it would pose even greater problems for theirs, since they would be forced either to permit far more people from far more places in the USSR than they could effectively control to experience the United States for themselves or to be put in the position of refusing to let their own people take advantage of an educational opportunity of immense inherent appeal.[7]

Such an offer was indeed made to the Soviets in 1987. A consortium of 18 eastern colleges, headed by Middlebury, expects to host up to 50 Soviet undergraduates in 1988–1989, with 2 to 3 students on each campus and no Soviet chaperones. The students will take half their courses in their major fields but must take the other half in liberal arts unrelated to their major. U.S. undergraduates, it is expected, will go to the Soviet Union in future years on similar terms.

PERFORMING ARTS

The most visible exchanges are in the performing arts—dancers, musicians, ice skaters, and even circus performers—who present the arts of one country to the people of the other. "Exchange" is perhaps the wrong term, because the performances are commercial and not numerically reciprocal.

In the United States there are many impresarios—concert agents— who compete in a free market, arranging tours for performing artists on a commercial basis. In the Soviet Union there is only one impresario, the State Concert Agency—*Goskontsert*—a state monopoly that arranges tours on a commercial basis but with profit going to the Soviet state.

When the Soviets send a ballet to the United States, they shop among impresarios for the best financial terms, and they take home a profit in dollars. When a U.S. ballet goes to the Soviet Union, it must negotiate with *Goskontsert* for a fee paid mostly in rubles. Rubles cannot be exported from the Soviet Union and have very little value, since there is little that foreigners can purchase with them. *Goskontsert* is able to pay in foreign currency, but it seeks to keep that portion of its fee as low as possible.

U.S. artists usually need subsidies to perform in the Soviet Union at least to cover costs. Salaries and international transport must be paid in dollars. Until 1980, subsidies were paid by the U.S. government. Recently private benefactors have helped to fund some tours.

Under this unequal arrangement, the Soviet Union earns dollars for performers it sends to the United States, while the United States pays dollars to send its performers. Since there is a large market for Soviet performers, the number who come to the United States each year is high and the profit in dollars to the Soviet state is substantial. Exact earnings are difficult to ascertain, but estimates in 1978 were as high as $1 million annually. Estimates for 1988 are considerably higher. By contrast, since subsidies to Americans are limited, the number going to the Soviet Union is small and the earnings, if any, meager.

Despite unequal conditions, artistic exchanges have brought something of each country's culture to the other. Americans have thrilled to performances of Soviet orchestras and virtuoso soloists, and U.S. ballet got a boost from visits of the Bolshoi and Kirov ballets. U.S. artists, in return, have brought a breath of fresh air as well as new concepts in music, dance, and theater to the Soviet Union, where orthodoxy and conservatism have long ruled the performing arts. Jazz, once considered decadent, has now become fashionable, thanks in part to tours by Benny Goodman, Earl Hines, Duke Ellington, the Preservation Hall Band, and other U.S. jazz greats. And rock, prohibited in the past, is now reluctantly recognized.

In a new and unprecedented development, Boston held a three-week festival of Moscow's arts and culture in the spring of 1988. Musicians, composers, dancers, and choreographers of the two countries worked together, preparing and staging performances that emphasized contemporary trends in the arts. The Boston festival, ten years in the making, was conceived and directed by Boston Opera director Sarah Caldwell and Bolshoi ballerina Maya Plisetskaya and her husband, composer Rodion Shchedrin. Moscow will hold a similar festival for Boston in the fall of 1989.

EXHIBITIONS

Exhibitions have been a recurring feature of cultural relations since 1959, when the two countries traded national exhibitions showing commercial products. The U.S. exhibition had displays by some 700 firms as well as Edward Steichen's "Family of Man" photo exhibit; Circarama; Buckminster Fuller's geodesic dome; IBM's RAMAC, which answered questions about the United States; and free Pepsi Cola (which paved the way for Pepsi's entry into the Soviet market in later years).

It was at the 1959 U.S. exhibition in Moscow that Vice-President Richard M. Nixon engaged Soviet Premier Nikita S. Khrushchev in the famous "kitchen debate" in a model U.S. home. Since 1959, there have been 18 major U.S. exhibitions in the Soviet Union and an equal number of Soviet exhibitions in the United States.

The U.S. exhibitions, prepared by USIA, have focused on such areas as transportation, medicine, education, graphic arts, outdoor recreation, photography, agriculture, and information. Staffed by 20 Russian-speaking U.S. guides, the exhibitions have been shown for one month in each of three or more Soviet cities. The total Soviet audience for all exhibitions since 1959 is more than 18 million, averaging 250,000 in each city. Soviet exhibitions in the United States, staffed by Soviet guides, have covered similar areas but have attracted far smaller audiences. Whatever their subjects, these exhibitions enable people of each country to see something of the other—its products and way of life—and to talk with the guides. For most visitors, it is a first opportunity to speak with someone from the other country.

Art exhibits began during détente when museums such as New York's Metropolitan Museum of Art and Washington's National Gallery of Art, and private collector Armand Hammer began exchanges with Soviet museums. After the Soviet invasion of Afghanistan in 1979 and the lapse of the cultural agreement, all exhibitions were suspended. When they were resumed in 1985, the first major event was an exhibit in Leningrad of 40 French impressionist paintings from the National Gallery of Art. A USIA exhibition, "Information USA," opened a nine-city tour of the Soviet Union in June 1987.

MOTION PICTURES, RADIO, TELEVISION, AND PUBLICATIONS

Cooperation by the media is ideologically difficult because it challenges the Soviet monopoly on what is said or written. Media cooperation, moreover, is mostly commercial, since the products exchanged are actually sold by both countries and the objective of each is to maximize its profit in dollars. Here again the problem is how a free market relates to a state monopoly.

Both countries have large motion picture industries and huge domestic audiences. Sales are limited, however, by ideology, audience interest, and price. U.S. films, no matter what their subject, are very popular in the Soviet Union, where there is an insatiable curiosity about the United States. The Soviets, however, generally purchase films that are in some way critical of Western society, and the United States in particular, or are ideologically neutral.

U.S. film distributors, not bound by ideology, purchase films that will be successful at the box office. Since many Soviet films, especially in earlier years, had an ideological message and were didactic in the tradition of Russian literature, they have been of little interest to the U.S. mass audience. Although some Soviet films have received good reviews, they have not done well at the box office. Currently the two countries sell each other only a handful of films each year.

Attempts to exchange radio and TV programs face similar ideological and cultural barriers. U.S. radio and TV programs present a picture of the United States that does not conform to Soviet ideology and, for the most part, they are not acceptable. And Soviet TV films have been difficult to place in the United States because they either carry a political message or are not of sufficient interest to the U.S. mass audience.

The American-Soviet Film Initiative is an attempt at cooperation between U.S. and Soviet film and television producers. At a meeting in 1987, ten Soviet film directors, actors, and writers and their U.S. counterparts studied how film and television have reinforced the stereotypes each country has of the other. The new initiative's goal is to serve as a channel for communication between filmmakers of the two countries in order to encourage coproductions, film screenings, festivals, and marketing.

Television space bridges—linkups between Americans and Soviets via satellite broadcasts—are a new and promising form of communication. Pioneered by the Esalen Institute of San Francisco in 1983, this people-to-people effort has been encouraged by the Gorbachev government under its policy of *glasnost* (openness). In 1986, U.S. TV star Phil Donahue and Soviet TV commentator Vladimir Pozner began a series of space bridges with live debate between U.S. and Soviet studio audiences. And U.S. members of Congress and deputies of the Supreme Soviet (parliament) have begun a series of "Congress bridge" TV debates aired in the two countries on subjects ranging from differences between the two political systems to human rights. The first U.S. presentation was broadcast on Soviet TV in April 1987.

U.S. books in translation are very popular in the Soviet Union, where there is a veritable book hunger. Whatever U.S. authors the Soviets publish are sold out quickly. Soviet authors, by contrast, face the demands of the U.S. market, where a book will be published if it can sell. Since Soviet books are not usually popular successes, the result is an imbalance in sales. Scientific and technical books and journals fare better. What each country produces is of interest to scientists of the other, and sales of rights to translated editions are brisk.

Publishers of the two countries met in Moscow and New York in the mid–1970s to seek ways to increase cooperation. This U.S. initiative, however, was only partially successful. It served to acquaint each country with the publishing practices of the other, thus helping to overcome one obstacle to increased trade. It failed, however, to overcome the major impediment—limitations on what the Soviets can sell in a free market.

Librarians collect books, and neither ideology nor the free market has prevented bilateral cooperation between libraries. The Library of Congress has been exchanging materials with the Soviets since the 1920s. It currently has more than 70 Soviet partners, including Moscow's Lenin Library, with which it trades government documents, scientific periodicals, and newspapers. Most U.S. research libraries also trade books with Soviet counterparts. The University of Illinois, for example, has arrangements with more than 100 Soviet libraries and forwards requests from other U.S. libraries for Soviet holdings.

PUBLIC DIPLOMACY

The Dartmouth Conferences, suggested by President Eisenhower and initiated in 1960 by Norman Cousins, then editor of *The Saturday Review*, bring together prominent U.S. and Soviet citizens for off-the-record discussions on public issues of mutual interest. Similar meetings are held by the United Nations Association of the United States. In recent years many other U.S. public policy institutes have made similar arrangements. For example, young politicians of the two countries (age

40 and under) have held joint meetings since 1971. These have been organized by the American Council of Young Political Leaders, for those of the Democratic and Republican parties, and the USSR Committee on Youth Organizations, representing Komsomol and other Soviet youth groups.

Similar meetings between U.S. and Soviet citizens proliferated between 1980 and 1985, when private groups filled the gap created by the U.S. government's withdrawal from cultural exchanges. These private groups included the American Bar Association, the Center for U.S.-USSR Initiatives, the Esalen Institute, the Friendship Force, the League of Women Voters, Peace Links, Physicians for Social Responsibility, the Samantha Smith Foundation, the U.S.-USSR Bridges for Peace, and the Young Astronaut Council. More than 250 U.S. private institutions are known to be involved in projects whose major focus has been peace issues—arms control, disarmament, and prevention of nuclear war.

The U.S.-Soviet "town meetings" held by the Chautauqua Institution are an example of what is now possible. The first week-long meeting, held at Chautauqua, New York, in 1985, featured discussions by day and performances in the evening. A second meeting, held at Jurmala, Latvia, in 1986, was attended by 250 U.S. and 2,000 Soviet citizens. Covered extensively by Soviet press and TV, it was the first public meeting in the Soviet Union between U.S. and Soviet citizens and officials in which major issues of bilateral concern were publicly debated with simultaneous interpretation. Among the topics discussed were arms control, regional issues, the role of the press in shaping public opinion, and the forcible incorporation of Latvia, Lithuania, and Estonia into the Soviet Union—a move not recognized by the United States. A third meeting, held at Chautauqua in 1987, was attended by 240 Soviets, most of whom lived with U.S. families while there.

As part of the people-to-people movement encouraged by President Reagan, new life has been infused into sister city pairings. Five pairings had been arranged in 1972 but only one, Seattle-Tashkent, remained active. Sister Cities International, the U.S. organization that arranges pairings, reported that in early 1988 there were 19 active U.S.-Soviet city relationships and another 44 were under discussion.

SPORTS

Athletic competitions have worked well, perhaps because ideology is not involved. In the 1960s, binational athletic events were negotiated by the State Department and listed in the cultural agreement. Currently, U.S. national sports federations (basketball, boxing, gymnastics, swimming, track and field, and wrestling, among others) deal directly with Soviet counterparts in arranging team competitions and invitations to individual athletes. Such meets succeed because they draw large crowds in both countries and are financially lucrative.

TOURISM

Tourism is a cultural as well as a commercial activity that permits private citizens of each country to get a firsthand look, albeit a limited one, at the other. According to Soviet estimates, more than 100,000 U.S. citizens visited the Soviet Union in 1987, most of them tourists who were a source of much-needed dollars for the Soviet state. Soviet visitors to the United States for the same year, based on U.S. visas issued, were about 11,000. Most of the Soviets came on official business or exchange visits. Several thousand came on family visits, with costs borne by U.S. relatives. Only a few hundred came as tourists.

The imbalance in tourism is not due to lack of Soviet interest but to Soviet controls on travel abroad. Soviet citizens, in addition to receiving government permission for travel, must be able to pay the dollar costs of a stay in the United States. In exchanges, these costs are paid either by the U.S. host organization or by the Soviet government. For tourists there is a Catch–22 situation: Soviet citizens are not allowed to possess foreign currency, the ruble is not freely convertible in the Soviet Union, and rubles cannot be taken out of the country. A Soviet citizen wishing to travel as a tourist, and lacking an invitation from a U.S. host, must join an organized tour group. The number of such tours to the United States is small, however, because the Soviet government has a limited amount of dollars it is willing to make available for tourism. Thus, only a few hundred Soviet tourists are able to visit the United States each year.

PROBLEMS IN EXCHANGES

How does an open society relate to a closed society? How does a pluralist society with a mix of private sector and governmental activity cooperate with a country where practically all activity is governmental? How does a culture based on individual rights and free choice relate to one that is collectivist, with individuals subservient to the state? How does the United States cooperate with a government that preaches peaceful coexistence but declares that the ideological struggle must continue? How do we reconcile U.S. interests in mutual understanding and constructive changes in the Soviet Union with Soviet interests in technical training and technology transfer? How do we cooperate with an authoritarian government without allowing it to set the agenda? And how do U.S. administrators of exchanges, private as well as governmental, coordinate their efforts to ensure that they are conducted "on the basis of equality, mutual benefit and reciprocity," as stipulated in the cultural agreement? These questions and contrasts are at the heart of difficulties that have persisted through 30 years of U.S.-Soviet cooperation.

Day-to-day irritants, such as access and travel controls, affect all foreign visitors to the Soviet Union. Access is the ability of visitors to see persons and institutions of choice; and for students and scholars this includes research archives. Soviet visitors to the United States are able to arrange meetings with most Americans, and U.S. archives and library holdings are open. This is not generally true in the Soviet Union, due to traditional Soviet secrecy and suspicion of foreigners, as well as a cumbersome bureaucracy. Difficulties in access to Soviet scientific institutions led to U.S. reassessment of the 11 cooperative agreements in the late 1970s. In the last year of the Carter administration, more cooperative research projects were terminated than were initiated, and U.S. government agencies began to evaluate individual projects more strictly on criteria of scientific merits and mutual benefits.

Travel controls for foreign visitors are another troublesome issue. Approximately 20 percent of each country's territory is formally closed to citizens of the other. Actually, because of inadequate transportation and accommodations for travelers, more than 90 percent of the Soviet Union is effectively closed. Closed areas, first imposed by the Soviet Union during World War II, were maintained after the war. Foreigners also cannot travel more than 40 kilometers from places of residence or study without approval of Soviet authorities, which is not always given. In retaliation, the United States in 1955, after the Soviets refused to lift their controls, imposed similar restrictions on Soviet citizens.

Soviet students and scholars in the United States must inform the State Department in advance of travel beyond 25 miles from their places of study. They are free to travel, however, unless the government objects, which may occur when a projected visit is to an industrial or scientific facility. U.S. closed areas, moreover, apply to Soviet diplomats, journalists, and other Soviets resident in the United States, but not to Soviets on exchange visits. The United States has offered to eliminate closed area restrictions on a mutual basis but so far has been rebuffed.

In reciprocal programs it has been customary for the sending side to select people to represent it abroad. When the Soviets wish to invite a particular American, they extend a direct invitation, and it is up to the invitee to accept. When a U.S. institution invites a Soviet, there is no assurance that he or she will receive permission to accept. In recent years the Soviets have become more flexible in approving such "name requests," as they are known. The 1985 cultural agreement, for example, permits universities to name professors they wish to invite under the Fulbright program, and in many cases Soviet authorities permit them to accept. The 1986 agreement between the National Academy of Sciences and the Soviet Academy of Sciences similarly permits each academy to name the scientists it wishes to invite.

It is disappointing to U.S. partners when the same Soviets come year after year—those who have political clearance for travel, are fluent in English, are deemed qualified to represent their country, and are well connected. Soviet authorities, rather than broaden opportunities for travel abroad, maintain control by supporting trusted and dependable persons, and this means sending repeaters. It also explains why so many U.S. initiatives are channeled to a few Moscow institutions, such as the Soviet Peace Committee, the Union of Friendship Societies, and the Institute for U.S. and Canadian Studies.

Human rights violations and restrictions on Jewish emigration have limited, and at times curtailed, exchanges. In past years, some members of the National Academy of Sciences have called for a boycott until Soviet performance improves, and some Americans will not participate for this reason.

Soviet bureaucracy is perhaps the greatest handicap. Because officials, as a rule, do not reply promptly to written proposals, a visit to Moscow is often the most effective way to reach agreement on a new proposal. Even after agreement is reached, a long lead time is usually required before anything begins. Soviet arrivals in the United States are often postponed for no apparent reason, or people do not arrive when expected. Patience is required. The wheels of Soviet bureaucracy turn slowly.

Finally, the state of bilaterial relations determines the degree of cooperation. In 1968, the Soviets cut back academic, cultural, and scientific programs because of U.S. involvement in Vietnam. The United States, after the Soviet invasion of Czechoslovakia in 1968, took similar action. After the Soviets invaded Afghanistan in 1979, the United States did not renew the cultural agreement, suspended most cultural exchanges, withdrew from the Moscow Olympics, and let agreements lapse in science and technology, space, and energy. After the Soviets shot down Korean Airlines flight 007 in 1983, the transportaiton agreement was allowed to lapse as a show of U.S. displeasure and disapproval.

Reducing the U.S. government role in collaborative projects would help to ensure that they continue when U.S.-Soviet relations are strained. Indeed, it can be argued that exchanges and cooperation are most useful, and even necessary, when relations are tense and dialogue between governments is reduced.

TECHNOLOGY TRANSFER

Critics charge that the Soviets use exchanges to acquire high technology with military applications. It is a Russian tradition, dating back to Tsar Peter the Great, to send scientists and engineers abroad to learn from the West, and the Soviet Union continues that tradition. Due to the potential for technology transfer through academic and scientific cooperation, the U.S. government has taken measures to limit Soviet access. For example, the Export Administration Act of 1979 regulates all exports of advanced technology, in particular those with military applications or dual use (commercial and military). The Committee on Exchanges, a U.S. government group that includes the intelligence community, reviews all proposed Soviet visits to the United States by persons in science and technology, including those for study, research, and attendance at scientific meetings. For each Soviet scientist applying for a U.S. visa, the committee assesses the potential for technology transfer and whether the visit is permissible under the Export Administration Act. A recommendation may be made to the State Department that the visa be denied, or no objections may be registered, provided the scientist is denied access to certain scientific facilities. Finally, Soviet scientists are routinely denied access to research, including unclassified material, funded by the Department of Defense; and their travel within the United States is controlled to ensure that they do not depart from proposed itineraries without prior approval.

Several panels have been convened over the years to review U.S.-Soviet cooperation and assess the effect on national security of technology transfer through open scientific communication. The most recent was the Corson panel, convened by the National Academy of Sciences in 1982. It concluded that the evidence reviewed failed to reveal specific evidence of damage to national security caused by information obtained from academic sources. The panel found that while academic exchanges have potential for technology transfer, only a very small part of lost technology can be attributed to the scientific tradition of open communication.

CIA Deputy Director Bobby Inman, testifying before the Senate Governmental Affairs Subcommittee on Investigations on May 11, 1982, estimated that 70 percent of Soviet bloc acquisitions of Western high technology is made through their intelligence services. Another 20 to 30 percent is made through legal purchases and Western publications.

"Only a small percentage," he concluded, "comes from direct technical exchanges conducted by scientists and students."[8]

WHAT IS TO BE DONE?

If the United States is to broaden cooperation, there is one basic and urgent task—the teaching of Russian. Meaningful student exchanges and people-to-people programs require ability to communicate directly in Russian rather than through interpreters. The place to start is the schools.

In 1986–1987, only 10,000 Americans were enrolled in precollege study of Russian, and only 2,100 were beyond the second-year level.[9] In Soviet schools, by contrast, English is studied by millions of students and there are special schools where English is the language of instruction.

For college students, statistics are little better. In 1986–1987, only 7.8 percent of U.S. college students were studying a foreign language, and only 33,961 were studying Russian, which was fifth in enrollment beyond Spanish, French, German, and Italian.[10]

It makes little sense to talk about large-scale student exchanges if the Americans do not speak Russian. Years are required to develop fluency, and the earlier study starts, the easier it is and the sooner the United States will have people for future cooperative efforts. Language skills are a basic requirement for communication and mutual understanding. Without them, we will merely be exchanging people to look, see, and tell, as in earlier years.

WHO WINS?

Who wins, Americans or the Soviets? The question is asked by those who regard U.S.-Soviet encounters as competitions in which points are scored and tallied, and one side or the other must win.

Tallying the score in academic and cultural exchanges is difficult on several counts. Objectives of the two governments are markedly different. They are long range, moreover, and results are not easily measured over the short term, especially since Americans cannot conduct polls in the Soviet Union. Nevertheless, there is sufficient experience to assess some results.

Winston Churchill in 1939 described Russia as a riddle, wrapped in a mystery, inside an enigma. Thanks to increased knowledge derived from 30 years of academic and cultural cooperation, Churchill's eloquent remark is no longer valid. In each country there is now a considerable body of experts who have spent time in the other country. They have met with counterparts, seen how they work and live, speak the language, and have a good understanding of attitudes toward their own country and the world.

Almost every U.S. university and college with a Soviet studies program has faculty members who have studied in the Soviet Union. They have a knowledge of Soviet society—its strengths and weaknesses—that comes from having lived there, and they are able to separate fact from fiction. Under their tutelage a new generation of Americans will have a more accurate and realistic understanding of the Soviet Union. American studies in the Soviet Union are not so widespread, but there are scholarly centers where, due to academic exchange, there is a more realistic understanding of the United States. At Moscow State, for example, there is an American studies program where a U.S. Fulbright lecturer in American history has been in residence each year since 1973, helping to train future Soviet Americanists. The Americans report that they lecture to Soviet students as they would to U.S. students. In the 1986–1987 academic year, there were 13 Fulbright lecturers at Soviet universities in a variety of disciplines.

In neither country is there assurance that expertise will reach top decision makers, but it is there for those wise enough to draw on it. In the United States, alumni of IREX, Fulbright, and other exchanges are found in the executive and legislative branches of government; in the arts, humanities, and social sciences; in natural and technical sciences; in business; in law; in state and local government; and in the media. In the Soviet Union, former exchange participants are in universities, the research institutes of the Soviet Academy, and all levels of government, as well as among top economic and political advisers to General Secretary Gorbachev. Their firsthand knowledge of the United States provides Soviet leaders with a basis for making better-informed decisions.

A new Soviet leadership has come to power in the 1980s. Better educated, it has traveled abroad and has a better understanding of other countries than previous leaders had. Exchanges have played no small part in this. For example, Politburo member Aleksandr Yakovlev was an exchange student at Columbia University in 1959 and ambassador to Canada from 1973 to 1983. Although he is no friend of the United States, Yakovlev has a better understanding of it than any other Soviet leader except perhaps former ambassador to Washington Anatoly Dobrynin.

As IREX Executive Director Allen H. Kassof puts it:

... looking through the window of scholarly exchanges, it is hard to avoid the conclusion that the old rules are bending, that patterns entrenched for many decades may at last be eroding, and that years of contacts [with the United States] are finally leaving their marks.[11]

Gorbachev's *glasnost* (believed to be Yakovlev's idea) and his relaxation of controls over creative arts, publishing, and the media are in part a result of exchanges with the West. For 30 years an entire generation of scientists, writers, journalists, motion picture and theater directors, and other cultural figures has traveled to the West. They have seen the creative freedoms enjoyed by their Western colleagues and have made the inevitable comparisons. When Gorbachev found that he needed the support of this creative intelligentsia in order to sell his *perestroika* (restructuring) of the Soviet economy to an entrenched bureaucracy and the Soviet public, he was able to offer the intelligentsia, in return, some of the freedoms they had witnessed in the West.

Gorbachev himself is the beneficiary of what might be called an exchange visit. Soviet Ambassador to Washington Yuri Dubinin, himself one of the first Soviet students to study in France in 1958, relates how Gorbachev and his wife Raisa, after an official visit to Paris in the 1970s, rented a car and drove unescorted as tourists around France, a country with a strong central government like the Soviet Union, but a nation of individualists and democratic traditions. They undoubtedly saw their own country in a different light after their return home.

Whoever is elected U.S. president in 1988 will most likely have visited the Soviet Union. The new president will not have driven around unescorted but will have had long talks with high Soviet officials and gained a better understanding of the issues they, and we, face. A brief visit does not make an expert, but it does make it easier to understand the divisions between the two countries that cultural cooperation attempts to bridge.

Exchanges with the Soviet Union, begun as an elite program, are now open to a broad range of citizens. To U.S. participants they provide access to the outside world as well as to the Soviet Union. They increase understanding of international relations, where Americans in general have much to learn, and they produce an increasing pool of U.S. speakers of Russian, who are vital to expanding U.S.-Soviet relations.

The quest for peace, an issue of prime importance to Americans, Soviets, and all peoples of the world, is furthered by exchanges. As President Eisenhower said when he initiated the People-to-People program in 1956:

If we are going to take advantage of the assumption that all people want peace, then the problem is for people to get together and leap governments—to work out not one, but thousands of methods by which people can gradually learn a bit more of each other.[12]

Twenty-nine years later, the message from another president, Ronald Reagan, was the same. In his address to the Congress on November 21, 1985, after the Geneva summit, Reagan reported:

... we discussed the barriers to communication between our societies, and I elaborated on my proposals for real people-to-people contacts on a wide scale. Americans should know the people of the Soviet Union—their hopes and fears and the facts of their lives. And citizens of the Soviet Union need to know of America's deep desire for peace and our unwavering attachment to freedom.[13]

Americans should have no illusions that people-to-people contacts will bring about rapid changes in the Soviet Union, where change comes slowly. Academic and cultural cooperation, however, can be a catalyst for change, if sustained over the years with patience and persistence, when relations are *not* good as well as when they *are* good.

NOTES

1. For a detailed account of the origins of U.S.-Soviet academic and cultural exchanges, see J. D. Parks, *Culture, Conflict and Coexistence: American-Soviet Cultural Relations, 1917–1958* (Jefferson, N.C., and London: McFarland, 1983).

2. *New York Times,* November 15, 1955, p. 1.

3. *United States Treaties and Other International Agreements* [hereafter TIAS], 3975, vol. 9 (Washington, D.C.: U.S. Government Printing Office, 1958), pp. 13–39.

4. TIAS, 4362, vol. 10, pt. 2 (1959), pp. 1934–1977.

5. *Weekly Compilation of Presidential Documents* 21, no. 47 (Washington, D.C.: Office of the Federal Register, 1985), p. 1424.

6. *Open Doors: 1985/1986, Report on International Educational Exchange* (New York: Institute of International Education, 1986).

7. James H. Billington, "American Foreign Policy and the New Isolationism," in Richard F. Staar (ed.), *Public Diplomacy: USA Versus USSR* (Stanford, Calif.: Hoover Institution Press, 1982), p. 10.

8. *Scientific Communication and National Security* (Washington, D.C.: National Academy Press, 1982), p. 140.

9. See *Russian Language Survey, 1986/1987* (Wallingford, Conn.: Russian Studies Center, Choate Rosemary Hall, 1987).

10. These statistics were provided by the Modern Language Association, New York.

11. *International Research and Exchanges Board Annual Report, 1985–1986* (Princeton: International Research and Exchanges Board, 1987), p. 7.

12. Dwight D. Eisenhower, *Waging Peace, 1956–1961, the White House Years* (New York: Doubleday, 1965), p. 411.

13. *Weekly Compilation* 21, no. 47 (1985), p. 1428.

FOR FURTHER READING

Comstock, Craig (ed.). *Global Partners: Citizen Exchange with the Soviet Union.* Lafayette, Calif. Ark Communications Institute, 1987.

English, Robert D., and Jonathan J. Halperin. *The Other Side: How Soviets and Americans Perceive Each Other.* Washington, D.C.: The Committee for National Security, 1987.

Newsom, David D. *Private Diplomacy with the Soviet Union.* Lanham, Md.: University Press of America and Georgetown University, Institute for the Study of Diplomacy, 1987.

Richmond, Yale. *U.S.-Soviet Cultural Exchanges, 1958–1986: Who Wins?* Boulder, Colo.: Westview Press, 1988.

Richmond, Yale (ed.). *Hosting Soviet Visitors: A Handbook.* Washington, D.C.: Delphi Press, 1988.

Surviving Together: A Journal on Soviet-American Relations. Washington, D.C.: Institute for Soviet-American Relations, published triannually.

Warner, Gale and Michael Shuman. *Citizen Diplomats: Pathfinders in Soviet-American Relations—and How You Can Join Them.* New York: Continuum Press, 1987.

3

U.S.-SOVIET COOPERATIVE DIPLOMACY: THE CASE OF ANTARCTICA

Christopher C. Joyner

Since World War II, the United States and the Soviet Union have enjoyed an impressive diplomatic relationship in dealing with Antarctic matters. Though little noticed in the mainstream of international politics, their cooperative effort has been markably successful in resolving a mix of issues affecting the political, legal, economic, and environmental status of the continent and the use of its circumpolar waters.

This chapter examines, first, the historical background and genesis of the 1959 Antarctic Treaty; second, its practical applications and influences on relations in the area; third, the national interests of each power in contemporary Antarctic affairs. Finally, an assessment is made of current joint superpower interests, motives for cooperation, and the price of future conflict.

HISTORICAL BACKGROUND

The political history of Antarctica is notably brief. Even so, it has been extraordinarily complicated by the remoteness of the region, the harshness of its physical environment, and the problematical claims by seven states of national sovereignty, not legally recognized by the rest of the international community.

It is interesting to note that prior to this century, both the United States and the Soviet Union made allegations that their nationals discovered Antarctica. The United States maintains that in late 1820,

Nathaniel Palmer, captain of the sealing vessel *Hero,* was first to sight the mainland when he discovered the extensive peninsula protruding north from the continent. Likewise, the Soviets assert that Admiral F. Bellingshausen, commanding two ships of the Russian Imperial Navy, deserves that honor because on January 27, 1821, he reported sighting a vast "ice field," which, one could argue, may have been the Antarctic mainland. Though this controversy remains unresolved—and is further complicated by a British discovery claim as well—the Soviets are quick to use Bellingshausen's voyages around the Southern Ocean as support and justification for their historical interest and presumed priority in Antarctic affairs.[1]

Sovereignty claims to the frozen continent have confounded its political and legal status throughout this century. In 1908, the United Kingdom issued letters patent declaring that it claimed sovereign rights over certain territory in Antarctica. Claims were subsequently posited by New Zealand in 1923, France in 1924, Australia in 1933, Norway in 1939, Chile in 1940, and Argentina in 1943. Political and legal complexities were compounded during the 1940s and 1950s. First, legal rationales for claims were open to serious challenge and therefore were regarded by nonclaimant governments as suspect. Second, no state in the international community—including the United States and the Soviet Union—recognized their legal validity or any purported attendant rights of sovereignty. Third, as indicated by Figure 3.1, three claims—those by the United Kingdom, Argentina, and Chile—overlapped substantially throughout the Antarctic Peninsula region, thus further eroding each claim's legitimacy. Each factor contained the potential for exacerbating legal ambiguities and diplomatic tensions over the status of the continent. Curiously, neither the United States nor the Soviet Union asserted a claim to Antarctica, although both governments reserved the right to do so on the basis of discovery and substantial past involvement in the region.[2]

Between 1928 and 1948, the United States assumed a prominent, if not dominant, role in Antarctic exploration. Major U.S. expeditions were undertaken by Richard E. Byrd in 1928–1930, 1933–1935, 1939–1941, and 1946–1947, and Lincoln Ellsworth led four U.S. expeditions between 1933 and 1937. During the summer of 1946–1947, the United States sponsored Operation High Jump, the most massive sea and air exploratory expedition ever attempted in Antarctica. Thirteen ships, 25 aircraft, and some 4,000 persons were involved. Though not directly related, concurrent with Operation High Jump was another U.S. expedition led by Finn Ronne during 1946–1948. During this 20-year period, the Soviet government remained wholly aloof from scientific and exploratory matters in the region.

By the late 1940s, U.S. concern mounted over the Soviet Union's

Figure 3.1
Antarctica: Claims and Jurisdictions in the Southern Ocean

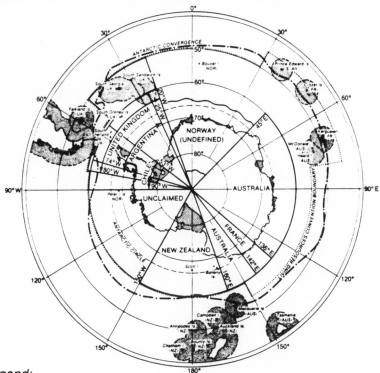

Legend:

▨ 200 Nautical Mile Zones

▨ Ice Shelves

Antarctica is claimed by seven states, although no other state recognizes
the legitimacy of those claims. One-fifth of the continent remains
unclaimed. Australia's sector is divided by the French claim, and
Norway's claim has no defined terminal demarcations. The claims by
Chile, Argentina, and the United Kingdom substantially overlap in the
Antarctic Peninsula region.

The area covered by the Antarctic Treaty extends to 60° south latitude (solid
line). The Living Resources Convention applies to the area inside the
Antarctic Convergence as defined in Article I (dotted line), which
corresponds to the area of the natural Antarctic Convergence (dot-dash
line). The 200-nautical-mile zones extending seaward from islands and
South America (dotted areas) indicate states' declared fishing or economic
jurisdictions.

Source: © Christopher C. Joyner, Woods Hole Oceanographic Institution, 1987.

emerging interest. Prompted by the escalating Cold War, the United States had become wary about Soviet aspirations—not only their desires to exert more influence in international affairs generally, but also the possibility that Antarctica might be of geostrategic importance. U.S. policy came to embrace the two objectives of ensuring that "no occasion should be given to the Soviet Union to participate in an Antarctic settlement or administration" and of "forestall[ing] any Soviet attempt to become a territorial claimant" on the continent. This latter concern of the United States was plain: "[T]here is nothing to prevent the Russians from sending an expedition to the unclaimed sector of the Antarctic continent between 90° and 150° west longitude, establishing a permanent base there, conducting explorations and laying official claim to territory on the basis of these activities."[3] No doubt any such Soviet action would have been particularly upsetting for the U.S. government, since the "unclaimed sector" was the precise region on the continent where the United States had conducted most of its activities during the 1930s and 1940s, and it would have been the most logical site for a possible future U.S. claim.

U.S. policy toward Antarctica was officially set forth in a paper issued on June 9, 1948, by the Policy Planning Staff of the Joint Chiefs of Staff.[4] Designated PPS–31, it represented the first policy statement made by the U.S. government on Antarctica, and its core features contained much of the substance that later came to comprise a treaty.

PPS–31 was designed to dispense with the sovereignty issue, reserve the continent for scientific purposes, and protect U.S. national interests. Three issues were dominant. First, on the territorial issue, PPS–31 espoused the nonclaims principle (that is, the United States recognized no claim and made none, but reserved the right to do so at a later date). The paper acknowledged that claims disputes existed among the United Kingdom, Chile, and Argentina; noted that the Rio Treaty was a new consideration in those disputes; and posited that Antarctica was not a vital concern for U.S. national security. The second issue, pertaining to economics and resources, was marked by negative conclusions due mainly to environmental obstacles and logistical liabilities because of a massive ice cap superimposed over possible subglacial mineral wealth. In whaling, factory ships were being used, a procedure that largely obviated the need for any bases on the continental shore. Third, PPS–31 addressed the strategic issue. While control of the Antarctic was not critical to U.S. interests, denying access to the continent and circumpolar islands to adversaries—particularly the Soviet Union—was. The United States was especially concerned that the Soviet Union might set up camps in the unclaimed portion of the continent, where the United States had established the firmest basis for legal rights to assert a future claim.

PPS–31 also proffered recommendations in the form of a draft treaty. Perhaps most intriguing, the paper proposed that Antarctica be placed under United Nations auspices as a special trusteeship territory. The United States would then exercise its right of claim, and all eight claimant states would form a joint administrative authority over the continent. The claims conundrum would thus be resolved, not by renunciation but by merger into a condominium arrangement. This U.N. trusteeship scheme, however, was forthrightly rejected by the claimants, and U.S. concerns became even further exacerbated by a pointed shift in Soviet policy. In 1950, the Soviets, as outsiders, sent a diplomatic note to the United States and six other claimants—Chile was excluded—demanding that the Soviet Union be included in any resolution of the Antarctic situation.[5]

During the Korean War, the anti-Soviet theme appeared fixed as a core strand in U.S. Antarctic policy. Throughout the early 1950s, the United States and Soviet Union increasingly turned their geopolitical attentions toward the poles. It appeared that East-West rivalry, with its inherent tensions, might come to generate Cold War politics in Antarctica, a development that would have complicated the already tedious geopolitical problems over sovereignty and overlapping claims. Even more ominous, it was believed that U.S.-Soviet rivalry in the Antarctic might precipitate an arms race, leading to testing and implanting nuclear weapons on the continent.

By the mid–1950s, U.S. policy had softened, as the opportunity for Soviet involvement in Antarctic matters was opened through a scientific door. The Comité Spécial de l'Année Géophysique Internationale, created by the International Council of Scientific Unions to manage the details of a "Third Polar Year," broadened its scope in 1955 to encompass the entire world and renamed its program the International Geophysical Year (IGY). In the July plenary meeting for planning the IGY, participants drew up a gentleman's agreement not to engage in political or legal argumentation during the IGY, in order that scientific progress might proceed unimpeded. Among the delegations intending to participate in the IGY and attending the Paris planning session was the Soviet Union. This occasion marked the Soviet Union's first formal international involvement in Antarctic affairs. The Soviets were persuaded to accept the geomagnetic South Pole (called the Pole of Inaccessibility because of its harsh, remote location) as the site for one of their IGY bases.[6]

In preparation for the IGY, the Soviets in 1956 established Mirnyy, their first base in Antarctica, on the coast of the Australian sector claim. By February 1957, the Australians had grown acutely sensitive about Soviet geopolitical intentions. Speculation suggested that following the IGY, Mirnyy might be transformed into a submarine base, which could pose a threat to Australia's territorial interests, as well as to shipping lanes in the Indian Ocean.[7] Yet, firm Soviet determination to participate made it difficult to exclude them. The linkage of science and politics in the IGY had permitted their entrance through the opening afforded by science.

During the IGY, July 1, 1957 to December 31, 1958, Antarctica was treated as a scientific laboratory. Twelve governments—Argentina, Australia, Belgium, Chile, France, Japan, New Zealand, Norway, South Africa, the Soviet Union, the United Kingdom, and the United States—and some 5,000 scientists and support personnel working at 55 base locations were officially involved. Scientists were permitted to manage affairs with a minimal degree of governmental interference, in effect settling issues among themselves. This was a new notion in Antarctic diplomacy, one that proved both managerially and politically successful.[8]

More broadly, the IGY set the stage for international cooperation in scientific research and world peace. There evolved an understanding that governments should put aside their differences regarding the legal status of Antarctica and agree to the principle of free access for everyone to the entire continent for purposes of scientific inquiry. This mindset helped to realize a special international treaty to regulate international activities.

Soviet participation in the IGY was principally motivated by scientific interests and opportunities for cooperative research with Western scientists. In the course of those activities, the Soviet Union established an impressive continental presence and constructed 6 of the 40 main research stations used by visiting scientists. Through the IGY the Soviets gained a respected scientific standing in the Antarctic and secured a recognized political role in administering the region. One expert commentator concluded, ";[T]he Soviet Union's entry into Antarctic politics and consolidation of its presence on the continent were the most significant aspects of the IGY."[9]

It was the launch of Sputnik on October 4, 1957, that probably supplied the strongest motivation for the United States to call for post-IGY conference negotiations. Sputnik demonstrably underscored for all claimants the Soviet Union's technological ability to launch missiles over intercontinental distances and the threatening implications—particularly for Latin American states—if the Soviet Union were to deploy them in the Antarctic. The idea of a treaty to stave off Soviet moves in that direction took on serious appeal.

DIPLOMACY

Cooperation between the United States and the Soviet Union in Antarctic matters came neither easily nor quickly. It evolved over three decades of mutual dealings, including tortuous negotiations and eventual promulgation of the Antarctic Treaty in 1959.[10]

On May 2, 1958, the United States issued letters of invitation to the 11 other Antarctic IGY governments for preparatory talks aimed at negotiating a treaty. All accepted. From June 1958 through early 1959, representatives of the 12 governments met once or twice weekly at the National Acadamy of Sciences in Washington, D.C. A formal negotiating conference was convened from October through November in Washington, and the final document was signed there on December 1, 1959. Protracted discussions during preparatory sessions revealed much about U.S.-Soviet policy positions, their difficult negotiations, and the manner in which diplomatic cooperation was forged.

The first meeting of the delegates convened on June 13, 1958, under the chairmanship of Paul C. Daniels, head of the U.S. delegation. As Ambassador Daniels later recalled, these preparatory meetings were held "in the strictest of secrecy, to avoid the disadvantages which would ensue if the controversial subjects under discussion were to be debated publicly by the news media and the politicians in various countries."[11] The chairmanship of the meetings rotated in alphabetical order to foster a sense of joint participation. Similarly, working papers on treaty proposals were drafted as joint multilateral documents in order to preserve the sense of concerted diplomacy and cohesiveness.

Strong divergent opinions arose over the extent to which preliminary discussions should clarify fundamental treaty principles. The United States and the majority of the other states endorsed a two-pronged strategy whereby polemical points would be identified for negotiation and satisfactory wording fashioned for points on which there was substantial agreement. Ambassador Daniels favored not only drafting agendas for preparatory talks and the conference, but also the preparation of a draft treaty, thus permitting the preliminary conversations to make a rich, constructive contribution toward producing a treaty. The Soviet delegation took strong exception. Andrei Ledovski, head of the Soviet group, maintained that talks should be concerned only with procedural issues—time, place and procedures for formal conference proceedings. The Soviet delegation, in short, favored general discussions on conference procedure, not substantive resolution of worrisome critical issues. At the very outset, Soviet suspicion and distrust surfaced over U.S. intentions in calling the conference.[12]

In discussing location and date, preferences were mixed. Australia, Belgium, Chile, Japan, South Africa, and the United Kingdom favored Washington, D.C., where their embassies could readily accommodate staffing needs; New Zealand, Norway, and the United States leaned more toward Paris; and the Soviet Union suggested Geneva with its United Nations facilities. Washington was eventually agreed upon.

The question of participation also prompted divergent opinions. All delegations, except the Soviet, favored a treaty negotiated only by the 12 governments active in the Antarctic phase of the IGY and invited to the preparatory talks. The Soviet delegation argued for a conference of all interested countries. The Soviets contended that an exclusive number of governments should not decide the future of Antarctica, a region where all humanity shared common interests. In the end, it was decided that the 12 participating governments would negotiate a treaty representing and serving the interests of all states.

In voting, the Soviets favored unanimity; the United States and the other delegations preferred majority rule. The Soviet position was accepted on practical political grounds: policies would function more effectively if approved by the entire treaty membership. The principle of unanimity was thus adopted as the core of treaty unity and efficacy. It would have been difficult to square the Soviet position for unanimity with its early insistence upon universal participation because the greater the number of governments, the more difficult it would have been to achieve consensus and the more encumbered the policymaking process would have become. In any event, consensus decision making in the Antarctic Treaty system remains a fundamental institutional contribution made by the Soviet Union.[13]

Substantive issues also came into play during preliminary informal meetings, notwithstanding Soviet protestations. Regarding the jurisdictional ambit of the treaty, Chile proposed that 60° south latitude should be set as the uniform northernmost reach. The Soviet delegation proposed instead that the Antarctic Convergence, the biological boundary of the antarctic, should be adopted as the treaty boundary. In fairness to the Soviet proposal, the convergence is a more scientific demarcation of the northern parameters of the antarctic, both in oceanography and in marine biology. The chief problem with the convergence, as shown in Figure 3.1, is that it meanders around the Southern Ocean, varying at points from 65° to 45° south latitude. Lack of consistency could have posed legal difficulties in administering the treaty. Eventually, the Soviets were convinced that the 60° jurisdictional boundary was the more practical of the two options.

Disagreement between the U.S. and Soviet delegations also arose over how to handle the issue of sovereignty. The United States favored shelving legal claims in order to make progress on other issues. A formula was presented with three criteria:

Nothing in the treaty should be interpreted as depriving a party of a claim or basis thereof secured through its activities or those of its nationals, nothing was to be interpreted as a recognition of any claims, and the legal status quo was to be preserved for the life of the treaty and could be affected by acts performed during this period.[14]

This proposal for the claims freeze was a modus vivendi, and did not furnish a permanent solution to the sovereignty conundrum.

The Soviet delegation rejected the suggestion that such a freeze be agreed to at preliminary meetings. They objected to working group sessions being used to settle questions of territorial sovereignty; in their opinion, this was a crucial, complex legal issue more properly reserved for the major diplomatic conference, not informal discussions for preparatory sessions.

On November 18, 1958, U.S. Ambassador Daniels submitted drafts of 12 articles that subsequently became the essence of the agreement. The Soviet delegation, however, persisted in its refusal to discuss these substantive matters until well into April 1959; then, for some reason still unknown, they adopted a more conciliatory tack. This shift in Soviet attitude toward the preliminary talks expedited the preparation of working documents for an Antarctic Treaty conference, which convened in October 1959 in Washington.

The lessons for U.S.-Soviet cooperation to be drawn from early treaty negotiations must be viewed cautiously, because the full record has not yet been made public. Most of the information about the preliminary negotiations is derived from personal papers and recollections and memoirs of the principals. Attitudes, opinions, and perceptions vary in degree, content, and scope. Nevertheless, a persistent common theme is that of Soviet intransigence on negotiating substantive issues, intransigence that at times assumed an obstructionist, even antagonistic, tone. Given the political climate of the times, this attitude can be explained by a Cold War mind-set. Of 12 participants in treaty negotiations, the Soviets stood alone in their ideological aspirations, governmental structure, and economic system. No other Eastern bloc member was participating. Suspicion, mistrust, and perhaps even paranoia may have skewed Soviet perceptions concerning the true motivations of the United States and West European states.

Nonetheless, during some ten months of preliminary discussions, a sense of unmistakable trust evolved among all the delegations. No less important was the emergence of a common purpose: to fashion an international legal instrument that would serve individual national interests by ensuring that "Antarctica shall continue forever to be used exclusively for peaceful purposes and shall not become the scene or object of international discord."[15] To this end, the United States and the Soviet Union found reason to cooperate as partners in fulfilling the purposes of the treaty. They worked as coarchitects in designing the family of attendant multilateral agreements, promulgated since

1959, to manage resource conservation and regulate environmental protection in the Antarctic.

THE ANTARCTIC TREATY

The eventual success of protracted treaty negotiations hinged largely on the relationship between the U.S. and Soviet governments. It turned out that the relationship was sufficiently strong to yield strikingly impressive provisions, particularly when seen within the broader context of their disagreements since World War II. The treaty is a preclusive agreement, specifically designed to forestall activities that might spawn conflict. It contains features that engender confidence building, including scientific and military cooperation rather than competition; a specifically defined nonmilitarized zone; free access and open inspection of all government facilities; and special provisions for settling disputes.

The Antarctic Treaty, signed on December 1, 1959, entered into force on June 23, 1961, with ratification by all 12 members of the Washington conference. Its provisions, though simple, are still profound. Article I declares that "Antarctica shall be used for peaceful purposes only." Prohibited are military bases and fortifications, military maneuvers, and weapons tests. By prohibiting military activities on or around the continent, the treaty is a model for arms control and furnishes a regime for treating the continent as a nonmilitary zone. The ban on military activities is neatly complemented by Article V, which prohibits nuclear explosions and the disposal of radioactive wastes. The ocean space, land area, and ice formations south of 60° south latitude thus became a nuclear-free zone, thereby distinguishing the treaty as the first international nuclear test-ban agreement. That it pertains to nearly 10 percent of the earth's surface is also very significant.

The treaty was spurred on by the desire for continued scientific cooperation. Article II stresses the principles of freedom of scientific research and investigation. Article III goes on to require that, "to the greatest extent feasible and practicable," all parties should exchange information regarding plans for scientific research, and the results of scientific observations should be "made freely available." Indeed, both the United States and Soviet Union have used these provisions for a broad range of scientific research: the United States, under the auspices of the National Science Foundation; the Soviet Union, under the sponsorship of the Institute for Arctic and Antarctic Research, Leningrad.

There is no reason to suspect that deliberate treaty violations are occurring. Even so, routine inspections serve to promote mutual confidence. Article VII provides for a comprehensive system of open, on-site and aerial inspections to be performed by designated observers with freedom of access at any time to any area on the continent. All stations, installations, equipment, ships, and aircraft are susceptible to spot checks. The United States (as well as New Zealand, Australia, the United Kingdom, and Argentina) has performed such operations periodically since 1961. Although its permanent stations have always been the object of inspection teams, especially those of the United States, the Soviet Union has refrained from conducting inspections of its own.[16]

Critical to the operation of the treaty is a provision that freezes the status quo ante of territorial claims. Article IV provides that no acts should constitute a basis for asserting, supporting, or denying a claim to territorial sovereignty or for creating any rights of territorial sovereignty on the continent. Moreover, this proviso stipulates that no new claims, or enlargement of an existing claim, may be asserted while the treaty remains in effect. Article IV states that nothing contained in the treaty should be interpreted as a renunciation or diminution by any party of previously asserted rights, claims, or basis of claim to territory in the Antarctic. This provision thus allows for claimant states to retain claims, and for nonclaimant states to persist in not recognizing their legitimacy.

Article IV has often been criticized for being legally ambiguous, vague, and unsatisfactory. Nonetheless, it is very comprehensive in the political sense. It balances the complex national interests of claimants and nonclaimants, of the United States and the Soviet Union, and of the larger industrial powers and the smaller, less developed ones. The treaty's creative ambiguity and ability to preserve equilibrium among the conflicting and competitive interests of its various signatories is the preeminent reason for its success.

Since the 1970s, Article IX has proven to be very important in highlighting U.S.-Soviet cooperation by establishing a mechanism for convening periodic consultative meetings. These Antarctic Treaty Consultative Party (ATCP) meetings are attended by the 12 founding members, as well as any other contracting party that has "demonstrate[d] its interest in the Antarctic by conducting substantial scientific activity there, such as the establishment of a scientific station or the dispatch of a scientific expedition."[17] Meetings occur every biennium and function as the treaty's decision-making apparatus.

Treaty policies take the form of recommendations adopted at ATCP meetings. As policy statements, recommendations tend to be formal and inflexible, and enter into force upon unanimous approval by participating governments. In the 13 ATCP meetings convened since 1961, some 160 recommendations have been adopted by consensus, an achievement plainly dependent upon continuous, close, constructive collaboration between the United States and the Soviet Union. Recommendations have addressed meteorology, telecommunications, tourism, postal services, facilitation of scientific research, nongovernmental expeditions, logistics, rescue operations, specially protected areas, historic sites, and, most recently, environmental protection and resource conservation and management. Many valuable ancillary multilateral agreements thus have served to augment and supplement the 1959 accord.

The treaty also contains provisions pertaining to peaceful settlement of disputes. These provisos contain legal incentives for resuming peaceful conditions in the region. Article XI calls upon parties to "consult among themselves with a view to having ... dispute[s] resolved by negotiation, inquiry, mediation, conciliation, arbitration, judicial settlement or other peaceful means of their own choice." Referral to the International Court of Justice is also suggested as an appropriate recourse for resolving disputes. During the 26 years in which the Antarctic Treaty has been in force, no major disagreement requiring any of these settlement recourses has occurred among the parties. That is a record of success that few international arms control agreements can claim.

THE ANTARCTIC TREATY SYSTEM

Continued commitment to the Antarctic Treaty by the United States and Soviet Union rests upon achievements and sustained cooperation, rather than conflict and confrontation. A family of protective measures known collectively as the Antarctic Treaty System has evolved for addressing certain resource-management issues not covered by the treaty power.

The first of these was the Agreed Measures on the Conservation of Antarctic Fauna and Flora, approved as Recommendation III–8 in 1964.[18] This agreement was designed to protect native birds, mammals, and plant life on the continent; to safeguard against the introduction of nonindigenous species; and to prevent water pollution near the coast and ice shelves. In addition, the Agreed Measures were undertaken to preserve the unique character of natural ecological systems. Measures are overseen by the Scientific Committee on Antarctic Research, on which both the United States and the Soviet Union have standing representatives with leading roles.[19]

The Convention on the Conservation of Antarctic Seals was promulgated in 1972 and entered into force in 1978.[20] It seeks to limit the vulnerability and commercial exploitation of six species of seals in order to maintain an optimal level of their populations. Since the early 1970s, sealing in the southern circumpolar waters has radically diminished. The United States and the Soviet Union—two of the most prominent sealing countries—are parties to the Seals Convention, and since the late 1970s both have redirected sealing practices to conform with this convention's purposes.

A third facet of the Antarctic Treaty System is the Convention on the Conservation of Antarctic Marine Living Resources (CCAMLR).[21] The CCAMLR accord, negotiated in 1980 and entered into force in 1982, applies to the region south of 60° south latitude, though it also encompasses certain areas south of the Antarctic Convergence that meander as far north as 45° south latitude. As implied by its name, CCAMLR has as its principal purpose the preservation of all living resources, which include fish, crustaceans (especially krill), creatures on the continental shelf (such as mollusks), and bird life. The fundamental principle underlying the "ecosystemic" conservation approach in CCAMLR is the need to maintain the ecological balance between harvested species and dependent predators. The key to this balance is krill. This two-inch-long, shrimplike crustacean plays an especially important role in the circumpolar marine ecosystem by being the principal link in the Antarctic food chain. It contains the protein equivalent of beefsteak or lobster, and thus may hold great potential for augmenting human foods. The need for conservation grew largely because of the unregulated fishing of krill during the late 1970s, mainly by the Soviet Union. Notwithstanding its major fishing interests in distant waters, the Soviet Union was quick to become a party to the CCAMLR convention (after hard negotiations), as did the United States. The benefits of long-range ecosystemic conservation were deemed to outweigh the gains of immediate krill exploitation.

The latest effort to augment the treaty system is the creation of an Antarctic Minerals Convention completed in June 1988. Although the extent of mineral wealth in the continent is unknown and speculative, having a regime in place would furnish regulatory predictability, should recoverable deposits someday be discovered. Since 1982, the consultative parties were engaged in a series of negotiations aimed at establishing a treaty-based minerals regime. A draft has been the focus of intense discussions and negotiation, and the institutional framework for such a mineral regime is apparent. The special regime is designed to administer and regulate prospecting, exploration, and exploitation of mineral resources on-shore and offshore. Membership will be restricted to the ATCP governments, and special voting modifications in the regime's institutions accommodate interests of the claimant states. Because both the United States and the Soviet Union assumed prominent positive roles in fashioning the consensus process in the minerals regime, a completed convention became available for signature before the end of 1988.[22] There will be no viable minerals treaty without their concurrence, or that of the other ATCPs.

The mineral potential of the Antarctic is wholly speculative. Trace amounts of cobalt, nickel, tin, platinum, copper, and chromium have been found. Also, sizable deposits of iron and low-grade coal are known. No discoveries thus far, however, have suggested that recoverable quantities of petroleum or natural gas might exist in or around the continent. Hence, the real value of Antarctic minerals remains far from certain, especially given the tremendous logistical, climatic, environmental, and financial obstacles that would have to be overcome to permit commercial exploitation. Nevertheless, having a regulatory regime in place will supply a ready institutional framework for managing those activities should minerals development in Antarctica ever become feasible.

MUTUAL NATIONAL INTERESTS

Cooperation between the United States and Soviet Union has been essential for the extensive expansion of the Antarctic Treaty System. Both governments have national interests in the Antarctic, and both have come to realize that much more stands to be gained by working together than by competitive politics. Participation in the Antarctic Treaty regime came about with the recognition by both powers that neither would make a formal claim to Antarctica, though each would continue to reserve the right to do so. Both also decided to press for unimpeded scientific opportunities, as well as the creation of the Antarctic as a zone of peace, a region nonmilitarized, nonnuclearized, and subject to unannounced on-site inspection. Both came to accept the premise that the treaty would be a limited-purpose agreement, dedicated to scientific investigation and the maintenance of the Antarctic for exclusively peaceful purposes. Special consultative machinery was invented to deal with problems not envisioned when the parties began deliberations.

Simultaneous involvement of Americans and Soviets in Antarctic matters has produced a catalog of mutual national interests. First and foremost, there are political and security interests. Both superpowers have found it valuable to reserve the Antarctic exclusively for peaceful purposes; to ensure that it is free of international discord; to continue a peaceful and constructive relationship with all states active in the region; and to keep the continent unmilitarized and nuclear-free. That no violation of treaty provisions has ever been reported strongly suggests that both governments have succeeded in keeping these policies on course. The ecosystem of both the continent and its surrounding ocean has survived. Fostering freedom of scientific research and the exchange of scientific personnel and data have been positive accomplishments. Natural resources in the Antarctic have been conserved. At the same time, both governments—especially the Soviet Union—

are keen on preserving access for their nationals to exploit living marine resources and minerals. They have made it clear during negotiations that ensuring nondiscriminatory access for their miners to all areas where mineral extraction may one day be environmentally permissible stands as priority policy.[23]

The United States and the Soviet Union have parallel and, indeed, symbiotic interests in sustaining the viability of the Antarctic Treaty System, thus allowing for easier agreement. The critical consideration is how their delegations to ATCP meetings can best understand and productively reinforce each other. The treaty is a framework for promoting opportunities and improving working relationships. Of great significance is the recognition that policies and influence are oriented more toward regional activities than toward the promotion of ideological objectives. Although the United States and the Soviet Union have starkly different political and economic systems, producing disparate approaches to foreign policy issues, Antarctic diplomacy has largely superseded the polemics and ideological predispositions that proved to be such stubborn obstacles for so many aspects of their relations. More constructive and substantive objectives in Antarctic policy have been pragmatically pursued, instead of quibbles over procedural or ideological problems. In sum, the Antarctic Treaty System has promoted a temperate diplomatic atmosphere between the superpowers; for the most part, it has moderated disagreement and sources of tension.

SCIENTIFIC BENEFITS

Antarctica presents a unique laboratory setting for scientists. Its remarkably pristine quality and remoteness from civilization make the ice-clad continent an ideal place from which to monitor critical global environmental variables. Scientists there have been especially interested in glaciology, geology, volcanology, meteorology, biology, astrophysics, and geomagnetics.

Nearly every year since 1961, the United States and the Soviet Union have exchanged scientists who winter over at each other's research stations.[24] Scientists work with counterparts in conducting experiments and research on a wide variety of subjects. There have been joint medical studies concerning the physiological adaption to isolation and climate; the petrology of geological formations; glaciology; geologic mapping; geochemical sampling; magnetic and radiometric surveys; and the hydrology of freshwater lakes. In the process, exchange scientists serve as ambassadors of goodwill and better understanding. They personify the benefits to be gained from cooperation in Antarctic affairs.

Polar-oriented government agencies and scientific communities of

Figure 3.2
United States and Soviet Stations in Antarctica

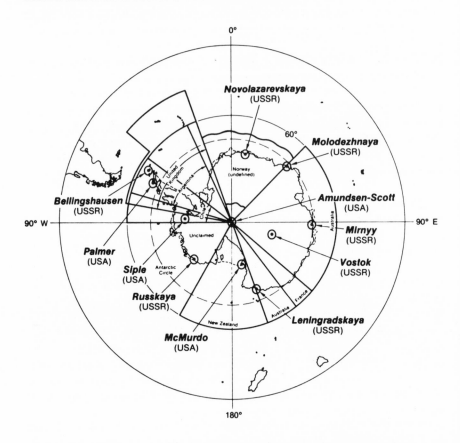

Source: © Christopher C. Joyner, Woods Hole Oceanographic Institution, 1987.

both countries engage in a broad program of information exchange. The Division of Polar Programs of the National Science Foundation sends to the Soviet Union's All-Union Research Institute of Hydro-meteorological Information scholarly U.S. publications, including the *Antarctic Journal of the United States,* the *Antarctic Bibliography, Current Antarctic Literature,* and the *Antarctic Research Series.* In exchange, the NSF receives the *Proceedings of the Arctic and Antarctic Research Institute,* the *Soviet Antarctic Expedition Bulletin,* and *Antarctica Commission Reports.*[25] Such information sharing not only enhances scientific knowledge about Antarctica for both scientific communities; it also fosters goodwill and strengthens the cooperative relationship between the two governments, particularly since much of the scientific effort and interest in Antarctica are generated by national government agencies.

A number of joint research activities have been organized on a large scale. During 1975–1978, a series of cooperative studies investigated the Southern Ocean. The first full-scale exercise of the Soviet Union's Polar Experiment (POLEX) in the South Polar region was conducted in the Drake Passage during December 1974–February 1975 on board the *Professor Zubov.* The purpose of this collaborative investigation was to study the structure and dynamics of the Antarctic Circumpolar Current for indicators of atmospheric-oceanic interaction. Scientists in POLEX South–75 studied the spatial variability of water circulation, time variability of currents, the structure and dynamics of the Polar Front Zone, and the processes of air-sea interaction—useful information for hydrometeorologists interested in the Southern Ocean.[26]

The success of this joint effort led to a 1975 planning session of the Soviet-American Commission on Collaboration in the Southern Ocean and its decision to combine efforts for further investigation. In 1976 a joint expedition performed experiments in the Drake Passage and the eastern Bellingshausen Sea. During the austral summer of 1977–1978, a full-scale U.S.-Soviet team sponsored by POLEX South–78 traveled to the Southern Ocean and monitored hydrological phenomena in the Scotia Sea and Drake Passage.[27]

Similarly, during October–November 1981, a joint scientific expedition was organized to investigate the Weddell Polynya under winter conditions. The Weddell Polynya is an ice-free region of some 250,000 square kilometers in the frozen Weddell Sea. Scientists were uncertain of the geophysical causes and circumstances that allowed such a vast opening to occur in an otherwise ice-covered ocean area. Plans for the expedition were developed by a U.S. coordinator (A. L. Gordon) and the national coordinator for the Soviet Union's POLEX-South program (E. I. Sarukhanyan) during June 1980 in Leningrad. Scientific and logistical details were worked out in February and April 1981 at the Lamont-Doherty Geological Observatory of Columbia University.

The expedition's principal objective was to penetrate as far as possible into the Weddell Sea during maximum ice cover in order to obtain data on physical, chemical, and biological processes relating to oceanographic, sea ice, and atmospheric conditions in and around the polynya. The vessel for the expedition, the *Mikhail Somov,* was supplied by the Arctic and Antarctic Research Institute of Leningrad; the United States furnished most of the instrumentation, including computers, autoanalyzers, and other specialized measurement devices. Twenty-six scientists participated, 13 from each country, in integrated teams to conduct joint experiments in physical oceanography, atmospheric physics, and marine biology. These concerted efforts have been widely praised, not only for their scientific results but also for the genuine cooperation evinced between Soviet and U.S. scientists.[28]

An incident in late 1978 further substantiates U.S.-Soviet cooperation in the Antarctic. In November 1978, a Soviet plane crashed while attempting to land at the base in Molodezhnaya. Three people were killed and 19 injured, necessitating a call for medical assistance. The United States was the first to respond, dispatching a Hercules transport plane from McMurdo station, some 1,800 miles away. The rescue mission flew five seriously injured Soviets to a medical facility in Dunedin, New Zealand, a truly remarkable evacuation covering some 5,600 miles, a record in the annals of transcontinental rescues. It was, as chronicled by the U.S. Navy in an official report, a "rescue mission [which] attested to the spirit of international cooperation in antarctic exploration."[29] More than this, it exemplified the humanitarian extent of U.S.-Soviet cooperation in the region.

Yet another joint project has focused on an investigation of the ozone hole in the atmosphere above Antarctica. The joint ozone study is part of a ten-year program, the progress of which has vacillated according to the status of bilateral relations. While this project is not a specific outgrowth of the Antarctic Treaty mechanism, it is fair to say that cooperative relations between the superpowers in the region since 1959 certainly have contributed to the project's feasibility. A monitoring and research program was agreed to in June 1987 under the auspices of Working Group VIII of the U.S.-Soviet Bilateral Agreement on the Protection of the Environment. The agreement calls for the United States to supply the Soviets with up to 50 small instrument packages (balloons and oxone sondes for ozone measurements), worth about $30,000. After being assembled at the Soviet Antarctic base of Novolazarevskaya, the packages will be launched aboard weather balloons from another permanent Soviet station at Molodezhnaya.

The ozone hole, amounting to a depletion of 35–50 percent of normal ozone levels, was first noticed in 1985 and appears to develop each September and October, the spring season in the Southern Hemisphere. The U.S.-Soviet study intends to produce detailed profiles of ozone readings slated to be interpreted simultaneously with U.S. satellite observations, thus providing a continent-wide view of the phenomenon's occurrence. The joint ozone study illustrates how diplomacy and science interact so closely in Antarctic affairs, and how success in one area can facilitate cooperation in the other.[30] As a case in point, U.S.-Soviet cooperation on the ozone issue carried over to promulgation in September 1987 of an international treaty specifically aimed at protecting the stratospheric ozone layer from destructive chemicals. The agreement, when ratified, will reduce by as much as one half the world's consumption of chlorofluorocarbons, the primary chemical agent believed responsible for eroding the ozone layer that shields Earth from harmful ultraviolet rays. The United States and the Soviet Union were active participants in the successful negotiation of this treaty. By January 1, 1988, both superpowers were signatories to the agreement.

THE BALANCE SHEET

Diplomatic and scientific cooperation continues to characterize the relations between the United States and the Soviet Union in Antarctic matters. The fulcrum on which cooperative enterprises turn is the Antarctic Treaty, an agreement that has mollified political concern about Soviet presence on the continent and has channeled earlier rivalries in the region toward more constructive activities, particularly those in scientific research. As the scope of the treaty has broadened, so has U.S.-Soviet cooperation, from science, arms control, and environmental management to more extensive resource exploration.

Over the past quarter-century the treaty has resolved long-standing dilemmas. It has removed the question of whether either superpower would make a claim to part of the Antarctic continent; it has made scientific exchange and cooperation the mainstay of diplomatic relations; and it has demilitarized and denuclearized the area—one-tenth of Earth's surface—and created confidence and predictability by providing for a unique on-site inspection system to calm anxieties on both sides. The experience has become an exemplar of post-World War II international diplomatic cooperation, especially in multilateral arms control.

The price of future conflict between the United States and the Soviet Union over Antarctica would be politically, scientifically, and environmentally extravagant. Clearly, both governments view such a prospect as undesirable. Not only would conflict unravel the neat tapestry of cooperation woven by the superpowers over three decades; it also might prompt a nationalistic rush to grab resources, without regard for preserving or protecting the region's fragile ecology. Such a scenario would mark a sad end to what thus far has been such a successful, productive U.S.-Soviet relationship in Antarctica.

As political relations between the United States and the Soviet Union improve, it seems natural that cooperative scientific efforts in the Antarctic will grow. More comprehensive research on the ozone problem ranks as a global priority, and further collaboration between the superpowers offers real possibilities for gathering new data more quickly to redress depletion. Opportunities for greater cooperation also lie in joint projects concerning Antarctica's geomagnetism, meteorology, and glaciology, as well as in surface mapping and sea ice studies.

The prospects for future U.S.-Soviet cooperation in Antarctica appear bright. Given the often tense strains in relations on other issues, impressive accommodation between the superpowers in the southern circumpolar region surely should be heralded. For in truth, the Antarctic diplomatic experience clearly ranks as an epic account in the untold story of genuine U.S.-Soviet cooperation during the past 30 years. This special experience must not be lost in analyzing global political events.

NOTES

1. "Question of Antarctica, Study Requested Under General Assembly Resolution 38/77, Report of the Secretary General," pt. 2, "Views of States", vol. 3, U.N. Doc. A/39/583 (pt. 3) (Nov. 9, 1984), pp. 82–83. [Hereafter cited as U.N. Antarctica Study: Views of States.] Regarding the question of credit for discovery of Antarctica, compare E. M. Suzymov, *A Life Given to the Antarctic* (Adelaid, Australia: Libraries Board of South Australia, 1968), translated from Russian by Tina Tupikina-Glaessner, p. 3; and T. Armstrong, "Bellingshausen and the Discovery of Antarctica," *Polar Record* 15 (1971): 888. For an account of the U.S. discovery, see Kenneth J. Bertrand, *Americans in Antarctica, 1775–1948* (New York: American Geographical Society, 1971), pp. 72ff. The British position on discovery of Antarctica is well told in Walter Chapman, *The Loneliest Continent* (Greenwich, Conn: New York Geographical Society, 1964), pp. 37–44.

2. On the merits and circumstances of the claims generally, see F. M. Auburn, *Antarctic Law and Politics* (Bloomington: Indiana University Press, 1981), pp. 23–61. The fundamental official policy adopted by the United States may be summed up thus: "The United States does not recognize any claims to territorial sovereignty in Antarctica and does not assert any claims of its own, although it reserves its basis of claims" (U.N. Antarctic Study: Views of States, p. 101). In responding to the U.S. invitation for an Antarctic treaty, the Soviet note of May 2, 1958, "stressed that the Soviet Union retained for itself all the rights arising from the discoveries and research of Russian navigators and scientists, including the right to lay claim to the corresponding territory in Antarctica." Marjorie M. Whiteman, *Digest of International Law*, vol. 2 (Washington, D.C.: U.S. Government Printing Office, 1963), pp. 1254–1255. See also U.N. Antarctica Study: Views of States, p. 85.

3. "Paper Prepared by the Policy Planning Staff," June 9, 1948, in U.S. Department of State, *Foreign Relations of the United States, 1948*, vol. 1, pt. 2 (Washington, D.C.: Congressional Information Service, 1980), pp. 977–980.

4. Ibid., pp. 977–987.

5. See "Draft Agreement on Antarctica," in ibid., p. 985. The text of the Soviet note is appended to Peter A. Toma, "The Soviet Attitude Toward the Acquisition of Territorial Sovereignty in Antarctica," *American Journal of International Law* 50 (July 1956): 611–626.

6. Walter Sullivan, *Assault on the Unknown: The International Geophysical Year* (New York: McGraw-Hill, 1961), pp. 292–293.

7. See "Russian Base in the Antarctic: Australian Concern," *The Times* (London) , Feb. 7, 1957, p. 7.

8. One commentator has asserted that the success of these "scientists-diplomats" in producing cooperation in Antarctic affairs has had spillover effects in moderating relations of the superpowers in general. See F. Michael Maish, "U.S.-Soviet Exchange Program at Vostok," in Richard S. Lewis and Philip M. Smith (eds.), *Frozen Future: A Prophetic Report from Antarctica* (New York: Quadrangle Books, 1973), p. 349.

9. Auburn, *Antarctic Law and Politics,* p. 89.

10. The Antarctic Treaty, 12 U.S.T. 794, T.I.A.S. no. 4780, 402 U.N.T.S. 71. [Hereafter cited as The Antarctic Treaty.] For representative accounts of the Soviet Union's appreciation of the value of the Antactic Treaty, see Ye. K. Federov, "Antarctica: Experimental Proving Ground for Peaceful Coexistence and International Collaboration," in Lewis and Smith, *Frozen Future,* pp. 64–85; Y. Deperov, "Antarctica: A Zone of Peace and Cooperation," *International Affairs* (Moscow) (November 1983) no. 11:29–37 and O. Khlestov and V. Golitsyn, "The Antarctic: Arena of Peaceful Cooperation," *International Affairs* (Moscow) (1978) no. 8: 61–66.

11. Paul C. Daniels, "The Antarctic Treaty," in Lewis and Smith, *Frozen Future,* pp. 38–39.

12. Peter J. Beck, "Preparatory Meetings for the Antarctic Treaty, 1958–59," *Polar Record* 22 (1985): 653, 656. The essence of Professor Beck's analysis, and hence much of the following discussion, is drawn from the papers of Admiral George Dufek, former Antarctic projects officer of the U.S. Department of Defense. These papers, which are now housed at Syracuse University, supply new insights into the preliminary negotriations that eventuated in the Antarctic Treaty Conference. For the official U.S. view at that time, see U.S. Department of State, *Conference on Antarctica* (Washington, D.C.: U.S. Government Printing Office, 1960).

13. Peter J. Beck, *The International Politics of Antarctica* (Cambridge: Cambridge University Press, 1985), p. 63.

14. Beck, "Preparatory Meetings," pp. 658–659.

15. The Antarctic Treaty, Preamble.

16. The U.S. government believes that inspection rights are "important and precedent-setting provisions," especially given the arms control features of the treaty. Accordingly, the United States has deemed it important to practice periodic exercise of these rights (U.N. Antarctic Study: Views of States, p. 111). Inspections have been carried out by the United States on eight occasions since the treaty entered into force in 1961: in 1964, 1967, 1971, 1975, 1977, 1980, 1983, and 1985. These inspections involved a total of 58 station visits and 2 visits to ship facilities. Of these, at least 12 visits were made to Soviet stations on the continent. Findings of these inspections have been uniformly positive. As generally stated by the U.S. government, "[T]here has been no evidence of any violation of either the provisions or the spirit of the Antarctic Treaty. All of the information gathered during these visits corroborates the fact that Antarctica is being used solely for peaceful purposes." Ibid., p. 113.

17. The Antarctic Treaty, Art. IX, para. 2. Since the treaty entered into force, ten additional states have applied for and been granted consultative party status: Poland in 1977, the Federal Republic of Germany in 1981, Brazil

and India in 1983, the People's Republic of China and Uruguay in 1985, the German Democratic Republic and Italy in 1987, and Spain and Sweden in 1988. All of these new entrants participate as full-fledged members of the ATCP decision-making group.

18. Agreed Measures for the Conservation of Antarctic Flora and Fauna, June 2–13, 1964, 17 U.S.T. 996, 998, T.I.A.S. no. 6058, modified in 24 U.S.T. 1802, T.I.A.S. no. 7692 (1973). For discussion, see Auburn, *Antarctic Law and Politics*, pp. 270–273.

19. Created in 1958 by the International Council of Scientific Unions, the Scientific Committee on Antarctic Research (SCAR) is actually an appendage of ICSU that is charged with continuing the international scientific cooperation in the Antarctic in the aftermath of the IGY. Besides originally formulating the agreed measures, SCAR designed the original sites of special scientific interest and drew up the Code of Conduct for Antarctic Expeditions and Station Activities. SCAR has served the Antarctic Treaty System in various capacities as an advisory agency, especially in fashioning policies affecting telecommunications, logistics and transport, marine living resources, and mineral resources.

20. Convention for the Conservation of Antarctic Seals, June 1, 1972, 27 U.S.T. 441, T.I.A.S. no. 8826, entered into force Mar. 11, 1978.

21. Convention on the Conservation of Antarctic Living Marine Resources, May 20, 1980, 80 Stat. 271, T.I.A.S. no. 10240, entered into force Apr. 7, 1982.

22. The Convention on the Regulation of Antarctic Mineral Resource Activities, done at Wellington June 2, 1988, opened for signature November 25, 1988. Doc. AMR/SCM/88/78 (June 2, 1988), reprinted in *International Legal Materials* 274 (July 1988): 859–900. Various versions of the Antarctic Minerals Treaty negotiating text were sometimes referred to as "Beeby texts," named after the chairman of the negotiations, Ambassador Christopher Beeby of New Zealand. For substantive treatment, see Christopher C. Joyner, "The Evolving Antarctic Minerals Regime," in Christopher C. Joyner and Sudhir Chopra (eds.), *The Antarctic Legal Regime* (The Hague: Martinus Nijhoff, 1988); and Christopher C. Joyner, "The Antarctic Minerals Negotiating Process," *American Journal of International Law* 81 (October 1987): 888–905.

23. David A. Colson, "The United States Position on Antarctica," *Cornell International Law Journal* 19 (Summer 1986): 291–300.

24. For representative experiences of scientists participating in these exchanges, see E. S. Grew, "An Austral Summer Field Season with the 30th Soviet Antarctic Expedition, 1984–1985," *Antarctic Journal of the United States* 21, no. 1 (1986): 17–19; E. S. Grew, "With the Soviets in Antarctica, Austral Summer 1976–1977," *Antarctic Journal of the United States* 12, no. 4 (1977): 86–88; E. S. Grew, "With the Soviets in Antarctica, 1972–1974," *Antarctic Journal of the United States* 10, no. 1 (1975): 1–8; F. Michael Maish, "U.S.-Soviet Exchange Program at Vostok," in Lewis and Smith, *Frozen Future*, pp. 344–350; and B. G. Lopatin, "Soviet Exchange Scientist at McMurdo," in Lewis and Smith, *Frozen Future*, pp. 350–352.

25. Letter from Guy Gutheridge, manager, Polar Information Program, National Science Foundation, to V. I. Smirnov, head of the All-Union Research Institute of Hydrometeorological Information, Nov. 2, 1984 (on file with the Division of Polar Programs, NSF).

26. A. F. Treshnikov (ed.), *Investigations of the POLEX South–75 Program* (New Delhi: Oxonian Press, 1979).

27. E. E. Sarukhanyan and N. P. Smirnov, "Main Results of Soviet-American Studies during the POLEX South and F. Drake Programs in the Drake Passage and the Scotia Sea (1975–1978)," in E. I. Sarukhanyan and N. P. Smirnov (eds.), *Investigations of the POLEX South–78 Programs* (New Delhi: Oxonian Press, 1985), pp. 1–10.

28. James M. O'Leary and Kenny L. Watson, "U.S. Navy Antarctic Development Squadron Six (VXE–6) Activities, 1978–79," *Antarctic Journal of the United States* 14, no. 5 (1979): 234–235.

29. "Introduction," in Bruce A. Huber and Sarah E. Rennie (eds.), *Reports of the U.S.-USSR Weddell Polynya Expedition, October–November 1981*, vol. 1 (New York: Columbia University Press, 1983), pp. 1–10; and Arnold L. Gordon, "The US-USSR Weddell Polynya Expedition," *Antarctic Journal of the United States* 17, no. 5 (1982): 96–98.

30. Letter from Peter Wilkness, director, Division of Polar Programs, National Science Foundation, to Ye. S. Korotkevish, deputy director of the USSR Arctic and Antarctic Institute, July 31, 1987 (on file with the Division of Polar Programs, NSF). Also see Robert Gillette, "U.S., Soviets to Study Ozone," *Los Angeles Times,* June 19, 1987; and Glenn Garelik, "A Breath of Fresh Air," *Time,* September 28, 1987, p. 35.

FOR FURTHER READING

Bush, W. M. (ed.) *Antarctica and International Law*. New York: Oceana Publications, 1982.

Charney, Jonathan I. (ed.) *The New Nationalism and the Use of Common Spaces*. Totawa, N.J.: Allan and Osmun, 1982.

Orrego Vicuna, Francisco (ed.) *Antarctic Resources Policy*. Cambridge: Cambridge University Press, 1983.

Peterson, M. J. *Managing the Frozen South: The Creation and Evolution of the Antarctic Treaty System*. Berkeley: University of California Press, 1988.

Quigg, Philip W. *A Pole Apart. The Emerging Issue of Antarctica*. New York: McGraw-Hill, 1983.

Shapley, Deborah. *The Seventh Continent: Antarctica in a Resource Age*. Washington, D.C.: Resources for the Future, 1986.

Wolfrum, Rudiger (ed.). *Antarctic Challenge*, 3 vols. Berlin: Duncker & Humblot, 1984–1988.

4

U.S.-SOVIET TRADE: CONFLICT AND COOPERATION

Gary K. Bertsch

The Government of the United States of America and the Government of the Union of Soviet Socialist Republics,

Considering that the peoples of the United States of America and of the Union of Soviet Socialist Republics seek a new era of commercial friendship, an era in which the resources of both countries will contribute to the well-being of the peoples of each and an era in which common commercial interest can point the way to better and lasting understanding,

Having agreed at the Moscow Summit that commercial and economic ties are an important necessary element in the strengthening of their bilateral relations,

Noting that favorable conditions exist for the development of trade and economic relations between the two countries to their mutual advantage,

Desiring to make the maximum progress for the benefit of both countries in accordance with the tenets of the Basic Principles of Relations Between the United States of America and the Union of Soviet Socialist Republics signed in Moscow on May 29, 1972,

Believing that agreement on basic questions of economic trade relations between the two countries will best serve the interests of both their peoples,

[Have agreed to enter into the 1972 U.S.-Soviet Trade Agreement]

Preamble of the 1972 Trade Agreement

HISTORICAL BACKGROUND

Despite the statements noted above, the world's two superpowers have had, at least until recently, rather little to do with each other economically in the postwar period. Although there have been some efforts to expand U.S.-Soviet trade and technological cooperation, and although some rewarding examples of cooperation have taken place, the postwar era has seen as much, or perhaps more, economic warfare than cooperation. This was not always the case.

For example, even though the U.S. government was reluctant to recognize the world's first Communist state following the Bolshevik takeover, and did not do so until 1933, when President Roosevelt finally accorded diplomatic recognition to the Soviet Union, the United States led the world in exports to the Soviet Union during much of the 1920s and 1930s. Subsequently, the United States became a major supporter of the Soviet effort in World War II through an extensive program of lend-lease assistance. Food, clothing, machine tools and other equipment, military aircraft, ships, vehicles, and even an oil refining plant were provided. Stalin reportedly told the president of the U.S. Chamber of Commerce that approximately two-thirds of the large industrial enterprises in the Soviet Union had been built with U.S. technical assistance.[1]

Although some thought that Soviet-U.S. economic ties would continue and expand after the war, trade deteriorated sharply along with the worsening political relationship. The Cold War period saw the growth of economic sanctions and export controls; economic warfare replaced opportunities for economic cooperation.

With the rapid deterioration of U.S.-Soviet relations in the late 1940s and early 1950s, plus the rise of antitrade forces within the U.S. system and the self-imposed economic isolation of the Soviet Union, trade relations took a significant turn for the worse. It was during this period that the U.S. Congress passed restrictive legislation like the Export Control Act of 1949, which embargoed exports thought to contribute to Soviet military or civilian economic performance, and the 1951 Trade Agreement Extension Act, which withdrew most-favored-nation (MFN) treatment from the USSR and all East European countries except Yugoslavia. Tariffs were high, trade facilities and credits were restricted, and export controls were tight. The primary goal of U.S. policy was to deny the Soviet Union the benefits of commerce with the West. The U.S. government was opposed to doing business with the Stalinists in the Soviet Union. During the ensuing Cold War period of economic warfare, U.S. policy was clearly antitrade and most Americans supported it.

What appeared to some in the United States to be a Cold War consensus supporting economic warfare was, however, relatively short-lived. First to challenge the consensus were U.S. allies in Europe, who in the mid–1950s began to resist the U.S.-imposed embargo and sought to expand economic relations with the Soviet Union and their traditional East European trading partners. Support for the embargo policy also weakened in the United States as U.S. business and some of its representatives came to recognize and calculate the costs of lost markets in the Soviet Union and Eastern Europe. By the 1960s, the Cold War consensus began to wane, and more protrade attitudes, actions, and policies emerged in the U.S. political system. For example, in 1964 the United States decided to sell large quantities of grain to the Soviet Union. In the mid–1960s, more business representatives, government officials, congressmen, and others came to speak in favor of expanding U.S.-Soviet commerce. In 1969 the U.S. Congress replaced the embargo-oriented Export Control Act with the somewhat more trade-oriented Export Administration Act.

Although President Richard M. Nixon, a perceived "Cold Warrior," entered office in 1969 initially reluctant to expand U.S.-Soviet commerce, substantial congressional support for trade expansion was demonstrated at hearings held from April to July of that year. Senators Walter Mondale, Edmund Muskie, and William Fulbright, among others, argued that the Cold War was over and that the restrictive U.S. trade policy was counter to U.S. economic interests and was causing unnecessary suspicion and tension in East-West relations. On June 3, 1969, the *New York Times* described U.S. policies as "self-defeating," "cold war policies," and "inconsistent with the Nixon administration's theory that it is time to move from an era of confrontation into one of negotiations and cooperation."[2]

Subsequently moving in this direction, President Nixon went to Moscow in 1972 and signed the Basic Principles of Relations, which noted:

The U.S.A. and USSR regard commercial and economic ties as an important and necessary element in the strengthening of their bilateral relations and thus will actively promote the growth of such ties. They will facilitate cooperation between the relevant organizations and enterprises of the two countries and the conclusion of appropriate agreements and contracts, including long-term ones.

In July 1972, the two countries moved further to liberalize trade relations: (1) they signed a three-year grain agreement covering the sale of up to $750 million of grain; (2) the United States undertook to make credit available through the Commodity Credit Corporation; and (3) the first session of the U.S.-USSR Joint Economic Commission was held in Moscow. On October 18 of the same year, President Nixon and Soviet Trade Minister Patolichev signed a comprehensive agreement that called for an expansion of trade and included a settlement of the Soviet lend-lease debt to the United States in exchange for the granting of MFN status.[3]

The 1972 U.S.-Soviet trade agreement was expected to provide a major boost for expanded trade. More specifically, it was intended to provide a framework of rules within which U.S. companies and Soviet foreign trade organizations (FTOs) could negotiate contracts to their liking. Such a framework was considered useful because, in the absence of such an agreement, commercial relations between U.S. companies and Soviet FTOs were conducted according to regulations laid down separately by the U.S. and Soviet governments. These regulations were not always in agreement and represented systemic impediments to Soviet-U.S. trade. Supporters of détente and expanded trade considered the agreement a significant breakthrough for improved U.S.-Soviet relations.

In order for the agreement's extension of MFN status to Soviet exports to take effect, U.S. congressional authorization was required. There were some in the Congress who wanted to link the MFN authorization to a guarantee that the Soviets would provide freedom of emigration. Specifically, in October 1972, Senator Henry Jackson introduced an amendment—later known as the Jackson-Vanik amendment—to the U.S. trade bill, making the Nixon promise of MFN status contingent upon a liberalization of Soviet emigration policy. Senator Jackson and his supporters wanted the Soviets to give specific assurances about the number of Jews who would be allowed to emigrate. In contrast, President Nixon and Secretary of State Kissinger wanted to conduct "quiet diplomacy," using trade to build "a web of constructive relationships" with the Soviet Union. There were many fiercely competing groups trying to influence U.S. policy. The protrade business groups wanted the government to stay out of trade, and the U.S. Jewish groups wanted the government to use trade to force the Soviets to open the gates to Jewish emigration. Important and powerful groups in U.S. society wanted very different things.

After interminable negotiations among these groups and lengthy congressional hearings, the issue came to a head in the summer and fall of 1974. Following an exchange of letters between Secretary Kissinger and Senator Jackson in which conditions concerning Jewish emigration were spelled out, members of the incoming Ford administration and Congress worked out a set of principles that empowered the president to grant MFN status and credits to the Soviet Union for an initial period of up to 18 months. On December 20, 1974, the House and Senate passed the trade act, but with an additional amendment by Senator Adlai Stevenson.

This amendment placed a limit on Export-Import Bank credit to the Soviet Union of $300 million for a four-year period. The Soviet leaders were offended, and reacted harshly to the Stevenson amendment and to the public assertions in the United States that they had agreed to increase Jewish emigration in exchange for MFN. On January 10, 1975, the Soviets stated that because of the added conditions, they would not carry out the provisions of the 1972 trade agreement with the United States. In response to the Soviet nullification of the trade agreement, Kissinger announced that the United States would not take steps to expand trade with the Soviet Union as called for in the agreement.[4]

Some viewed the nullification of the agreement as the "beginning of the end" of Soviet-U.S. détente. The Soviets saw the Nixon administration's inability to win passage of the agreement as a lack of good faith. And the Americans saw Soviet adventurism in Angola and other Third World nations in the mid–1970s as evidence that trade could not be used as a lever to tame the Soviets. In reality, part of the theory behind détente—that increased economic ties might produce favorable changes in Soviet domestic and foreign policy—was never put to the test in the 1970s because of the failure of the U.S.-Soviet trade agreement.

U.S.-Soviet commerce suffered further setbacks in the late 1970s and early 1980s. The Carter administration sought to use trade as an instrument to affect Soviet domestic and foreign policies. For example, trade and credits were to be expanded in response to favorable Soviet actions. On the other hand, negative actions by the Soviets would be met with cutbacks in trade and credits. The Carter administration's desire to use trade as a "carrot" and "stick" later assumed a more restrictive approach designed to punish Soviet misbehavior. U.S. denials of certain export licenses (for instance, for the Sperry-Univac computer system for TASS, the Soviet news agency) and the addition of oil and gas exploration and production equipment to the Commodity Control List were early attempts to punish the Soviets. Later, in response to the Soviet invasion of Afghanistan, President Carter imposed controls on grains, phosphates, and assorted items for the 1980 summer Olympics; temporarily suspended and subsequently tightened controls on the sale of high technology; and undertook other economic sanctions to signal U.S. displeasure with Soviet behavior. As a result, U.S.-Soviet trade dropped sharply in 1980.

At the onset of the next administration, President Ronald Reagan took an important protrade action by honoring his campaign pledge to rescind President Carter's grain embargo. However, most other actions taken during the first term of the Reagan administration were clearly antitrade. President Reagan and most of his advisers were highly critical of U.S.-Soviet trade and felt that the Soviet Union was enjoying most of the benefits while the United States was bearing most of the costs. Then, in response to Soviet complicity in the December 1981 imposition of martial law in Poland, the Reagan administration imposed a number of restrictive controls (involving, most importantly, controls on oil and gas transmission and refining equipment and technology, and suspension of the issuance of all licenses for exports to the Soviet Union, including not only security commodities and oil and gas items but also unpublished technical data related to industrial processes).

In the summer of 1982, the Reagan administration took these controversial sanctions a step further by expanding oil and gas controls to West European subsidiaries and licensees of U.S. firms involved in business with the Soviet Union. This led to an outburst of European criticism, forcing the United States to withdraw these controls in November. Although the United States pushed for sanctions in response to the Afghanistan and Poland crises, the NATO allies remained highly skeptical about, and generally opposed to, using trade to influence Soviet foreign policy. In contrast with the protrade attitudes of the European allies, prevailing U.S. opinion about U.S.-Soviet trade during this period was extremely critical and generally assumed that such relations meant lopsided advantages for the Soviet Union.[5]

As a result of these and related events and opinions, the U.S. government has placed important constraints upon economic and technological relations with the Soviet Union. The most important of these relate to (1) the denial of MFN on the basis of the Jackson-Vanik amendment to the Trade Act of 1974; (2) the restriction of official export credits, as specified in the amendments to the Export-Import Bank Act of 1974; and (3) the control of trade and technology transfer through the Export Administration Act of 1969. Each of these will be briefly described.

MFN Status

MFN status allows a country's exports to the United States to be subject to relatively low tariff rates. Without such rates, tariffs are high and exports to the United States are more difficult. The U.S. denial of MFN status for the Soviet Union continues to be an important issue affecting trade relations. It is important for both economic and political reasons. Politically, the Soviet Union feels that the absence of MFN status discriminates unfairly against its exports to the massive U.S. market. It believes it deserves the same treatment that the United States provides to almost all other countries, including such Communist states as the People's Republic of China and Poland.

Economically, the U.S. decision not to grant the Soviet Union MFN status has had an impact on the Soviet Union's ability to export to the U.S. market. The Soviets find it difficult to compete with countries receiving the tariff benefits of MFN status. Although it has been difficult to calculate the real economic significance of this loss of exports to the United States, it is fair to say that it has been rather sizable and that it will probably grow in importance in the future. Certainly, because of the size and significance of the U.S. market, MFN status is important symbolically and practically to the Soviet objective of becoming an international exporter of manufactured goods to the world's major markets.

Official Export Credits

As with MFN, there are political and economic reasons why the Soviet Union desires official U.S. export credits. Credits are basically loans to foreign countries—in this case loans to the Soviet Union given by the U.S. government or U.S. banks. Official credits involved loans from government banks (like the U.S. Export-Import Bank) or government insurance of private bank loans (as is done by the Commodity Credit Corporation). The Soviet Union has a special need for export credits because of its inconvertible currency. (The ruble is only a domestic currency and is currently useless on international markets. It is inconvertible because the Soviet economy is not based on rational prices and exchange rates.) Only three options exist for importing goods: (1) export products to earn "hard currency" such as yen, dollars, or pounds, and use this hard currency to pay for imports; (2) sell Soviet gold for hard currency import payments; (3) receive export credits from governments and private banks. Certainly, official credits are viewed as a normal feature of international trade. The West Europeans and Japanese offer the Soviets very favorable terms on export credits, thus facilitating sales to the Soviet Union.

In his 1985 address to the U.S.-USSR Trade and Economic Council, General Secretary Gorbachev noted that "there can be no serious trade without credits."[6] The U.S. credit restrictions are seen by the Soviets as a sign of U.S. unwillingness to grant them recognition as an equal trading partner. Although the extension of official export credits would not result in a major increase in U.S.-Soviet trade, it would be a significant political step connoting U.S. interest in normalizing the relationship.

Export Controls

Since World War II the United States has placed restrictive controls on exports to the Soviet Union. Although intended primarily to control the export of goods and technologies that might contribute to Soviet military capabilities, controls have an impact on the economic and technological relationships that goes far beyond militarily significant goods. The Soviet Union contends that the United States has controlled not only items of military relevance but also many nonmilitary goods, such as important energy equipment and technology needed to promote Soviet economic development. In addition to controls on such items, the United States has exerted considerable pressure upon allies not to engage in such trade with the Soviet Union. Furthermore, the United States has been eager to restrict exports in order to signal displeasure with Soviet actions at home (the treatment of dissidents) and abroad (the invasion of Afghanistan). The use of export controls for these and other purposes has done much to limit the expansion of U.S.-Soviet trade and technological relations. Because of controls and other impediments, a mixed picture emerges when we review the specifics of U.S.-Soviet economic and technological cooperation.[7]

AREAS OF TRADE AND TECHNOLOGICAL COOPERATION IN THE 1980s

Because of the many political impediments, Soviet-U.S. trade never approached its potential. Trade between the superpowers in the 1980s represented less than 2 percent of each country's international trade turnover. After bilateral trade reached a postwar high of almost $4.5 billion in 1979, it fell to below $2 billion in 1980 and has not yet regained its earlier status (see Table 4.1).

The United States has been exporting primarily food, crude materials, and manufactures, including chemicals (see Table 4.2). Continuing the pattern established in the 1970s, agricultural exports represent the bulk of total exports, approximately 75 percent. However, this has been a highly variable category of trade. When Soviet grain purchases dropped significantly in 1986, this share fell to below 60 percent.

Soviet-U.S. trade in grain has been governed since 1975 by long-term agreements (LTAs) that establish floors and ceilings for Soviet purchases. According to the 1975 LTA, the Soviets agreed to buy 3

Table 4.1
U.S.–Soviet Trade: 1979–1987
(millions of dollars)

	1979	1980	1981	1982	1983	1984	1985	1986	1987
U.S. EXPORTS									
TOTAL	3604	1510	2339	2589	2002	3283	2422	1248	1480
Agricultural	2855	1047	1665	1855	1457	2817	1864	648	923
Non-Agricultural	749	463	674	734	545	466	558	600	557
U.S. IMPORTS									
TOTAL	873	462	387	248	367	602	441	605	470
Agricultural	15	10	12	11	11	11	9	16	22
Non-Agricultural	858	452	375	237	356	591	432	589	448
Gold Bullion	549	88	22	4	2	2	1	154	-
U.S.-U.S.S.R. TRADE TURNOVER	4477	1973	2726	2837	2369	3885	2863	1853	1950
U.S. TRADE BALANCE (+)	2731	1047	1952	2341	1635	2681	1980	643	1010

Source: U.S. Census Bureau, U.S. Department of Commerce.

million tons of corn and 3 million tons of what; the United States agreed to permit the sale of another 3 million tons of each without the need for additional consultation and agreement. The LTA signed in 1983 committed the Soviets to buy 4 million tons each of corn and wheat annually, and expanded the range of purchases to 9–12 million tons.

These agreements have not been completely successful in stabilizing U.S.-Soviet grain trade. As noted in Table 4.3, the U.S. embargo in response to the Soviet invasion of Afghanistan resulted in a precipitous decline in the U.S. market share of Soviet corn and wheat imports. After the embargo was dropped, the Soviets limited their purchases from the United States to the minimum required by the LTA. In 1981/1982 and 1983/1984, however, U.S. exports shot up to record levels as the Soviets attempted to make up their wheat shortfalls by taking advantage of low prices and the U.S. interest in expanding sales. In 1984/1985, the Soviets decided to conserve hard currency and buy lower-priced Argentine and subsidized French wheat; U.S. market shares declined again, and the U.S. government accused the Soviet Union of breaching the LTA. U.S.

Table 4.2
U.S. Exports to Soviet Union, 1981–1987
(thousands of dollars)

Description	1981	1982	1983	1984	1985	1986	1987
Food and live animals	1,600,423	1,642,161	1,194,970	2,585,154	1,728,525	318,242	859,909
Beverages and tobacco	400	2,979	954	1,264	8,732	497	144
Crude materials, inedible	59,350	214,250	264,594	224,263	90,450	328,102	56,549
Mineral fuels, lubricants, etc.	62,840	90,013	22,571	30,045	54,538	56,312	54,131
Oils & fats, animal & vegetable	56,089	40,565	21,506	38,872	63,927	15,470	18,787
Chemicals & related products	180,223	287,861	239,534	208,151	281,634	288,373	263,859
Manufactured goods	32,019	29,110	29,749	17,450	9,587	14,159	23,452
Machinery & transport equipment	301,223	225,788	149,718	110,252	112,106	156,329	87,695
Miscellaneous manufactured	47,126	59,233	76,815	66,276	71,309	68,411	113,763
Not classified elsewhere	722	614	2,461	2,205	2,017	1,618	1,476
Total of Above	2,340,415	2,592,574	2,002,872	3,283,932	2,422,825	1,247,513	1,479,765

Source: Compiled from official statistics of the U.S. Department of Commerce.

Table 4.3
U.S.–Soviet Grain Trade, 1976/1977–1987/1988

Year 1/	USSR purchase from U.S.		
	Wheat	Corn	Total
	Million tons		
1976/77	3.1	3.0	6.1
1977/78	3.5	11.1	14.6
1978/79	4.0	11.5	15.5
1979/80	2.2	5.8	8.0
1980/81	3.8	5.7	9.5
1981/82	6.1	7.8	13.9
1982/83	3.0	3.2	6.2
1983/84	7.6	6.5	14.1
1984/85 2/	2.9	15.8	18.6
1985/86	0.2	6.8	7.0
1986/87	4.1	4.1	8.2
1987/88 3/	9.0	4.2	13.2

[1]Grain agreement year—October/September.
[2]Total does not add due to rounding.
[3]As of May 5, 1988.

Source: U.S. Department of Agriculture, Economic Research Service, Situation and Outlook Series.

sales declined again in the next two years before increasing significantly in 1987/1988.

The United States also was once a major supplier of soybeans to the Soviet Union. In fact, in 1978–1979, the United States supplied 96 percent of Soviet soybean imports! However, after the invasion of Afghanistan and U.S. sanctions, U.S. sales declined significantly while those of alternative suppliers (including Argentina, Brazil, and China) climbed.

Fertilizer is also a significant, yet sometimes troublesome, component of bilateral trade. In 1973 Armand Hammer, the colorful head of Occidental Petroleum, concluded a major compensation agreement involving the construction of ammonia production, storage, and pipeline facilities in the Soviet Union and exchanges of Soviet ammonia and urea for U.S. superphosphoric acid.[8] Although U.S. sanctions and charges of Soviet "dumping" (selling fertilizer at a lower price in the U.S. market than in other markets) complicated this area of super-power commerce, fertilizer remains a significant component of two-way trade.

U.S. manufactures constitute the major portion of nonagricultural exports and averaged around $500 million in the 1980s. The composition of this category underwent considerable change, however, as chemical sales (mostly fertilizers) rose and machinery and transportation equipment sales declined in the first half of the 1980s. The decline in U.S. industrial exports during this period was partially the result of growing political tensions. Many potential exports were lost due to the denial or suspension of export licenses, the imposition of sanctions relating to the Afghanistan and Poland affairs, and the resulting cancellation of major U.S.-Soviet projects. These political developments proved to be major impediments to economic relations and had a considerable impact.

Consider, for example, the experience of the Caterpillar Tractor Company, which had established itself as a major supplier of heavy construction equipment to the Soviet Union. In 1978 the U.S. government reacted to Soviet human rights violations and decided that track-type tractors and pipe layers could no longer be exported without a validated export license. Although this raised new licensing impediments and brought about considerable delay, Caterpillar tried to continue its business and was successful in obtaining a Soviet order for 200 pipe layers in 1981. Because the export license for the deal got caught up in U.S. sanctions surrounding the Polish affair, Caterpillar lost the deal. The company's former market share of 85 percent of Soviet imports in this area dropped to minuscule amounts and Komatsu, its Japanese competitor, established its own 85 percent market share. It has been estimated that in 1981 and 1982 alone, Caterpillar lost as much as $400 million in exports and 12,000 man-years of employment, at the very time the company had 15,000–20,000 employees on indefinite layoff.

This was one of many unfortunate developments resulting from political tensions that impacted on both nations. The Soviets needed equipment to develop their energy resources, and the Caterpillar Company and workers of Peoria, Illinois, needed business. An ideal opportunity for economic cooperation benefiting both countries existed. Political tensions and economic sanctions intervened, however, and numerous opportunities for economic cooperation were lost. Interestingly, the Reagan administration dropped licensing requirements in 1987, concluding that they had been to no avail. The Soviet Union was able to use indigenous and non-U.S. technology and equipment, and completed its pipeline with little delay.

Table 4.4
U.S. Imports from the Soviet Union, 1981–1987
(thousands of dollars)

Description	1981	1982	1983	1984	1985	1986	1987
Food and live animals	2,955	5,632	18,078	17,477	12,834	2,969	3,283
Beverages and tobacco	6,072	10,876	21,154	7,839	13,278	16,401	20,138
Crude materials, inedible	19,522	10,049	12,098	19,353	15,895	37,831	49,676
Mineral fuels, lubricants, etc.	115,913	10,946	59,158	202,563	106,876	89,911	106,990
Oils and fats, animal & vegetable	25	6	1	12	44	8	0
Chemicals and related products	112,839	131,684	160,559	235,029	217,792	185,435	118,208
Manufactured goods	91,369	61,758	91,202	107,826	64,849	105,644	141,526
Machinery & transport equipment	2,677	1,659	3,721	2,874	4,695	5,028	8,355
Miscellaneous manufactured	2,889	9,171	6,295	4,605	3,556	4,436	9,157
Not classified elsewhere	22,762	5,268	2,402	2,524	3,693	157,792	10,546
TOTAL	377,023	247,049	374,668	600,102	443,512	605,455	467,879

Source: Compiled from official statistics of the U.S. Department of Commerce.

U.S. imports from the Soviet Union also remained low during this period, influenced by pressing political and economic realities (see Table 4.4). Political factors included the continuing denial of MFN status, which subjected Soviet products to tariff rates higher than those on imports from other countries. Other politically motivated impediments targeted nickel and furs. U.S. allegations that Soviet nickel exports to the United States contained nickel of Cuban origin resulted in a ban in November 1983. There was also continued refusal to import seven types of fur skins, which meant no trade in an area of economic interest to both countries.

Economic factors are probably more significant in explaining the low level of U.S. imports from the Soviet Union (less than 0.2 percent of total U.S. imports and 0.5 percent of total Soviet exports between 1982 and 1986). There are various reasons for this, including the economic facts that (1) the United States is itself a major producer of many of the goods that the Soviet Union is prepared to export; (2) the United States has long-standing trade relationships with countries that export most of the goods it might otherwise buy from the Soviet Union; (3) Soviet exports have a hard time in the highly competitive U.S. market in view of their questionable quality and the lack of Soviet marketing skills.

Yet everyone agrees that bilateral trade remains far below its potential. Many also wonder if the will exists to expand it in the future. Some reasons for optimism, however, developed in the mid–1980s.

FUTURE EXPANSION OF U.S.-SOVIET TRADE AND TECHNOLOGICAL COOPERATION?

> Durable, stable trade and economic ties . . . should become a positive
> factor in relations between the Soviet Union and United States.
> Mikhail Gorbachev, written statement to
> U.S.-USSR Trade and Economic Council, 1986

> I encourage you to explore possibilities for increasing trade and
> commercial exchanges that will benefit the people of both countries.
>
> Ronald Reagan, written statement to
> U.S.-USSR Trade and Economic Council, 1985

In the mid–1980s, President Reagan reevaluated U.S. objectives and policies toward the Soviet Union and considered the possibility of an expansion of trade relations. Concerning his stated objective of building a more constructive working relationship, President Reagan suggested that increased trade would be of benefit to both the United States and the Soviet Union. The president's statement provided justification for renewing and sustaining the 1974 Agreement on Economic, Industrial, and Technical Cooperation (EITCA), the only accord covering general commercial relations in the 1980s. It calls for the two governments to use their influence to promote and facilitate commercial, industrial, and technical cooperation between the superpowers.

The renewal of the EITCA led to the convening of the Joint U.S.-USSR Commercial Commission (JCC) in Moscow in May 1985. Chaired by Secretary of Commerce Malcolm Baldridge and Soviet Foreign Trade Minister Nikolai Patolichev, the meeting was the JCC's first in over six years. Prior to the invasion of Afghanistan, the commission had met seven times to monitor U.S.-Soviet commercial relations and deal with a wide variety of bilateral trade issues. To help overcome past difficulties, Secretary Baldridge and Minister Patolichev agreed to put trade on a better footing. Baldridge made a public affirmation of the U.S. government's support for peaceful trade, and Patolichev pledged to improve U.S. access to the Soviet market.

Although economic relations were not an item on the 1985 Gorbachev-Reagan summit agenda in Geneva, subsequent reports and statements raised further optimism about possible improvements. Secretary Baldridge reported that President Reagan expressed his support for an expansion of trade and, at a press conference following the summit, General Secretary Gorbachev noted Soviet readiness to consider cooperative projects with U.S. firms.

Discussion of Soviet trade reforms in the mid–1980s also raised optimism for better economic relations. Statements by Secretary General Gorbachev, resolutions of the top organs of the Communist Party, and the twelfth Five-Year Plan (1986–1990) outlined measures intended to improve economic performance and management of foreign economic relations. Among the significant reforms were efforts to decentralize the foreign trade system, thus providing greater access for U.S. and other foreign firms. Perhaps the most dramatic innovation authorized, for the first time since the 1920s, joint ventures with foreign firms. Foreign firms were encouraged to develop cooperative ventures on Soviet soil, as long as they allowed for 51 percent Soviet ownership and agreed to be governed by Soviet law. Although details remain to be worked out, many U.S. companies have signed letters of intent and some have undertaken joint projects. These include the joint enterprises of such companies as Archer Daniels Midland, Monsanto, and Occidental Petroleum in projects involving soybean processing, plastics, and chemicals.

In another interesting step, on July 24, 1987, Soviet authorities spent $300,000 for an unprecedented nine-page special advertising section in the *Wall Street Journal* to describe their economic reforms and convey their interest in doing business with the United States.[9] Under the heading "New Opportunities for Cooperation," the advertising included articles by leading officials and economists. An article titled "Soviet Technology Aids Western Production" began with the following paragraph:

Most Americans don't know that the rails of the Washington, D.C. subway are welded by machines developed and built in the USSR; that American physicians are using "surgical guns" made under Soviet licenses; that by 1990 three-fourths of the steel output in the U.S. will be based on the original Soviet technology of continuous casting; that among others, Soviet licenses are purchased by G. R. McDermott, Bristol Myers, American Home Products, Du Pont, 3M, and the like.

As the research of John Kiser has observed, all of this is true. He shows that major U.S. companies have purchased licenses for the following forms of Soviet technology: electromagnetic aluminum and copper casting, psychotropic and anti-cancer drugs, flash butt welding, magnetic impact bonding, titanium nitriding of steel tools, and in situ coal gasification. He and others validate Soviet claims that technology transfer is not totally a one-way street. There is indeed evidence that the United States and other industrialized Western nations benefit from Soviet technology.

THE IMPORTANCE OF U.S. POLICY: PAST AND FUTURE

There are, of course, a host of factors that will determine the course of U.S.-Soviet economic and technological cooperation. Much has to do with Soviet domestic and foreign policies, and with U.S. policy.

U.S. policy in the 1980s was a complicated mixture of past policy and American political culture; contemporary pressures resulting from competing protrade and antitrade centers of power; and a reaction to global economic and political forces, not the least of which were declining U.S. trade and technological performance and the changing superpower relationship. The ostensible values of economic warfare and latent Cold War impulses continue to affect and to be reflected in the 1980s. There were many such examples, including U.S. efforts to expand controls on bilateral trade, the continued denial of MFN status to the Soviet Union and extension of it to other Communist countries with poor human rights and emigration records, and continuing restraints on public lending. Economic warfare was clearly evident in these and other examples of recent U.S. policy.

While many in the United States reflected an economic warfare mentality and worked to restrict economic and technological relations in the 1980s, others sought to facilitate them. In agricultural trade, for example, pragmatic economic interests often transcended political and ideological ones. Due to pressure from U.S. grain growers and congressional supporters, the limited embargo was dropped in 1981 and a new LTA on grain was signed in 1983. In another policy area, many in the private sector and Congress sought in the 1980s to liberalize U.S. export controls in order to facilitate U.S.-Soviet trade and restore U.S. credibility worldwide as a reliable supplier. As a result of protrade forces, the Export Administration Amendments Act of 1985 (the primary U.S. legislation authorizing controls on trade with the Soviet Union) contained a number of relaxations, including additional requirements that the president consult with Congress before the imposition of new restrictions, such as a grain embargo. It also prohibited the president's use of foreign policy controls that would break contracts previously entered into, except in cases where a "breach of the peace" posed a serious and direct threat to the strategic interest of the United States, and it terminated U.S. foreign policy controls on items that are available from foreign sources.

As U.S.-Soviet political relations began to thaw in the mid–1980s, more protrade policy changes unfolded. In May 1985, Secretary Baldridge went to Moscow to cochair the eighth session of the JCC. In a letter to the U.S. business community, Baldridge encouraged U.S. exporters to explore opportunities in the Soviet Union, noting that they would find the business climate improved. In June 1985, there was the renewal of the U.S.-Soviet Agricultural Cooperative Agreement, calling for scientific and technological cooperation through the exchange of information and teams of specialists in 20 different agricultural areas. The environment of economic and technological relations warmed further in November 1985 as a result of the Reagan-Gorbachev summit in Geneva. When asked if the climate of trade relations had changed for the better following the summit, Baldridge replied: "Yes, it's a different ballgame."[10] In the summer of 1986, the United States and the Soviet Union announced 13 exchange programs in education, science, and culture, raising them to their highest levels since the cuts attending the imposition of sanctions for the invasion of Afghanistan in the early 1980s.

In the December 1986 meeting of the JCC in Washington, Secretary Baldridge urged both governments to take steady steps to expand trade. In line with his urging, the U.S. government supported the U.S. pavilions in the Soviet Union at the food industry show in September 1986 and the construction exhibition in May 1987. Other positive steps were taken, including the introduction of legislation to end the longstanding embargo on imports of Soviet fur skins; attempts to reach an agreement to end the embargo on imports of nickel; and the addition of a second commercial officer to the Commercial Office attached to the U.S. embassy in Moscow.

Trade relations continued to improve in 1987 and 1988. In 1987 the U.S. government removed controls on the sale of oil and gas equipment to the Soviet Union and undertook other measures to expand trade with the Soviet Union. Later in the year, William Verity, former cochairman of the U.S.-USSR Trade and Economic Council, a private organization intended to promote trade between the two countries, was named secretary of commerce. Known for his longtime support for U.S.-Soviet trade, Verity worked quietly to lay the foundation for further expansion of U.S. economic relations with the Soviet Union.

In April 1988, Secretary Verity, other government officials, and over 500 U.S. business executives went to Moscow to undertake further efforts to promote trade between the superpowers. The trip involved meetings of the JCC and the U.S.-USSR Trade and Economic Council. The meetings resulted in a number of new initiatives, including the formation of a trade consortium intended to facilitate expanded U.S. participation in joint ventures in the Soviet Union. Called the American Trade Consortium, Inc., and including Archer Daniels Midland, Chevron, RJR Nabisco, Eastman Kodak, Ford, Johnson & Johnson, and the Mercator Corporation, the consortium was intended to promote more intensive economic and technological relations, and the sale of goods ranging from floppy disks and medical equipment to trucks and automobiles.

The Trade Consortium may signal exciting new areas of superpower cooperation. Although much remains to be seen, at the time of this writing Archer Daniels Midland was involved with its Soviet counterparts in negotiating joint ventures covering agricultural areas such as oilseed processing and the production of starch and sweeteners. Chev-

ron was involved in discussing joint oil exploration and development.
RJR Nabisco was discussing the production of cookies, crackers, break-
fast cereals, and cigarettes. Eastman Kodak expected to set up a joint
venture to manufacture and market floppy disks for personal computers
and blood analysis equipment. Ford was carrying on discussions related
to plants to manufacture cars, light trucks, and vehicle components.
Johnson & Johnson was interested in the joint manufacture of many
of its pharmaceutical, medical, and consumer products. In addition,
Occidental Petroleum announced a joint venture with the Soviet Chemical Industry Ministry to construct and operate two petrochemical
plants in the Ukraine to make PVC, a widely used plastic. These and
related developments suggested the potential for the highest level of
superpower economic cooperation in history. Many directly involved
in the meetings spoke of a new era in U.S.-Soviet trade and technological relations.

Although more cooperation appears to be in the future of U.S.-Soviet
relations, the likelihood for fully normalized economic relations—including MFN tariff treatment, governmental credit, and a major relaxation of export controls—still appears unlikely. Normalization
would require important political preconditions plus major breakthroughs on arms control, a code of conduct governing superpower
involvement in regional disputes, and greater agreement concerning
human rights.

Also unlikely, but not inconceivable, is a return to a more restrictive
policy. If agreements in the above areas elude the superpowers, and if
new areas of confrontation come to the fore, antitrade forces could
spring back into action. Their activities could take a number of forms.
With reduced Soviet income from declining oil and gas revenues, additional restraints on private lending could tighten commercial bank
credits and lessen the Soviet ability to buy from the United States even
further. It is also plausible that the LTA for grain may not be renewed,
causing Soviet grain imports from the United States to fall markedly.
Finally, some U.S. policymakers might undertake another major effort
to tighten trade controls.

Another future policy scenario is a continuation of the past—a com-
bination of conservative and liberal policies reflecting complex forces
in the domestic U.S. and international environments. In the area of
U.S. export control policy, we might see conservatives resisting further
attempts to reduce export controls or to limit the role of the Defense
Department in export licensing. On the other hand, liberals might
succeed in removing unsophisticated technology from the control list
or speeding up the licensing process.

The issue of MFN and U.S. import restrictions on the Soviet
Union will also remain controversial. Some policymakers will seek

to provide the Soviets with more access while others will seek further to restrict it. Although repeal of the Jackson-Vanik amendment is unlikely, there may well be efforts in Congress to circumvent obstacles through a waiver of the amendment in return for some improvement in Soviet emigration policy. We might also see efforts to tighten and enforce provisions of the 1930 Smoot-Hawley Tariff Act, halting millions of dollars' worth of imports from the Soviet Union (including petroleum products, gold ore, agricultural machinery, tractor generators, and tea) that some consider to be processed or manufactured with forced labor.

There will also be continuing debate on loosening or tightening credit controls. Some in Congress and the executive branch continue to be concerned with Western lending to the Soviet bloc. It is interesting to note that in 1985, the Reagan administration opposed a Senate bill (the Financial Export Control Act) that would have put greater pressure upon U.S. allies to restrict credits to the Soviet bloc, and noted that the bill reflected "capricious political decisions which may damage the international image of U.S. credit markets, create disputes within the Western alliance, and run counter to the spirit of Geneva." However, in March 1987 Senator Jake Garn and eight Democratic and Republican cosponsors reintroduced financial export control legislation to grant the president the authority to regulate the transfer of money and other financial resources to U.S. adversaries. When introducing the legislation, Senator Garn noted that he had received thousands of cards and letters urging that "the United States stop providing money and other financial resources to the Soviet Union." The issue of government credit control will continue to be controversial as the U.S. government wrestles with the problems surrounding declining U.S. trade performance.

The development of integrated, coherent U.S. trade policies toward the Soviet Union based upon broad political consensus appears unlikely in the foreseeable future. It will be difficult to forge an integrated antitrade policy of economic warfare. It will be equally difficult to develop an integrated cooperative trade policy with the Soviet Union because of lingering Cold War images in U.S. political culture. In all scenarios, economic and technological relations are likely to be significantly affected by, and remain a hostage to, both U.S. domestic and superpower politics.

NOTES

1. W. Averell Harriman reporting to the State Department, as quoted in Antony C. Sutton, *Western Technology and Soviet Economic Development*, vol. 2 (Stanford, Calif.: Hoover Institution Press, 1971), p. 3.

2. Noted in Henry Kissinger, *The White House Years* (Boston: Little, Brown, 1979), p. 152.

3. For a full statement of the agreement, see Nish Jamgotch, Jr. (ed.), *Sectors of Mutual Benefit in U.S.-Soviet Relations* (Durham, N.C.: Duke University Press, 1985), pp. 191–200.

4. For a full analysis of this episode, see Paula Stern, *Water's Edge: Domestic Policy and the Making of American Foreign Policy* (Westport, Conn.: Greenwood Press, 1979).

5. For a chronology of major U.S.-Soviet trade developments from 1971 to 1984, see Jamgotch, *Sectors of Mutual Benefit*, p. 201–208.

6. "Address by Mikhail S. Gorbachev," *Journal of the U.S.-USSR Trade and Economic Council* 11, no. 1 (1986): 6.

7. For more on these issues, see Gary K. Bertsch, "American Politics and Trade with the USSR," in Bruce Parrott (ed.), *Trade, Technology and Soviet-American Relations* (Bloomington: Indiana University Press, 1985), pp. 243–282.

8. For a autobiographical account of Armand Hammer's considerable experience in the U.S.-Soviet trade, see Armand Hammer with Neil Hyndon, *Hammer* (New York: G. P. Putnam's Sons, 1987). Hammer's business experience with the Soviet Union goes back to the time of Lenin. Having dealt personally with Soviet leaders from Lenin to Gorbachev, Hammer is the most successful of all U.S. businessmen in trading with the Soviet Union.

9. *Wall Street Journal,* August 24, 1987, pp. 9–17.

10. *Journal of Commerce,* May 19, 1986, p. 4C.

FOR FURTHER READING

Bertsch, Gary K. (ed.) *Controlling East-West Trade and Technology Transfer: Power, Politics, and Policies.* Durham, N.C.: Duke University Press, 1988.

Chapman, Margaret (ed.) *Forum on U.S.-Soviet Trade Relations.* Washington, D.C.: American Committee on U.S.-Soviet Relations, 1987.

Chapman, Margaret, and Carl Marcy (eds.) *Common Sense in U.S.-Soviet Trade.* Washington, D.C.: American Committee on East-West Accord, 1983.

Naylor, Thomas H. *The Gorbachev Strategy: Opening the Closed Society.* Lexington, Mass.: Lexington Books, 1987.

Parrott, Bruce (ed.) *Trade, Technology and Soviet-American Relations.* Bloomington: Indiana University Press, 1985.

Rode, Reinhard, and Hanns-D. Jacobson (eds.). *Economic Warfare or Detente.* Boulder, Colo.: Westview Press, 1985.

U.S. Congress, Joint Economic Committee. *Gorbachev's Economic Plans.* Washington, D.C.: U.S. Government Printing Office, 1987.

5

ENVIRONMENTAL PROTECTION AND CONSERVATION

Donald R. Kelley

U.S.-Soviet cooperation in the field of environmental protection and conservation has proven to be one of the most durable areas of scientific exchange between the two superpowers. Most joint activities are governed by the American-Soviet Agreement on Cooperation in the Field of Environmental Protection. Other related activities, such as cooperation to deal with the consequences of the Chernobyl disaster, have occurred through ad hoc activities, especially in the area of emergency medical aid, or under the auspices of the American-Soviet Agreement on the Peaceful Uses of Nuclear Energy or multilateral bodies such as the International Atomic Energy Agency. A product of the Nixon-Brezhnev summit in 1972, the environmental agreement has operated as an umbrella for a wide-ranging assortment of activities that have been maintained at a relatively high level even through the recent time of troubles between the two superpowers. It was also the first exchange to experience a resumption of near-normal activities as the Reagan administration sought in 1984 to signal its willingness to turn away from the level of confrontation that had marked U.S.-Soviet ties since 1979.

U.S.-Soviet collaboration on environmental protection and conservation has been the product of multiple motivations on both sides, some technical and scientific, as both nations have recognized their growing domestic environmental problems and realized their international implications, and some political and blatantly opportunistic, as top-level leaders and lesser bureaucrats have realized that cooperation would present them as political realists willing to work with the other side in the interests of environmental quality or would strengthen their hand in bureaucratic warfare at home over environmental priorities. This chapter will review both the scientific and the political aspects of that collaboration, as well as note environmentally relevant cooperation occurring through other channels.

HISTORICAL BACKGROUND

While both nations had begun to experience environmental problems in the 1960s, each faced a particular mix of technical, economic, and political issues that gave their own spin to efforts to strike a balance between developmental and environmental priorities. Each came to see the environment not only in light of historical and economic features that shaped current reality but also in light of contending political and institutional forces that sought to set the public agenda.

In the United States, environmental awareness came in connection with early scientific and subsequent public attention to nuclear fallout. This set the stage for scientists-cum-popular prophets such as Rachel Carson, Barry Commoner, and Paul Ehrlich to dramatize the dangers of pesticides and toxic wastes, and to note the synergistic effects of population growth, technology, and consumer affluence. Dramatic incidents such as the Santa Barbara oil spills in 1968 added emotional fervor to the issue, and mobilized both conventional proenvironmental and counterculture activists to add the question of environmental quality to their indictments of contemporary society.[1]

Economic and political considerations also shaped the initial response to environmental woes. Already part of a confirmed consumer economy, the average American found it difficult to surrender the notion that growth is intrinsically good, although a significant minority quickly endorsed the smaller-is-better point of view. Equally significant was the particular technological profile of the nation's environmental problems. As Barry Commoner observed, the mix of population growth, especially in urban areas, increasing consumer affluence (with its orientation toward planned obsolescence), and ever more toxic industrial technologies resulted in the exponential growth of environmental threats.

Political and institutional questions also played a role. Working within a historical framework that had stressed limited state control of the private sector, even the most concerned public officials found it both intellectually difficult and politically dangerous to take action. The first major national legislation came in 1969 with the passage of the National Environmental Policy Act, which provided a legislative umbrella under which limited centralized control could occur. That same year, Congress established the Council on Environmental Quality to monitor the environment and coordinate programs, only to yield to pressures for an even stronger federal presence and to create the Environmental Protection Agency (EPA) a year later.

In the Soviet Union, awareness came more slowly. While the quality of pure research on environmental questions remained high after the revolution, the regime's single-minded concern with industrialization, to say nothing of rebuilding the nation after two world wars and revolution, pushed the issue of environmental quality into the background. Devoted to a world view that it was man's task to reshape nature to his needs, and that economic growth and giantism are the highest achievements, Soviet leaders and citizens viewed the deterioration of the environment as an acceptable price to be paid for progress.

When environmental awareness came in the 1960s, it arrived as a consequence of growing public health problems and the deterioration of specific areas so severe that even the most growth-oriented leaders could no longer ignore the ecological and human costs. The selective, case-by-case responses that emanated from Soviet authorities throughout the 1960s and 1970s combined real concern and generally effective programs for high priority areas with seeming nonchalance about the deterioration of less important locations. General public concern came only in the 1970s, although earlier dramatic incidents, such as the pollution of Lake Baikal, did much to raise elite consciousness.

As in the United States, political and economic factors shaped Moscow's response. Because of the relatively low technological level of Soviet industry and its distinct lack of a proconsumer orientation, the nature of the environmental threat was far different from that in the United States. Water pollution associated with industry, mining, and agriculture loomed as the most serious issue, to be dealt with by specific programs for particular water basins or industries; the more generalized problem of air pollution was less serious, in part because of the more favorable siting of Soviet industries and in part because of the relatively fewer gasoline-powered vehicles.

The centralization of political and economic power in the hands of top party and government officials who shared a devotion to further industrialization and growth, as well as the absence of proenvironmental lobbies, made it doubly difficult to place the question of environmental quality on the political agenda. Moreover, Soviet officials had vested responsibility for protecting nature, conserving raw materials, and dealing with environmental problems in industrial ministries charged with exploiting such resources. Even with the dawning of greater awareness in the late 1970s, they pointedly avoided the creation of a single national ministry charged with environmental protection, although they did strengthen the hand of related agencies, such as the Ministry of Health and the Hydrometeorological Service. Only in 1988, under Gorbachev's bolder leadership, did they create the State Committee for Environmental Protection, centralizing the activities of nine state committees and seven ministries.

NEED FOR U.S.-SOVIET COLLABORATION

The fact that a formal agreement emerged in 1972 was as much a product of political factors at work in Washington and Moscow as it was of the objective need for collaboration. To be sure, there were strong reasons to begin cooperation quite apart from political concerns. The leadership of both nations had, however grudgingly, acknowledged the existence of worsening environmental problems, and scientists on both sides were eager to create a framework for future joint efforts. The idea that the effects of pollution were not limited solely to the nation that produced toxic wastes had also dawned on political leaders, and there were many efforts under way to find effective international forums that would address environmental problems. Moreover, in many areas U.S. and Soviet experiences tended to be complementary, especially in agreements broadened to include larger questions of conservation and ecosystem management. What the Soviets lacked in modern abatement technology and experience with certain pollution problems associated with advanced industry, they made up for with long-standing expertise on wildlife and preserve management, and in specific fields such as earthquake prediction. What the Americans lacked in conservation and pollution control procedures, they more than made up for in advanced technology and environmental impact assessment.

Technical issues aside, Washington and Moscow wanted the agreement to underscore the growing success of détente and to confirm the diplomatic skills of their respective governments. It is not accidental that Richard Nixon sought improved relations with the Soviets during his 1972 reelection bid. The Nixon-Brezhnev summit reflected the priorities of U.S. presidential politics as much as it did the superpower agenda, and the wide-ranging agreements on security and lesser questions of bilateral cooperation signed at the Moscow meeting were meant to signal to U.S. skeptics that the once staunch anti-Communist could deal productively with Soviet leaders. Almost as an afterthought, the environmental agreement was touted to U.S. audiences as proof of the administration's concern with environmental quality, an area of domestic policy in which it had received low marks. And to conservative audiences, it was presented as an opportunity to increase U.S.-Soviet trade in pollution abatement technology, where the United States unquestionably held a significant lead.

Moscow's agenda was equally political, although General Secretary

Brezhnev was in no danger of falling from power over the question of superpower ties. But the entire question of détente had been controversial within the Politburo. Certain elements, soon to be forced from office, had opposed the Nixon visit because of the resumption of U.S. bombing in North Vietnam. Nevertheless, agreements signed at the Moscow meeting were meant to remind Soviet audiences that détente brought not only a reduction of bilateral tensions but also a more open door for the acquisition of advanced U.S. technology and increased trade. Lower in Moscow's ministerial pecking order, Soviet environmental officials, whose agencies were political lightweights in comparison with the industrial ministries, hoped that the agreement would lend added legitimacy and bureaucratic clout to their efforts. The Hydrometeorological Service, or Hydromet, was particularly anxious to use the agreement to assert its claim to be the lead agency on environmental issues.

Other political considerations aside, three principles guided the comparatively short talks between U.S. and Soviet officials that resulted in the creation of the Moscow agreement. First, the pact was intended to establish a minimum of formal structures and, at the same time, to promote the greatest possible number of direct links between research teams and individual scientists. The lead agencies on both sides were to function essentially as coordinators of the activities of a diverse assortment of governmental agencies and research facilities.

Second, both sides accepted the principles that the mix of exchange activities—and any judgment of the success or failure of the program itself—would be guided by the desire for an overall balance of benefits to both sides. Reciprocity would be broadly defined to strike a balance of benefits from the agreement as a whole rather than from each of its categories of exchange activities. This approach both guided the selection of the original 11 areas of activity and provided a mix in which the strengths and weaknesses of each side were complementary rather than competitive; each side ensured the inclusion of subcategories in which its activities set world standards as well as subcategories in which it hoped to learn much from the other.

Third, each side accepted, perhaps even celebrated, the bellwether nature of the agreement. To both leaders who signed the 1972 agreement in Moscow, the political implications of the pact were an overriding concern. Although the agreement automatically renewed itself every five years unless either side chose to pull out, it was clearly placed within the broader context of superpower relations. At the very outset, Russell Train, who coordinated the agreement first as director of the Council on Environmental Quality and then as head of the EPA, spoke of it as "one of the most important outgrowths of our policy of détente with the Soviet Union," and Yuri Izrael, who became director of Hydromet shortly after the agreement was signed, referred to it as "an important part of the process in which relations between the two countries are being normalized."[2]

When U.S.-Soviet relations turned sour in the late 1970s and early 1980s, in connection with the Soviet invasion of Afghanistan, pressure on Poland to deal with its Solidarity movement, and repression of dissidents at home, exchange activities were purposely cut back to reflect U.S. displeasure. The agreement nevertheless fared better than many other scientific and cultural exchanges, and the pact was permitted to self-renew without U.S. objection. Similarly, movement to revitalize the agreement and set the groundwork for future expansion came in the mid–1980s at a time when the Reagan administration, confident that it could deal with Moscow from a strengthened position— or perhaps merely reacting to its domestic critics—wished to signal a more cooperative attitude.

INTENTIONS, GOALS, AND OBJECTIVES

In the short run, the agreement signed at the 1972 summit was intended to establish a minimal institutional structure to facilitate and coordinate exchanges across 11 areas of environmental and conservation activities. The initial U.S. lead agency was the Council on Environmental Quality, which was replaced by the EPA. On the Soviet side, the initial counterpart agency was the Hydrometeorological Service, which had functioned principally as a weather bureau, although it aggressively sought a broader mandate on environmental issues. In 1988, responsibility for the exchange passed to the newly formed State Committee for Environmental Protection. A Joint Committee composed of lower-level officials in the EPA and Hydromet was established as the de facto operational arm of the exchange, with the provision that the committee would meet annually, alternating in Moscow and Washington, to review activities and plan future exchanges.

The first meeting of the Joint Committee took place in Moscow on September 18–21, 1972. General guidelines were provided to govern exchange activities, preparing the way for individual working groups and team leaders to define specific areas of cooperation. Although the memorandum of implementation signed at this meeting called for working group meetings to begin by the end of the year, the Soviets requested postponements because of the difficulty of coordinating the many academic and governmental agencies involved. By 1973, organizational difficulties had been overcome, and the exchange of information on most of the 39 specific projects began. The exchange grew rapidly over the next few years, and by 1979, the last year of expanding activities prior to the Soviet invasion of Afghanistan, over 1,000 participants on both sides had taken part. In his summary report for 1976, EPA administrator Russell Train described the exchanges as "the world's largest bilateral environmental program."

In substantive terms, the agreement provided for joint symposia and research projects, the exchange of information and research findings (including joint publication), and the exchange of individual scientists and research teams in 11 different topic areas:

1. Prevention of air pollution (six projects)
2. Prevention of water pollution (four projects)
3. Prevention of agricultural pollution (six projects)
4. Enhancement of the urban environment (five projects)
5. Protection of nature and nature preserves (six projects)
6. Protection of the marine environment (two projects)
7. Biological and genetic effects of pollution (two projects)
8. Influence of environmental changes on climate (three projects)
9. Earthquake prediction and tsunami (tidal wave) warning (five projects)
10. Arctic and subarctic ecology (projects subsumed under other topic headings)
11. Legal and administrative measures for environmental protection (two projects).

In the longer term, the agreement set as its ambitious goals the creation of an ever-growing network of scientific and commercial ties that would benefit both the scientific community and the commercial and industrial consumers of pollution abatement technology. The technical, bureaucratic, and political problems aside—although they were considerable and are detailed below—the agreement achieved remarkable success on a number of fronts. By the mid–1980s, over 2,000 U.S. and Soviet scientists had participated in the exchange. Even more remarkably, collaborative activities survived in reasonably good order even after the worsening of U.S.-Soviet ties in the late 1970s. Exchange levels for 1977 through 1979 (before the Soviet invasion of Afghanistan) ran at roughly 300 participants a year; from 1980 through 1984, the level dropped by 50 percent. In comparison, most of the other bilateral scientific exchanges saw a drop of over 75 percent for the same period.[3] The resumption of Joint Committee meetings in 1985 paved the way for increased exchange levels, the curtailment or redirection of programs that had never gotten off the ground or had logically concluded without further guidance from the Joint Committee, and the addition of new projects.

Hopes that the agreement would facilitate a growth in U.S.-Soviet trade were less fully satisfied. Speaking to a congressional review committee in 1985, Fitzhugh Green, EPA's associate administrator for international affairs, concluded that total trade volume had amounted to "several million dollars" in pollution control and seismological equipment in the 1970s. Green indicated, however, that during a recent visit to the Soviet Union, Commerce Secretary Malcolm Baldridge had offered to reexamine U.S. restrictions on the sale of certain pollution control technologies, in the hope that the reactivization of the scientific exchanges might give impetus to improved commercial ties.[4]

PROBLEMS IN IMPLEMENTING THE AGREEMENT

The successes of the agreement have not been achieved without difficulties, some rooted in the nature of the scientific exchanges themselves, some coming from the "normal" problems of trying to coordinate U.S. and Soviet bureaucracies—"normal" in this case means a long list of red-tape and clearance issues that would not apply in dealing with other nations—and some inevitably flowing from the bellwether nature of the agreement linking the level of cooperation to the broader context of bilateral ties.

In some instances, problems arose because areas of potential collaboration were poorly defined or because exchange activities ran their natural course within the first few years and lacked subsequent redirection because of the long hiatus in Joint Committee sessions from 1979 to 1985. Certain programs, such as the enhancement of the urban environment, the protection of the marine environment, and the biological and genetic effects of pollution, saw only limited activity under the best of circumstances and quickly fell into dormancy during the long deterioration of relations. Yet other, more technical projects completed their research agendas and found it impossible to proceed without additional high-level direction.

The ebb and flow of exchange activities were also affected by administrative and budgetary difficulties. On both sides, the lead agencies were vested with the responsibility of coordinating a wide array of exchanges housed within different departments of their own agency, in other government entities, or in academic or research institutes. Coordination on the U.S. side proved fairly easy, given both the involvement of public and private sector actors and the propensity of research and academic institutions to take their own head on matters of research priority.

On the Soviet side, problems of coordination were more difficult, a not surprising finding, given the relatively low position in the bureaucratic pecking order of Hydromet, the initial lead agency. The creation of the State Committee for Environmental Protection offers at least the hope that problems of coordination may be less severe in the future, although it is too early to assess the new agency's bureaucratic and political clout. Rather pointedly the Soviet leadership chose not to offer the directorship to Yuri Izrael, who will remain at Hydromet; the new State Committee's director will be Fyodor Morgun, a specialist in agricultural pollution who reportedly is close to Gorbachev.

Inevitably adding to these administrative problems was the difficulty faced by Soviet scientists—indeed, by virtually all Soviet citizens—in securing permission to travel abroad, although clearance undoubtedly would have been easier to obtain for participants working in areas in which authorities hoped to gain access to more advanced U.S. technology. One suspects that program participants on the Soviet side were probably screened thoroughly in advance of their selection, thus avoiding embarrassing lapses in the actual exchanges themselves.

Budgetary problems also hampered the exchange program. On the U.S. side, both the budget-cutting zeal of the Reagan administration and its general inclination against promoting an activist role for the EPA led to substantial cuts. In the early years, annual U.S. government expenditures on the program for all federal agencies (excluding grants to universities and direct university or private-sector contributions) had risen to a high of $355,000 in 1979; by 1981, funding had fallen to $163,000. Much of this reduction can be explained by cuts in overall expenditures for environmental programs as well as by the obvious propensity to reduce relatively visible exchanges after the invasion of Afghanistan. Although direct federal expenditures rose with the acceleration of exchange activities after 1984, the EPA (perhaps with considerable political wisdom) has stressed its own efforts to cut waste and the cost-benefit advantages of requiring participating agencies to pay much of their own way. Program administrators have cautioned against making the exchange a direct line item in the federal budget instead of the recipient of funds provided under a variety of agency budgets. Their rationale is that such direct and highly visible funding would make the program an easier target for politically motivated cuts during periods of tension.

While no reliable figures for Soviet expenditures are easily available, it seems certain that many of the same problems arose in the Soviet Union. Operating funds for substantive exchanges come from participating agencies and ministries themselves, and, as in the U.S. experience, such international programs have always been a distinctly second-class priority except when boosted by Soviet hopes for immediate access to Western technology.

Larger political and bureaucratic issues unconnected with the tone of U.S.-Soviet relations also have affected the exchange. On the U.S. side, the question of environmental protection already had begun to slip as a domestic priority by the end of the 1970s because of the success of federal and local programs. Even before the Reagan administration, priorities within the EPA had begun to shift away from conventional pollution issues and toward more exotic problems, such as toxic wastes. Under the new administration, interest in environmental issues dropped considerably. Unlike her predecessors (and her successors, for that matter) Anne Gorsuch Burford, Reagan's first EPA director, declined to serve as the chief U.S. spokesperson for the U.S.-Soviet environmental agreement, a move intended as much to lower the profile of the agency as to signal displeasure with Moscow.

On the Soviet side, too, the agreement has been affected by the growing bureaucratic clout of its initial lead agency, Hydromet, which controlled the exchange until 1988. Paradoxically, its emergence as a key representative of environmental concerns and its designation as the agency responsible for pollution monitoring and air pollution abatement somewhat diminished its interest in the program. Both its own aggressive advocacy of and official acknowledgment of environmental problems throughout the 1970s made Hydromet a more effective player in the game of bureaucratic politics. Its broadened mandate was not accompanied by extensive funding increases, inevitably leading to a reordering of priorities within the agency itself. In addition, Hydromet was not able to profit politically from what it hoped would be its ability to facilitate high-technology trade that would make it valuable to a wide assortment of more influential ministries seeking such know-how. In some areas Soviet technology made sufficient advances so that it was no longer as dependent on the U.S. experience, while in others, hoped-for technology transfers were blocked by the Jackson-Vanik amendment denying most-favored-nation trading status or tight export controls.

Additional difficulties were created by Soviet reluctance to grant access to certain research facilities and geographic regions, and to supply certain data that would facilitate exchange activities. Research on air pollution issues was hampered by Soviet denial of access to the critically important Institute of Atmospheric Optics at Tomsk, which was developing laser technology for long-distance monitoring of pollution levels that also had important defense applications. Because of continuing Soviet refusals to admit U.S. scientists to the Tomsk facility, activities in this exchange area were curtailed. Access problems also beset activities conducted under the arctic and subarctic section of the agreement. Although a number of successful research projects and joint cruises took place, certain geographic areas continue to be closed to U.S. participants, presumably for national security reasons.[5]

There also have been occasional instances in which Soviet authorities have purposely withheld information relevant to exchange activities.

U.S. participants in the program on earthquake prediction complained that certain geological maps were withheld and that seismological data were edited or altered to remove information that might be useful in the detection and measurement of underground nuclear tests. Efforts to gain access to comprehensive studies of growing air pollution problems in major industrial cities prepared for the state planning agency, Gosplan, also have proven futile.

On the U.S. side, there have been no systematic attempts to withhold information from Soviet participants because of the classified nature of the data, although there have been isolated instances such as reciprocity concerning access to the Tomsk Institute of Atmospheric Optics noted above. To be sure, the politically motivated reductions that occurred from 1969 on had the effect of curtailing information flows, but these were initiated to signal overall dissatisfaction with Soviet behavior rather than to cut off information in particular areas.

Budgetary and administrative problems aside, there remains clear evidence that the ebb and flow of exchange activities have been determined—as they always were intended to be—by the overall tone of U.S.-Soviet relations. No description of the problems in administering the program can avoid the conclusion that politically motivated reductions have been the most serious impediment to the growth and scientific maturation of exchange activities. Without question, virtually all such reductions were initiated by the U.S. side as a means of indicating displeasure with Soviet activities at home and abroad, although it must be added that many individual U.S. participants questioned the wisdom of scientific collaboration because of the Soviet treatment of dissidents in general and the internal exile of Andrei Sakharov in particular. For their part, Soviet leaders as well as individual participants were cast, in the early 1980s, into a politically exploitable role of jilted suitor trying to preserve low-level exchange activities through surviving normal channels and informal networks that quickly arose between U.S. and Soviet scientists.

The first clearly politically motivated difficulties came in the late 1970s in connection with the Soviet treatment of dissidents and minorities at home. In 1978, a scheduled visit to Moscow by the EPA deputy administrator was canceled because of the dissident issue, although the annual Joint Committee meeting was held as usual and day-to-day exchanges continued without interruption. This largely symbolic action occurred at a time when many U.S. scientists were questioning the morality of business as usual on the whole range of technical and scientific exchanges, a posture that produced well-intentioned, if short-lived, reductions of activities in many other areas as well.

Far more serious was the effort of the U.S. Congress to restrict trade opportunities and to demand more liberal treatment of Soviet dissidents and virtually open-door emigration for Soviet Jews as the quid pro quo for granting most-favored-nation status to the Soviet Union. To be sure, agreement-inspired trade has never developed as either side had hoped; U.S. sales of pollution abatement equipment to the Soviet Union amounted to no more than $2 to $3 million, and Moscow had higher priorities on its shopping list in terms of the acquisition of advanced Western technology. But the broader significance of the denial of most-favored-nation status must also be seen in the context of bilateral ties, for there is convincing evidence that this setback to détente marked a major turning point in hardening Soviet attitudes toward collaboration with the United States and in emboldening Moscow to undertake actions certain to offend U.S. interests.

The most significant political watershed for the agreement predictably came as a consequence of the Soviet invasion of Afghanistan in December 1979. Occurring at a time when U.S.-Soviet relations had already begun to deteriorate because of the dissident and emigration issues, the invasion both confirmed the fears and suspicions of the growing U.S. conservative movement and placed the Carter administration, which was seeking to defend the SALT II agreement, in a difficult and eventually untenable position. The initial response was to curtail the most publicly visible aspects of environmental and conservation programs, and to place a freeze on new initiatives, such as the creation of a joint working group on environmental education. The EPA was instructed to lower the public profile of the exchange at home. More significantly, a ban was imposed on further meetings of the Joint Committee; the last regularly scheduled meeting occurred late in 1979, and a moratorium remained in effect until 1985. At the operational level, however, initially most exchanges went forward without interruption, although some individual projects were cut. For example, a visit to the Soviet Union by U.S. earthquake specialists initially planned for the summer of 1980 was canceled in protest, but arrangements were made so the exchange could be conducted at a later date. Similar postponements were reported for other sectors of the agreement. Within just over a year, however, the day-to-day programs experienced extensive cutbacks at the hands of the new administration.

While the inauguration of the Reagan administration is generally seen as a major watershed in U.S.-Soviet relations, it is clear that bilateral cooperation on the environment had begun to deteriorate in the last years of the Carter presidency. Perhaps more important, the bellwether nature of the agreement linking the overall tone of U.S.-Soviet relations with the fate of the environmental exchange was clearly demonstrated. Politics, rather than the scientific and technical merits of the program, would be the ultimate arbiter of its fate, leading the new Reagan administration first to reduce exchange levels ever further and then, when it wished to repair relations with Moscow and improve its image at home, to reactivate dormant or extensively cut exchanges.

ENVIRONMENTAL COOPERATION UNDER REAGAN

Even with the new administration's hard-line policies toward Moscow, it is difficult to tell whether its efforts to rein in the EPA or its natural inclination against collaboration with the Soviet Union was the principal cause of the deteriorating fortunes of the exchange. The ban on Joint Committee meetings was continued, and overall exchange levels fell dramatically. In 1979, before the December invasion of Afghanistan, the number of exchange visitors was 316, with 183 Americans visiting the Soviet Union and 133 of their counterparts journeying to the United States; in 1980 the total figure fell to 148 participants, with more Soviet scientists coming to U.S. research centers, a reversal of the normal flow pattern since the beginning of the pact. In 1982, the total was 123 exchangees; in 1983, 119; and in 1984, the last year before efforts to reinvigorate the program, an all-time low of 67 (61 Americans and 6 Soviets).[6]

While Soviet pressure on Poland to restrict the activities of the Solidarity trade union further contributed to the general deterioration of U.S.-Soviet relations, it had little direct impact on the exchange itself. Both politically motivated and general budgetary cutbacks had begun to affect exchange levels, and there was little need for additional measures unless U.S. authorities wished to restrict programs on a case-by-case basis. The only instances in which that occurred were linked to technology transfers that had potential application to cold-climate pipeline construction, an area in which the administration was attempting, with little final success, to block Soviet acquisition of Western technology, and to the sensitive issue of environmental law. Yet after a brief delay, the former program continued in modified form. The U.S.-ordered suspension of direct Aeroflot flights to the United States also added to the practical problems of the exchange. Intended to express displeasure over events in Poland, the suspension simply made it more difficult for economic, rather than political, reasons for Soviet participants to visit the United States.[7]

The reaction of U.S. participants reflected both their hopes that something could be preserved of the day-to-day activities begun so auspiciously nearly a decade before and their uncertainty about why certain programs had been chosen for reductions. During the early 1980s, some participants reported that exchanges continued virtually normally, while others observed that their activities "limped along" or suffered "definite contractions" not attributable to the scientific merits of the respective programs. There seemed to be no discernible pattern of conscious choices to preserve some programs at the expense of others. Many U.S. participants felt that program reductions were as much the result of budget cuts aimed at the EPA as they were of decisions to terminate or scale back specific exchanges.[8]

U.S. participants evidenced typical U.S. diversity as they reacted to the purely political nature of the problems facing the exchange. Most expressed gratitude that at least some exchange activities were permitted to continue, and noted the importance of the informal networking that had developed to link them to their Soviet counterparts. Many simply declared themselves apolitical on the question of the exchange and argued that scientific exchanges should be set apart from political considerations. Yet a significant minority expressed regretful support for the U.S. curtailment in terms of using the exchange as the political bellwether it had always been intended to be. At the purely personal level, comments about the politicization of the exchange ranged from one participant's support of the need to present a "solid front" against Soviet authorities to another's complaint about the "self-proclaimed patriotism" of his project leader, who had moved more rapidly than other team members would have desired to limit the scope of exchange activities.[9] The essential goodwill that remained despite these difficulties was expressed by the U.S. executive secretary of the Joint Committee, Gary Waxmonsky, who in 1982 commented, "The important bottom line, I think, emerged clearly enough: that sufficient interest and good will remains on both sides to sustain a selective program of high quality scientific and technical cooperation."[10]

While it was far more difficult to assess the attitude of Soviet participants, some indication can be obtained from the comments of Yuri Kazakov, Waxmonsky's Soviet counterpart. He repeatedly urged the resumption of annual Joint Committee meetings, which were necessary to evaluate ongoing exchanges and launch new initiatives, and he spoke of the harmful impact of what his government chose to term the "artificial restrictions" being imposed by Washington. Some part of his frustration undoubtedly stemmed from growing difficulty that Hydromet experienced in obtaining operating funds from other participating Soviet agencies because of the seeming deterioration of the program.

At the operational level, Soviet participants expressed the same sense of frustration that was felt on the U.S. side. U.S. respondents reported that Soviet colleagues found it difficult to understand—at least purported to find it difficult to understand—why politically inspired considerations were permitted to affect the exchange. The sense of scientific camaraderie and group identity, as well as the elaborate informal communications networks that had developed over the years, clearly had the cumulative impact of creating a community of dedicated participants on both sides. Thus U.S. scientists sensed that their Soviet counterparts had the same interest in getting on with business as usual, particularly in maintaining the relatively apolitical relationship that had developed among the working teams.[11]

Problems and frustrations aside, both sides were content to let the agreement automatically renew in 1982. According to provisions negotiated in 1972, the pact is self-renewing every five years, although either participant may withdraw with six months' prior notification. In this regard, the agreement on environmental cooperation fared far better than many of the other scientific and technological exchanges that did not provide for automatic renewal. In those instances, the Reagan administration refused to enter into new formal agreements with Moscow, while in the case of the environmental exchange, it was content to let the agreement roll over with little public fanfare.

The first indication that Washington would permit a reinvigoration of the exchange came in June 1984, at a time when the Reagan administration sought to moderate its public image. At a meeting at the Kennan Institute for Advanced Russian Studies of the Woodrow Wilson International Center in Washington, convened to discuss the fate of U.S.-Soviet exchanges, the president announced his intention to reopen negotiations on a number of lapsed cultural and technical exchanges, and to reactivate existing agreements on environmental protection, housing, health, and agriculture. The Kennan Institute conference had been called to increase the pressure on the president to take at least symbolic action to salvage what had been flourishing agreements in many areas, and to give an administration now anxious to prove its willingness to deal with the Soviets a podium from which to present its case. Perhaps to maintain his conservative credentials, President Reagan forcefully reminded his audience that the resurrection of such agreements should not be read as "a signal that we have forgotten Afghanistan" or that "we will ignore violations of the Helsinki Final Act or the plight of Andrei Sakharov, Yelena Bonner, Anatoly Shcharansky, Yuri Orlov, and so many others." But it also was obvious that he had not forgotten the approaching presidential election.[12]

Soviet authorities were quick to pick up on the president's pledge of renewed cooperation. Later that month, Yuri Izrael, the head of Hydromet, sought out EPA administrator William D. Ruckelshaus at an Economic Commission for Europe (ECE) meeting in Munich to invite him to discuss a renewal of exchange activities. U.S. observers left with the impression that Izrael's own commitment to the exchange "has not flagged in any way."[13] Later that summer Gary Waxmonsky journeyed to Moscow to discuss a resumption of Joint Committee meetings, although the next formal session was not held until November 1985, a gap of six years from the previous meeting.

When the Joint Committee reconvened, U.S. and Soviet officials faced the task of reinvigorating a badly damaged program. On paper it now included 42 separate exchanges encompassed under the original 11 major fields of activity. But in reality, nearly half of the 42 individual exchanges had proven unproductive or had lapsed because of the suspension of Joint Committee meetings.

By the time of the next Joint Committee session in December 1986, some progress had been made in discontinuing completed or stillborn projects and in providing new directions for inactive programs. The list of projects was pared to 38, including new areas of activity in environmental education, groundwater quality, and the development of waste-free and low-waste technologies. Many programs witnessed the elaboration of new research activities to continue fruitful collaboration or the selection of new topics. The research agenda for 1987 provided for the reactivation and/or extension of most of the areas of exchange activity, and meetings of working groups and on-site visits were planned for most exchanges.

In budgetary terms, too, the U.S. side devoted increased resources to the exchange. While no complete figures are available, direct EPA expenditures rose to the $200,000 to $300,000 range, a figure that excluded both indirect funding through grants to participating academic and research agencies (which, as noted, were expected to assume a greater share of the financial burden) and arrangements that provided private funding for Soviet exchange personnel in the United States. The increase in funding is all the more impressive in light of the EPA's efforts to be more cost effective in eliminating program duplication and needless travel.

AGENCIES AND ACTORS

The choice of lead agencies on both sides was made for political and well as environmental and scientific reasons. In the U.S. case, the initial lead agency was the relatively powerless Council on Environmental Quality, whose director, Russell Train, was placed in charge of the program. Both the creation of the EPA, whose broader legislative mandate suggested a greater national commitment to environmental protection, and the subsequent promotion of Train to the directorship of that agency led to the transfer of administrative control to the EPA.

In the Soviet case, primary responsibility initially was in the hands of the State Committee on Hydrometeorology, which in the mid–1970s was given greater responsibility for environmental questions and renamed the State Committee for Hydrometeorology and Control of the Natural Environment. Yet despite added responsibilities, its principal concerns lay with weather forecasting and related atmospheric tasks; environmental issues initially were a secondary priority, although the agency's aggressive administrator, Yuri Izrael, undoubtedly saw the opportunity to expand into environmental protection as a way of enhancing the visibility and powers of his bailiwick. Perhaps ironically, the very success of the agency in claiming new responsibilities for the environment—an issue that has risen in significance in both the Soviet Union and the United States—tended to draw it away from its international activities, at one time valued as highly visible mechanisms for raising the environmental consciousness of the Soviet elite. Despite its newfound role, however, Hydromet always lacked comprehensive authority over all aspects of environmental quality in the Soviet Union. Significant responsibilities were lodged in the hands of the Ministry of Health, the State Planning Committee (Gosplan), various water basin commissions, and production ministries.

In January 1988, Soviet authorities announced the creation of the State Committee for Environmental Protection, which was to assume the environment-related tasks previously performed by nine state committees and seven ministries, including all contact with foreign governments on related issues. Despite the formidable mandate given the new agency, only time will tell whether any meaningful centralization will take place.

In two very important ways, both the EPA and Hydromet have faced similar administrative difficulties. As noted, both are charged with coordinating the actions of other agencies that conducted the substantive activities of the exchange. While some working groups are housed in the operational branches of the EPA or Hydromet, others are located in different government ministries, research facilities, the academic community, or, in the U.S. case, in the private sector. Second, both agencies are heavily dependent on participating agencies for funds, a posture that puts them at the mercy of sometimes quite different priorities.

The quality of leadership at the top also has affected the exchange. Vigorous leadership provided by Ruckelshaus as EPA director, and the activist orientation of most other EPA chiefs, have lent positive force to exchange efforts. In contrast, the Reagan administration's first EPA director, Anne Gorsuch Burford, did not provide personal leadership in dealing with the Soviets and refused to serve as the de jure program coordinator. The predictable turnover of the EPA directorship also introduced an element of instability that Soviet officials frequently cite as one of the difficulties of administering the program.

On the Soviet side, the exchange was headed from 1974 to 1988 by

Yuri Izrael, whose ambitions for his agency and personal hope to emerge as the principal spokesperson for environmental concerns seemed intertwined. A member of the Central Committee of the Communist Party, he was an increasingly visible figure both at home and abroad, and his vigorous leadership can be credited with overcoming some of the typical administrative difficulties endemic to Soviet bureaucracy. His long experience at Hydromet and with the exchange itself contributed continuity. His failure to win appointment as director of the new State Committee for Environmental Protection is probably more a result of Gorbachev's interest in placing a former associate from the Agricultural Department, Fyodor Morgun, in the post than of any serious shortcoming in Izrael's performance.

The day-to-day management of the exchange is in the hands of the U.S.-USSR Joint Committee on Cooperation in the Field of Environmental Protection. Housed in the international departments of the EPA and of Hydromet/State Committee for Environmental Protection, the U.S. and Soviet sections of the Committee are headed by executive secretaries and served by very small staffs. The U.S. side has gone through nearly half a dozen executive secretries, either on lateral assignment from the State Department (usually for brief terms) or from the EPA staff itself. The longest-serving U.S. executive secretary has been Gary Waxmonsky, an EPA employee sent in 1987 on a two-year leave to fill the science counselor post in the U .S. embassy in Warsaw. His Soviet counterpart, Yuri Kazakov, has served as executive secretry since the beginning.

Exchange efforts are headed by jointly chaired working teams of U.S. and Soviet scientists. Under the best of circumstances, working teams were intended to meet at least annually, usually on an alternating basis in the United States and the Soviet Union, although longer gaps occurred for some teams from 1979 to 1985. Teams are charged with the administration of their exchange area, the planning of a research agenda and exchange visits, and the transfer and publication of research findings.

CHERNOBYL AND INTERNATIONAL COOPERATION

The reactor explosion at Chernobyl on April 26, 1986, dramatically raised the question of the environmental consequences of radiation pollution in ways not envisioned by the U.S.-Soviet agreement on environmental cooperation or a similar bilateral pact signed in Moscow at the Nixon-Brezhnev summit that provided for cooperation in the field of nuclear energy. The former did not include radiation contamination as one of the 11 categories for joint research, and the latter focused primarily on the development of the nuclear power industry rather than its potential dangers. Like the environmental agreement itself, it had fallen on hard times because of the chill in U.S.-Soviet relations, and exchanges were virtually suspended at the time of the Chernobyl disaster.

The picture was little better in multilateral international agreements to police the nuclear power industry and to deal with such catastrophic situations. There were no formal agreements under the auspices of the International Atomic Energy Agency (IAEA) dealing with the spread of radioactive pollutants or requiring prompt notification of other nations when they spilled over international boundaries. While the IAEA had been involved in investigations of lesser accidents elsewhere and international teams of experts had been consulted about such problems, there were no firm guidelines nor response mechanisms.

It is not surprising that the U.S.-Soviet agreements on environmental protection and nuclear power had avoided the question of potential environmental dangers. A difficult enough question for the United States because of vocal criticism of nuclear power at home, it was unthinkable in Moscow to acknowledge that the rapidly developing nuclear power industry could pose any serious threat to health or the environment. Problems that had arisen in the past, such as the explosion of a waste fuel storage facility in the late 1950s, has been concealed from the Soviet public and were only vaguely known to Western observers. When Soviet authorities spoke to both domestic and foreign audiences about nuclear power, it was to underscore its growing importance in the nation's energy profile and to reassure skeptics of its safety. Ironically, the Chernobyl power station was featured as a showcase development in the U.S.-oriented magazine *Soviet Life* a year before the disaster.

The explosion at Chernobyl and initial Soviet attempts to conceal the seriousness of the problem changed that. Whatever the human or technological causes of the accident, there is little doubt that Soviet authorities reacted slowly to order local evacuations and delayed notifying neighboring nations of the danger until many hours after Swedish monitoring devices had detected unacceptably high radiation levels. Despite their subsequent candor and willingness to report fully to the IAEA, Soviet officials were conspicuously silent in the critical early days following the explosion.[14]

The Chernobyl explosion resulted in a number of international efforts to deal with the immediate problem and the real danger that such a disaster might occur in the future. Most dramatic was the medical relief mission headed by Dr. Robert Gale, described in great detail in this book. After receiving a candid report about the causes of the explosion from Soviet authorities, the IAEA formulated a new set of guidelines requiring any country experiencing a major radiation leak from any civilian and almost any military nuclear installation immediately to inform other countries if there were a danger to neighboring states. Another agreement required all IAEA members to render assistance to a nation experiencing such problems, although no formal mechanisms were established.[15]

The Chernobyl incident also became an important element in the reinvigoration of the U.S.-Soviet agreement on cooperation in the field of nuclear energy, which had been signed in 1972 at the Moscow summit and had fallen into dormancy since 1979 because of the deterioration of relations. The Joint Committee on Cooperation in the Peaceful Uses of Nuclear Energy met in August 1986, after an eight-year suspension of activities, and signed a wide-ranging agreement providing for reciprocal on-site inspection of atomic research facilities, collaborative research on the development of breeder and liquid metal reactors, and cooperation in the development of safety standards for all types of reactors. While the talks leading to the resumption of exchanges had begun before Chernobyl, U.S. officials were quick to admit that the explosion increased mutual interest in the pact. In April 1988, two years after the Chernobyl incident, Washington and Moscow signed an agreement under the auspices of the 1972 pact creating the Joint Coordinating Committee for Civilian Nuclear Safety.

Chernobyl has had less impact on the environmental exchange agreement, which never envisioned research in this area as part of its original mandate. Hopeful that the improving tone of U.S.-Soviet relations in general, and the acceleration of exchanges in particular, would create a favorable atmosphere for expansion into this area, U.S. scientists plan to suggest several areas of joint research involving data on the short- and long-term effects of the explosion to their Soviet counterparts.

EVALUATION OF THE AGREEMENT

In both scientific and political terms, the 1972 agreement has fulfilled the expectations of those who designed it. While some technical areas have not lived up to expectations—a detailed examination of the individual programs is given below—others have produced exceptional scientific and technical payoffs in new research or the application of technologies or ecosystem management techniques. In political terms as well, the agreement has served as a bellwether of U.S.-Soviet ties, creating one of the most active and productive bilateral scientific exchanges linking the two nations, as well as illustrating the importance of the warmth or chill of superpower relations in setting the tone of scientific and technical exchanges. One of the keys to the agreement's success has been the effort on both sides to ensure an overall balance of benefits. In part because the agreement permitted each side to suggest areas of activity in which it would gain from the experience of the other, and also in part because each side was permitted to tout its successes in areas where it had achieved a scientific or technical lead, political leaders on both sides were able to picture the agreement as broadly equitable and profitable despite the inevitable failures of individual projects. Political wisdom, in this case, paved the way for continued scientific collaboration, and each side developed a vested interest in portraying the successes of the agreement in the best possible light.

Official proclamations of balanced benefits aside, assessments of individual U.S. project leaders have been more mixed. In the area of climate research, regarded initially as a field in which the Soviets could make contributions valuable to the U.S. effort, the hoped-for benefits to U.S. research programs have not been realized. Similarly, the assessment of water pollution projects is mixed, with some U.S. respondents describing the results as "one-sided" and others terming the exchanges "extremely productive." This pattern of conflicting assessments applies fairly consistently to the rest of the exchanges.

Yet despite these problems, an area-by-area review of exchange activities reveals numerous successes as well as failures. In the area of air pollution, for example, the United States enjoyed a strong technological lead in pollution measuring and abatement activities, causing the Soviets to press for an expansion of collaboration. By the early 1980s, however, the changing priorities of the EPA and the denial of access to the Tomsk Institute of Atmospheric Optics chilled exchanges. Nevertheless, there were a number of striking successes, including joint field monitoring of aerosol dispersal in ambient air conducted at a mountaintop observatory in Soviet Georgia. In addition, Soviet pollution abatement technology has been useful to specialists in the steel and coal industries, although a separate project on mobile source emission-control technology yielded little because the U.S. side saw it as a Soviet attempt to pirate auto engine data.[16]

Collaboration on water pollution control has produced mixed results. While some projects experienced difficulties because of changing priorities within the EPA and the bureaucratic fragmentation of responsibility for water quality in the Soviet Union, others yielded positive results. For the most active exchanges, the balance of benefits has been fairly even, with the United States receiving some innovative ideas from Soviet pollution control procedures and the Soviet Union benefiting from more sophisticated U.S. instrumentation and testing equipment. By the end of the 1970s, one U.S. team leader reported that Soviet technology had, on the whole, lagged only two to five years behind the U.S. equivalent and, in some select areas, it had risen to the state of the art. In other technical areas, such as cold weather biological treatment of wastes, the magnetic separation of sludge, the use of ultrasonics, and the application of ozone for the purification of water, more advanced Soviet experience has proved instructive to the Americans.[17]

In the area of agricultural pollution, three of the four projects never got off the ground or fell into disuse, although the fourth, on pesticides, became one of the most active exchanges.

The area of urban environmental problems has never been a successful aspect of the exchange. While a number of projects on the preservation of monuments and places of historical interest, solid wastes, urban land management, and recreation zones in urban areas were attempted, differing U.S. and Soviet priorities impeded progress from the beginning. U.S. team leaders continuously complained that their Soviet counterparts gave them access only to showcase urban projects, although they acknowledged that they could learn much from the Soviet greenbelt experience, in which urban areas are circled with belts of forests and parks.[18]

The area of nature conservation and the organization of nature preserves has been one of the most active aspects of the agreement. Over 500 U.S. and Soviet botanists, zoologists, and ecologists have taken part in laboratory work and fieldwork. One project resulted in the U.S.-Soviet migratory bird convention, and others have led to joint breeding efforts and animal stock exchanges. Unparalleled Soviet experience in the organization of preserves and conservation has been one of Moscow's proudest contributions to the agreement. Yet a shadow was cast over the agreement in the fall of 1984 when a Russian-speaking Interior Department official responsible for coordination of all exchanges was denied a visa. Shortly thereafter, he was slandered by name in *Izvestiia,* suggesting that certain quarters in Moscow wished to cast a pall over the exchange and warn their own scientists against close collaboration. Despite this difficulty, exchanges continued after the warming of U.S.-Soviet relations in 1985.[19]

Exchange activities in marine environmental protection have not lived up to U.S. expectations. One major project on the prevention and cleanup of pollution from shipping yielded an unsatisfactory balance of benefits, although it provided valuable information to Soviet participants. By the early 1980s, activity had virtually ceased, in part because of the lack of balance and in part because on the U.S. side the project was administered by the already overworked Environmental Affairs Office of the U.S. Coast Guard. Efforts have been made to revitalize this aspect of the exchange.

The area of biological and genetic effects of pollution has witnessed limited activity. Only two projects were attempted, the first dealing with the biological and genetic effects of specific pollutants and the second focusing on a comprehensive analysis of environmental ecosystems. The latter has been particularly closely tied to the politics of environmental protection in the Soviet Union, with Hydromet officials using it as a podium from which to lecture colleagues on the importance of a holistic approach to environmental affairs.

Studies of the impact of environmental changes on climate have been some of the most productive aspects of the program, especially the award-winning studies of paleoclimate and the impact of specific pollutants. According to U.S. participants, benefits clearly have been weighted toward the Soviet side, since they began the program "at least a decade behind the United States in the area of climate research."[20]

Earthquake prediction has emerged as one of the real showcase projects. In contrast with climate studies, Soviet scientists led the world in this area, although they have benefited from access to more modern U.S. monitoring technology and instrumentation. U.S. participants have frequently complained, however, that certain geographical maps and other data are withheld because of their potential value in detecting underground nuclear tests. A potentially useful program for tsunami (tidal wave) prediction in the Pacific basin became dormant in the early 1980s, although an effort is under way to reactivate joint research.

Although the programs dealing with arctic and subarctic ecological systems are subsumed under other administrative divisions of the exchange, some general conclusions can be offered. For the most part, U.S. participants report cooperative and productive work with their Soviet counterparts, especially in the areas of wildlife management and pollution monitoring. While numerous joint expeditions and cruises have occurred, especially in the late 1970s, Americans have still found some geographic regions off limits, presumably because of national security concerns.

Finally, concerning legal and administrative questions of environmental protection, activities have been successful in establishing contacts between U.S. environmental lobbies, such as the Sierra Club and the Environmental Defense Fund, and their less-than-independent Soviet counterparts, and in linking U.S. and Soviet legal scholars. However, there has been little concrete payoff. The U.S. side has learned much about Soviet environmental policymaking, and there are clear indications that the Soviets have used some U.S. legislation as models for their own laws and environmental impact studies. However, in the more technical area of the harmonization of water and air quality standards, little progress has been made, largely because Moscow has withheld information about its own standard-setting methodology.

RECOMMENDED IMPROVEMENTS

Any suggestions concerning improvements in the agreement must be informed by an understanding of the simultaneous political and scientific purposes of the accord. Simply to recommend the depoliticization of exchange programs would be to ignore political realities that attended their birth and to risk alienating broader political constituencies beyond the scientific community that supported their creation.

It must also be recognized that the most significant interruptions have occurred at the U.S. initiative. Whatever one's judgment about the moral or political merits of signaling U.S. displeasure over Soviet actions by curtailing cultural and scientific exchanges, the fact remains that the volatility and openness of the U.S. political process create a situation in which "nonpolitical" exchanges become targets for criticism and politically low-cost weapons for retaliating against Soviet behavior. Without large and politically powerful constituencies to defend them, and without significant trade with an important sector of the U.S. economy, they easily fall victim to the urge for symbolic, and yet politically risk-free, action against Moscow.

Given this basic political reality, what recommendations can be offered to reduce and rationalize political pressures on the level of exchanges? Perhaps the most important would be to resist suspensions of the annual Joint Committee meetings. As the reduction of exchange activities from 1979 to 1986 suggests, it was one thing to reduce or curtail separate exchanges on a case-by-case basis, and quite another to place the overall coordination and direction of the program in official limbo.

It is tempting to suggest that one simple yet significant improvement would be to increase overall funding. It is clear that reductions of the EPA budget in the early 1980s impacted negatively on the exchange. And yet it is difficult to argue that these cutbacks were aimed at the exchange agreement per se; rather, they represented the Reagan administration's diminished interest in the environment in general and its intention to put an overactive EPA in its place. The primary problems have been political rather than economic, and the U.S. program directors have shown considerable political wisdom in attempting to portray exchange activities as cost effective and to avoid the dangerous visibility of direct line-item funding. More for its political than for its economic significance, increased U.S.-Soviet trade in environmentally relevant technology should be vigorously pursued, and restrictive export controls should be reexamined, although it is likely that Soviet purchases would be limited by the generally low priority attached to environmental concerns.

On the Soviet side, greater efforts must be made to provide access to relevant research institutes or geographic regions, and to increase the flow of complete and unaltered data among exchange participants. Problems of access are not surprising to anyone who has dealt with what is still an essentially closed society, and it is hardly surprising that they should affect a seemingly apolitical exchange agreement carefully crafted to provide a balance of benefits to both sides. But despite our understanding of Soviet reluctance to deal openly on all questions, the United States must continue to articulate—and to restrict Soviet access to its research institutions and scientists to enforce—a policy of reciprocity.

SIGNIFICANCE OF THE AGREEMENT

Any assessment of the agreement must acknowledge the relative nature of such a judgment. To members of the scientific communities on both sides who have taken part, the agreement has proven to be a success in areas in which joint projects are flourishing, and an outright failure in areas in which collaboration has languished. For both sides, the achievements in showcase areas have been substantial. Joint research teams have developed a sense of community and mission that has provided the basis for fruitful collaboration in the best of times and created an all-important informal communications network in times of trouble.

In one sense, the agreement has lived up to its expectations as a bellwether of U.S.-Soviet relations. Whatever the scientific costs, the agreement has been used by three of the four U.S. presidents in office at the time of or since its creation as a way of indicating displeasure with Soviet actions or as a way of breaking the ice in times of difficulty. Despite technical successes, however, the agreement has not promoted increased trade and therefore has failed to build a broader constituency within the business community.

For the public as a whole, the agreement is largely invisible. Lacking the drama of joint missions in space and the human interest of collaborative achievements in medicine, it has risen to public visibility only when it has been a part of a broader political question, such as the Reagan administration's use of the accord in 1984 to indicate its willingness to improve relations with Moscow. But its relative anonymity may be as much an asset as a liability, making it less a target for constrictions and public pressures except in times of a serious deterioration in U.S.-Soviet relations.

Despite its relative invisibility to the man in the street, U.S.-Soviet cooperation on environmental protection and conservation has proven to be one of the most successful of the many technical and scientific agreements linking the two nations. Useful for both its intrinsic merits and as a bellwether of U.S.-Soviet relations reflecting—and, more important, sometimes influencing—the overall tone of bilateral ties, it has linked both nations' common concern with environmental quality to the broader issue of superpower relations. In doing so, it has both shown the way for fruitful collaboration and underscored the inexorable connection between scientific and political issues. To some small but, it is hoped, growing degree, each will now affect the other in ways not possible before the beginnings of such programs.

NOTES

1. For a comparative study, see Donald R. Kelley, Kenneth R. Stunkel, and Richard R. Wescott, *The Economic Superpowers and the Environment: The United States, the Soviet Union, and Japan* (San Francisco: W. H. Freeman, 1976).

2. "International Cooperation with the Soviets," *Environmental Science and Technology* 10, no. 5 (May 1976): 414–415; and Y. Izrael and B. Kuvshinnikov, "USSR-USA: Cooperation in Protection of the Environment," *International Affairs* (Moscow), March 1975, pp. 30–37.

3. Statement of Fitzhugh Green, in *Hearing Before the Special Subcommittee on U.S. Pacific Rim Trade of the Committee on Energy and Commerce, U.S. House of Representatives* (hereafter *Hearing*) (Washington, D.C.: U.S. Government Printing Office, 1985), p. 11.

4. Ibid., pp. 28–30.

5. Statement of Gary Waxmonsky, *Hearing,* pp. 26–27; *Report on the Implementation of the US-USSR Agreement on Cooperation in the Field of Environmental Protection During the Period February 1979 to December 1979* (Washington, D.C.: U.S. Environmental Protection Agency, 1979).

6. Green, *Hearing,* p. 10.

7. Gary Waxmonsky, "US-USSR Environmental Agreement: Recent Developments and Future Prospects," memorandum to U.S. participants, April 6, 1982.

8. Letters to the author from F. H. Wagner, College of Natural Resources, Utah State University, January 6, 1983; R. A. Schoettger, director of EPA Large Lakes Laboratory, Grosse Ile, Michigan, January 25, 1983; L. Gates, chairman, Department of Atmospheric Sciences, Oregon State University, January 10, 1983; J. W. Cook, National Park Service, January 3, 1983; and G. L. Baughman, EPA Environmental Research Laboratory, undated.

9. These comments aside, there was remarkably little concern with political issues other than to lament their impact on the exchange.

10. Waxmonsky, "US-USSR Environmental Agreement."

11. Letters from Gates, Schoettger, and P. L. Wise, acting director, EPA Office of Evaluation and Analysis, December 28, 1982.

12. Remarks of President Ronald Reagan to participants in the conference on U.S.-Soviet exchanges, June 27, 1984, in *US-Soviet Exchanges: A Conference Report* (Washington, D.C.: Woodrow Wilson International Center, 1984).

13. Green, *Hearing*, p. 3.

14. For a complete discussion, see David R. Marples, *Chernobyl and Nuclear Power in the USSR* (New York: St. Martin's, 1986).

15. *New York Times*, September 27. 1986.

16. Green, *Hearing*, pp. 12–13.

17. Letter from Schoettger.

18. Letters from Cook and J. L. Rogers, National Park Service, April 4, 1983.

19. Green, *Hearing*, p. 19.

20. Letter from Gates.

FOR FURTHER READING

Fullenbach, Josef. *European Environmental Cooperation: East and West.* London: Butterworth's, 1981.

Goldman, Marshall. *The Spoils of Progress: Environmental Pollution in the Soviet Union.* Cambridge, Mass.: MIT Press, 1972.

Kelley, Donald R., et al. *The Economic Superpowers and the Environment: The United States, the Soviet Union, and Japan.* San Francisco: W. H. Freeman, 1976.

Komarov, Boris (pseud.). *The Destruction of Nature in the Soviet Union.* White Plains, N.Y.: M.E. Sharpe, 1980.

Pryde, Philip. *Conservation in the Soviet Union.* New York: Cambridge University Press, 1972.

Volgyes, Ivan (ed.). *Environmental Deterioration in the Soviet Union and Eastern Europe.* New York: Praeger, 1974.

Ziegler, Charles E. *Environmental Policy in the USSR.* Amherst: University of Massachusetts Press, 1987.

6

THE UNITED STATES AND THE SOVIET UNION IN SPACE

David D. Finley

Many a child has turned the toy telescope around and made a nearby object tiny and distant. It is startling to make the baseball seem a marble. In the 1960s, when man reached space, he got a chance to turn the telescope around on his world for the first time, and the fascination was about the same. Those first color photos of earth from space made the planet, wrapped in cloud streams, look like an agate. Humankind shrank suddenly before its own eyes, newly set in cosmic scale. The habitats of Soviets and Americans seemed like squiggles on the surface of a small planet, inconclusive evidence for the likelihood of life.

Russians and Americans reached up into space independently, with a jealous eye cocked at each other, fired less by fundamental curiosity than by their apprehensions of the terrestrial adversary. Getting into space first meant a quantum leap in the hostile engagement, as a cat facing down a challenger suddenly gains the edge by springing to a table. But when both looked down together, their perspective changed.

Nearly a generation later—half the world's present population has been born since—space still makes an ambiguous promise: a new stalking ground and a stimulus to cooperation. Our immediate concern in this book is politics, the terrestrial interface of the United States and Soviet Union. So we shall adopt the closer perspective: to address the effects of space competition and cooperation on Soviet-U.S. relations. But while we do so, it might pay to keep the other, larger reality in mind.

COMPETITION, AND A LITTLE COOPERATION

Wary competition has been the larger part of the story of Soviets and Americans in space; that emphasis, which grew from the Cold War and the allure of exotic weaponry, has consistently dominated. It was the sudden fear of being left behind and vulnerable that galvanized the U.S. government and people when electronic beeps from the first Soviet Sputnik seemed to taunt them in October 1957. Thirty years later the vision of war in space rivets the attention of both governments and publics on the hucksters of the Strategic Defense Initiative (SDI). For a full generation space research has seemed inseparable from the maneuvers of the two superpower scorpions as they thrust and parry and feint on our planetary rock in the sunshine.

Cooperation has also been there from the outset, usually as a minor theme obscured by more dramatic manifestations of conflict. It is not just the tacit cooperation that proceeds from accumulation of custom in any enduring institutional conflict, but real reciprocity. Soviet-U.S. cooperation in space has depended on the ambivalent promise of the quest. That first Sputnik was launched during the 1957–1958 International Geophysical Year, a global period of cooperation in which both the United States and the Soviet Union participated and in which both had planned to launch artificial satellites.[1]

It has never been satisfactory to look at space research simply as a zero-sum game in which one side's achievement is the other's loss. As in the age of terrestrial exploration five centuries ago, every step forward in science and technology has opened new possibilities on all sides for practical application and new inquiries.

The dramatic public high point of Soviet-U.S. space cooperation occurred on July 17, 1975, when the U.S. Apollo and Soviet Soyuz spacecraft docked 225 kilometers up in orbit, displaying a jointly developed technology and the possibility of jointly conducted scientific experiments in space. Many millions watched cosmonauts Leonov and Kubasov and astronauts Stafford, Brand, and Slayton crawling through each other's modules.[2]

The Apollo Soyuz Test Project (ASTP) required gestation in a period of political relations that made overt cooperation acceptable to both governments. The event itself came to symbolize the détente of the mid–1960s to the mid–1970s. That it was dependent on the political environment to a much greater degree than it was a cause of that environment became very obvious soon afterward—when events far removed from science destroyed détente, and the support for space cooperation quickly withered.[3]

But taken in a broader perspective and over a longer time frame, the disproportionate effects of "high politics," those events at the top of the news, do not seem to be the whole story. The dramatic events of high politics do not occur in a vacuum. The conditions of the environment in which détente may deepen or disintegrate are themselves composed of routines of interaction; of public and private attitudes, visions, and expectations; of organizational structures; of perceptions of relative values, priorities, and possibilities. Cooperation affects the conditions of politics quite as actively as conflict and competition, but its increments of political relevance and success are smaller and the process of accretion slower and more fragile.

THE ASTP IN HISTORICAL CONTEXT

The background of the ASTP illuminates a generic process of Soviet-U.S. cooperation, its development, its fragility, and its promise for an enduring legacy in the political environment. Milestones along the way included a series of formal agreements, the most significant signed in Moscow by President Nixon and Premier Kosygin during their summit meeting in May 1972.

Earlier agreements had set the stage, particularly the multilateral Treaty on Principles Governing the Activities of States in the Exploration and Use of Outer Space, and the narrower bilateral Agreement on Rescue and Return of Astronauts. The preceding month the United States and Soviet Union had signed an extension of the Agreement on Exchanges and Cooperation in Scientific, Technical, Educational, Cultural, and Other Fields. The new agreement called for cooperation in the fields of space meteorology, study of the natural environment, exploration of near Earth space, the moon and planets, and space biology and medicine, all pursuant to earlier discussions and formal memoranda of the understanding generated by the National Aeronautics and Space Administration (NASA) and the Soviet Academy of Sciences over the prior 16 months. A separate article envisaged the ASTP, with a first experimental flight to be conducted during 1975. A subsequent article committed the parties to efforts to resolve problems of international law emerging in the new field of exploration and peaceful use of space. Final articles held open the prospect of mutual agreement to extend cooperation into other areas not explicitly provided for, and limited the agreement to a period of five years, subject to modification or extension thereafter by mutual agreement.[4]

The importance of formal agreements to initiate cooperative activity between the United States and Soviet Union must be underscored heavily. For the Soviet side in particular, legitimacy of cooperation depended (and depends) on an explicit foundation in international treaty law. The ideological justification for collaboration between Marxist-Leninist and capitalist worlds demands a specific coincidence of interests. It also demands avoidance of any implication that interests will indefinitely coincide. Insofar as nominal fealty to Marxist-Leninist orthodoxy remains essential, the formal paraphernalia of agreements is functional, even a prerequisite for interaction to proceed. Once in place, the domestic administration of Soviet participation can gain momentum.[5] For the U.S. side, too, specific agreements are important, if only to establish clear limits that mark off areas of cooperation that coexist with enduring conflict. Experience has shown that the illusion of general cooperation supplanting general conflict can be dangerous.

Discovering common interests in space that collaboration might advance came slowly for the United States and the Soviet Union. NASA itself was established in reaction to Sputnik, and to U.S. chagrin over the sudden challenge to its scientific and technological world leadership. Its task was to recover leadership in space for the United States and to catch up to and overtake the Soviets. National prestige was at stake; more important, national defense seemed jeopardized.

U.S. military superiority had driven Soviet space programs in the 1950s. When, after Sputnik, President Eisenhower wrote to Soviet Premier Bulganin in the spring of 1958, proposing that "outer space be dedicated to the peaceful uses of mankind and denied to the purposes of war," Bulganin replied that such a worthy commitment could come only in the context of general disarmament.[6] The Soviet Union could not afford to renounce the military potentials of space technology if they offered a chance to redress the military balance between the two countries.

The late 1950s and early 1960s were years of spectacular Soviet space achievements. Luna I first penetrated interplanetary space; Luna II reached the moon; Luna III rounded the moon to take photographs. Yuri Gagarin became the first man to orbit the earth on April 12, 1961. Meanwhile, the United States was embarrassed by frequent launch failures. There was glaring contrast between Soviet successes that captured the world's imagination and admiration, and the televised images of U.S. rockets exploding on the launch pad.

The Kennedy-Nixon presidential race in 1960 drew U.S. space shortcomings into domestic politics. Congressional struggles over budgetary priorities revealed pressure to fund U.S. space programs and related educational and scientific endeavors in order to catch up with the Soviets. Thus the peculiarly visible public dimension of space research, its integral association with military advantage, and its utility for political, sometimes partisan, battles all conspired to obstruct U.S.-Soviet cooperation in the field. Meanwhile, major political events in U.S.-Soviet relations—the Berlin Wall and the Cuban missile crisis— maintained an atmosphere in which it was hard to think positively about cooperation in either Moscow or Washington.

U.S. mobilization was dramatically successful. The latter half of the 1960s was as dominated by spectacular U.S. space achievements as the first half had been by Soviet progress. President Kennedy's call to send a man to the moon and return him safely to earth in the decade of the 1960s—to many an extravagant vision in 1961—was realized in 1969; and the series of Apollo missions to and around the moon absorbed the world's attention. Thereafter, no one doubted that projects Mercury, Gemini, and Apollo had given the United States clear leadership in the manned space exploration field.

NASA Administrator James Webb summarized the spirit of the U.S. commitment in May 1965:

The greater our lead in space, the more willing the Soviet Union may become to give up its hopes for world domination and the victory of communism everywhere. The greater our lead in space, the more ready the Soviet Union may become to cooperate with us in mutually beneficial ways that will lessen the dangers of nuclear war and advance the cause of freedom.[7]

But the hope that being behind would stimulate Soviet eagerness to cooperate was probably as unrealistic as it would have been to have expected such a reaction from the United States a few years earlier. A more promising approach was laid out by Webb's successor at NASA, Thomas Paine, after the success of Apollo II:

I decided—and I hope I made the right decision—that although Jim Webb certainly had done a tremendous job of building up NASA and the program on the basis of the Russian threat,... times had changed. The time had come for NASA to stop waving the Russian flag and to begin to justify our programs on a more fundamental basis than competition with the Soviets.[8]

Paine sought to move U.S. space exploration toward an international scientific undertaking whose dimensions would be so formidable that collaboration among nations, with the United States and Soviet Union in the lead, would be irresistible. Not only would costs be shared, and fruitless duplication of effort be avoided, but a common purpose might generate a rapprochement between adversaries that could extend beyond space research.

In the latter 1960s, despite the cloud of Vietnam, political relations between the United States and Soviet Union made a reduction of bilateral tensions and stabilization of what had become a complex matrix of interaction and joint interests more feasible. Formerly decisive margins of U.S. military superiority had shrunk, the reach of Soviet power had extended globally, and the danger of mutually catastrophic war had become unmistakable in the wake of the Cuban missile crisis. Peaceful coexistence and détente seemed more likely paths to a safer future. Managing and containing conflict, if not eliminating it, and exploring possibilities for mutually useful cooperation in economic, scientific, and cultural ways gained increasing political credibility.[9]

It was in this more moderate and open environment in U.S.-Soviet relations that Paine's conception of NASA's rationale drew support. The rationale was not enough to replace competition based on the Soviet threat, but it was enough to complicate the structure of motives and appeals, and to make approaches to the Soviet Union legitimate. Those approaches eventually led to the 1972 agreement and the drama of the ASTP three years later.

Although international public attention focused on the Nixon-Brezhnev summit at Moscow in May 1972, where the governing agreements were signed, the essential preliminaries had been in motion long before. These were of two sorts: the cultivation of interpersonal communication and the negotiation of explicit logistical understandings. Paine had opened informal contact with Mstislav Keldysh, president of the Soviet Academy of Sciences, and Anatoly Blagonravov, chairman of the Academy's Commission on Exploration and Uses of Space, in 1969. A January 1971 meeting between representatives of NASA and the Soviet Academy of Sciences had produced a summary statement of common purposes to be jointly pursued; and a crucial meeting between George Low, chief U.S. negotiator, and his Academy of Sciences counterparts in early April 1972 generated a detailed, 17-point memorandum of mutual commitments.[10] The program of educational, scientific, and cultural exchanges—waxing and waning over more than a decade—had provided some empathy and an understanding of respective national institutions and procedures, so that when political conditions made new steps possible, people and channels were available.

Prior exchanges had established "scientific bridges across political chasms."[11] But no one on either side doubted that using those bridges depended on political conditions entirely apart from inducements intrinsic to science. In 1972 conditions afforded a special opportunity.

Why then? First, Brezhnev's foreign policy of "peaceful coexistence" with the advanced capitalist countries linked progress in the domestic Soviet economy to increased economic interchange with the West. Highly visible space cooperation clearly would add symbolic reinforcement for other sorts of East-West interchange. Second, in the United States the Nixon-Kissinger administration, wrestling with the agonies of withdrawal from the decade-long misadventure in Vietnam, sought stabilized relations with the Soviet Union.[12]

More fundamentally, for both superpowers the decade after the Cuban missile crisis had been one of searching for a satisfactory replacement for the modus vivendi of the 1950s. U.S. deterrence of war, and regional containment of Soviet power on the basis of clear military superiority and NATO solidarity, no longer fit the facts of world power and politics. A compromise balance of power that managed limited conflict and recognized limited common interests appealed to the mood of realism on both sides.[13]

Other considerations helped. The long Soviet effort for international parity with its superpower rival found recognition in a new, formally equal ASTP partnership. No critical technologies were likely to transfer from one side to the other. Neither side had a clear advantage in relevant equipment, but both sides were likely to learn more about the other's capabilities and processes, a prospect that mollified both sets of military skeptics. For all these reasons, the window opened in the spring of 1972.[14]

ASTP: IMPACTS AND LEGACIES

There is no doubt that the respective scientific communities of both countries were attracted by the opportunity to collaborate. Beyond science per se, within the U.S. space program a new package of goals was needed to maintain the momentum established by the highly successful Apollo project. NASA still needed politically attractive hooks on which to hang its annual competition for federal funds in Congress, and the space shuttle program was still over the horizon. Although the annual budget struggle is much more overt in U.S. politics, it has its Soviet counterpart. Soviet space agencies recognized that the ASTP could be an effective budgetary bargaining lever. On the U.S. side the ASTP budget was $250 million. Soviet expenditures were probably comparable.

A product of external political circumstance and coincidence of many interests, the ASTP led to inspiring summer entertainment for millions, and then to an uncertain legacy for the scientific future and for the political systems that had created it. The collaboration was not without difficulties en route. Managerial styles and priorities required adjustment. Frequent bottlenecks that raised suspicions of obstructionism turned out to be attributable to disparate institutions. Over time, flexibility born of a genuine common purpose generated new teamwork, and with it the technical and managerial base for another "scientific bridge." In July 1975, when both Soyuz and Apollo modules had landed safely, it was, however, unclear whether the project had been an episode or a beginning.

From the perspective adopted by the NASA-Soviet Academy of Sciences meeting in January 1971, a broad range of space-related cooperation could be undertaken. Some of the new outlook had made its way into the 1972 agreement, which incorporated the ASTP as its centerpiece. Five joint working groups had been established between NASA and the Academy pursuant to the earlier interagency plan: meteorological satellites; meteorological rocket soundings; natural environment; exploration of near Earth, the moon, and the planets; and space biology and medicine. The political energy of ASTP derived from the summit meeting, setting the stage for a total of 11 bilateral agreements for scientific and technical collaboration over a two-year period, might reasonably be expected to spread beyond the ASTP itself and give vitality to the less dramatic cumulative activity of the two agencies.

On the other hand, one could observe that only $10 million of the $250 million ASTP budget on the U.S. side had gone to a mutual public relations venture of small scientific value. The ASTP was primarily of political value to the Soviet Union, too. Certainly there was no guarantee in the success of the public relations spectacle that scientific collaboration would be given a lasting impulse. And even if the motivation for expanded space research collaboration was reinforced, the political framework of U.S.-Soviet relations might over time cease to accommodate it.

The prospects envisioned by the 1972 agreement may be divided under three headings for analysis. First, the short-term specific commitments, which were predominant in Article 3:

The Parties have agreed to carry out projects for developing compatible rendezvous and docking systems of the United States and Soviet manned spacecraft and stations in order to enhance the safety of manned flights in space and to provide the opportunity for conducting joint scientific experiments in the future. It is planned that the first experimental flight to test these systems be conducted during 1975, envisaging the docking of a United States Apollo-type spacecraft and a Soviet Soyuz-type spacecraft with visits of Astronauts in each other's spacecraft.... [15]

These were fully implemented. But they contained no necessary followup commitment and implied only the establishment of an *opportunity* for subsequent collaboration.

It is relatively easy to evaluate the accomplishments subsumed under a second heading: the set of scientific categories in which the parties committed themselves to "develop cooperation." As indicated above, these included space meteorology; the natural environment; near-Earth space, space biology; and medicine—affirmed in Articles 1 and 2, and drawn entirely from the prior interagency agreement between NASA and the Soviet Academy. We shall come back to the record in these areas.

It is quite difficult to assess accomplishments in the third and most far-reaching category: the general vision of an enhanced legal order for space and the resolution of issues arising from exploration and efforts to preserve space for peaceful uses. These purposes are asserted in the Preamble and Article 4:

... Striving for a further expansion of cooperation between the U.S.A. and the U.S.S.R. in the exploration and use of outer space for peaceful purposes; ...

Desiring to make the results of scientific research gained from the exploration and use of outer space for peaceful purposes available for the benefit of the peoples of the two countries and of all the peoples of the world; ...

The Parties will encourage international efforts to resolve problems of international law in the exploration and use of outer space for peaceful purposes with the aim of strengthening the legal order in space and further developing international space law and will cooperate in this field.[16]

These principles and objectives are at the same time the most abstract commitments of the agreement, and in the long run the most significant for international political relations. General Secretary Brezhnev greeted the landing of Apollo and Soyuz as follows:

A relaxation of tensions and improvements in Soviet-American relations have created the conditions for carrying out the first international space flight. They are opening new possibilities for wide, fruitful development of scientific links between countries and peoples in the interests of peace and progress of all mankind.[17]

Were these new possibilities real? What happened to such far-reaching aspirations? We shall leave an assessment for last, after examining the relevant record of the years following the ASTP in U.S.-Soviet relations.

Seen in retrospect, the ASTP did indeed seem to stimulate an expansion in both breadth and depth of U.S.-Soviet space science collaboration. Talks about follow-up activity in both manned and unmanned space missions began soon after the completion of the ASTP. A package of jointly developed biological experiments was first flown on the Soviet Cosmos 782 in 1975, setting a precedent for subsequent U.S. participation in other biosatellite flights of the Cosmos series in 1977 and 1978. A three-volume joint publication, *Foundations of Space Biology and Medicine*, emanated from the joint working group in that field in 1976. Informal talks at NASA headquarters during the fall of 1976 projected the possibility of joint studies for a collaboration of shuttle, Soyuz, and Salyut spacecraft—exploiting the flexibility of shuttle resupply technology and the longer orbital stay-time of the Soviet Salyut—for scientific applications including identification and monitoring of atmospheric pollutants. An additional major project was assayed in the area of a jointly developed space platform. Simultaneously, multilateral cooperation involving the United States, the Soviet Union, Canada, and some European countries emerged on remote agricultural data sensing from space (such as moisture levels and other climactic indicators) and joint search and rescue programs utilizing U.S. and Soviet satellites (COSPAS/SARSAT).[18]

The momentum generated made it a foregone conclusion that the 1972 agreement would be renewed in 1977 for five additional years. The emphasis followed the same directions as the original agreement: delivery of Soviet lunar samples; mutual briefings on Soviet Venera 9 and 10 unmanned Venus missions and on the U.S. Viking landers on Mars; continued U.S. participation in Soviet experiments aboard Cosmos biosatellites; continuation of the joint agricultural sensing project; and tests to cross-calibrate NASA and Soviet meteorological rockets. The new agreement also included mutual consideration of the Shuttle/Salyut and space station projects as introduced the preceding year.

Shortly thereafter, in May 1977, another agreement between NASA and the Soviet Academy of Sciences established three new joint working groups, two oriented toward the operational and scientific dimensions of the Shuttle/Salyut project, and the third to consider the feasibility of an international space station on either a bilateral or a multilateral basis. The working groups, which began meeting soon after the agreement was concluded, proceeded on the assumption that the first Shuttle/Salyut flight would occur in 1981. Two years after the rendezvous of Apollo and Soyuz, there seemed to be abundant evidence of cooperation set in motion by the 1972 agreement.[19]

COLLAPSE OF DÉTENTE

Unfortunately for the proponents of space collaboration, the momentum of ASTP was not to last. U.S.-Soviet space programs withered as the supportive political environment of détente deteriorated rapidly in the late 1970s. Soviet-Cuban intervention in Angola and then the Horn of Africa, U.S. human rights initiatives targeting Soviet domestic practices, and Soviet perceptions of U.S. efforts to "play the China card" against them all cooled détente and delayed signing of the SALT-II Treaty for strategic arms control. Allegations of a "Soviet brigade" in Cuba, in violation of postmissile crisis understandings, frustrated the SALT-II Treaty in the U.S. Senate. Then the Soviet intervention in Afghanistan in December 1979 prompted President Carter to withdraw the treaty from Senate consideration and to resort to reprisals with respect to trade and the Olympics, thus marking the virtual demise of détente.

The changing political climate was reflected in a loss of momentum in space collaboration as well as in most other areas of U.S.-Soviet cooperation that had been building through the decade. The Shuttle/Salyut working groups fell into abeyance. No new projects were initiated. U.S. funding, already in decline for NASA in a period of retrenchment and lower public visibility, was withdrawn from joint working groups across the spectrum of cooperative activities. The punitive trend intensified when the Reagan administration came to office on a platform that disparaged the potential of all cooperative dimensions of U.S.-Soviet relations. The 1977 agreement was never canceled, but by 1982 there was no political possibility of renewal, and it expired. The Soviet Union expressed regret at the withdrawal of U.S. support for joint space activities and condemned the United States for sabotaging détente without cause. But by 1980, Afghanistan, a political crisis in Poland, and the twin perils of stagnant economy and the imminent prospect of a lengthy leadership succession crisis at home eliminated the likelihood of Soviet initiatives to reverse the trend.

U.S.-Soviet relations in the early 1980s revolved about the issues of a renewed arms race and the militarization of space. Competition reigned; cooperation was barely evident. Even arms reduction negotiations came to a halt in the wake of U.S. intermediate nuclear force (INF) deployments in Europe and Soviet rejection of President Reagan's 1983 "zero-option" proposals. For a year strategic, intermediate-range, and conventional arms talks were suspended, trade declined substantially, and a unilateral Soviet moratorium on underground nuclear tests was aborted in the face of U.S. refusals to join in. President Reagan's enthusiastic commitment to a vision of space-based strategic defense to change radically the long-standing equation of "mutual and assured destruction" elicited caustic Soviet denunciation. With contradictory estimates of SDI the chief focus of debate, space seemed to have become only a stalking ground for U.S.-Soviet rivalry. Little room seemed left for the cooperation that had blossomed a decade earlier.

The decade in which space cooperation had risen to unexpected degrees and then fallen back with surprising suddenness, despite tangible mutual payoffs, clearly demonstrated the dependence of Soviet-U.S. cooperation on the state of overarching political relations. As a 1981 U.S. Senate committee study observed:

Experience of the past bears out the generalization that in times of detente and easing of international pressures, space cooperation between the superpowers flourishes; in times of tension and cold war, cooperation deteriorates. Politics, in brief, is the thing: It determines the limits of space cooperation.[20]

THE LIMITS OF COOPERATION IN THE 1970s

The ASTP had been mainly a demonstration project, proving in a most unforgiving public forum the possibility of long-term, complex coordination for a common purpose between enduring political adversaries whose differences persisted. The ASTP also proved the viability of the demonstration project as a catalyst for associated scientific activity that promised mutually recognized payoffs to both sides. As science breeds unforeseen applications, so space research collaboration bred the impulse on both sides for unforeseen sorts of space collaboration and generated a growing self-interested community devoted to this activity across national frontiers.

None of this positive outcome established protective insulation against the vicissitudes of new political priorities. The benefits of collaboration in space were never great enough. Immediate political ends were more pressing. The U.S. government was quite ready to deny the Soviet Union the payoffs of collaboration as a punitive reprisal against Soviet policies it abhorred, simultaneously denying itself most of the same payoffs. The Soviet government was equally unwilling to modify political priorities or actions that would, quite predictably, incur that sort of U.S. opposition. The rise and fall of space research collaboration in the 1970s may thus be said to have shown both the intrinsic and the applied values and promise of such activity, and also their relative insignificance when arrayed against overriding political values.

Our understanding of "linkage politics," in this case the use of deprivations in one dimension of Soviet-U.S. relations as a conscious instrument to induce a modification of policy in another dimension, may profit from this interlude of space cooperation during the détente of the 1970s. One lesson might be that it is foolish for either the United States or the Soviet Union to expect to avoid "linkage" policymaking by the other. Certainly in the domestic politics of U.S. democracy it is difficult to undertake a sustained policy of visible cooperation with an adversary when punitive measures, even with sacrifices, seem readily at hand. The U.S. administration that seeks to compartmentalize its international connections is typically indicted for inconsistency and lack of principle rather than praised for its sophistication. It is frequently so indicted by constituencies it is powerless to resist.

But an equally evident lesson is the resistance that strongly maintained political priorities present to the costs as well as the benefits of scientific cooperation. The threat to suspend cooperation was notably ineffectual as a U.S. lever against Soviet behavior in Afghanistan, a decision-making arena in which other variables crowded out the potentially valuable returns of U.S. cooperation in space research. Nor did the United States hesitate to sacrifice self-interest in space collaboration for even the tenuous hope of political leverage.

But to generalize that the leverage of "linkage politics" is never effectual would be equally foolish. One need only contemplate the historical linkage between military force and political influence. The lesson, then, is limited but clear: in contemporary U.S.-Soviet relations neither the carrot of cooperative payoffs nor the stick of denial of ongoing payoffs can be expected significantly to moderate the winds of high politics directly.

SPACE COOPERATION IN THE 1980s

The détente of the 1970s proved fragile and vulnerable. But the deterioration of U.S.-Soviet cooperation appears to be reversible. Once again the macropolitical environment has changed to allow prospects for new cooperation to emerge. Neither Yuri Andropov nor Konstantin Chernenko occupied the office of Soviet Communist Party general secretary long enough to consolidate personal control fully and to give active new direction to Soviet foreign policy. But Mikhail Gorbachev, clearly impatient to put the floundering Soviet bureaucracy on a reform path, has moved quickly since the spring of 1985 to take the initiative in U.S.-Soviet relations. The recovery of détente is not a new theme, but Soviet opposition to SDI has given it renewed urgency and accorded the uses of space top billing. At the Geneva summit in November 1985, Gorbachev and Reagan agreed to reinvigorate programs of U.S.-Soviet educational and cultural exchange, signing formal agreements to pave the way. Subsequent Soviet initiatives in arms control negotiations, including those at the Reykjavik summit meeting in October 1986, contributed to a resumption of serious discussions that led to a major INF agreement, and thus a newly receptive environment for scientific and technological cooperation associated with détente in the 1970s.

The opportunities for intrinsically valuable scientific payoffs are still apparent to the respective scientific communities. Détente clearly serves both the declaratory long-term policy and the short-term priorities of the Gorbachev leadership. The attitude of the second Reagan administration has been less clear than the first about the appropriate balance of conflict and cooperation with the Soviet Union. Continuing commitment to SDI has been accompanied by declaratory efforts to associate new U.S.-Soviet cooperation with the SDI vision of a safer relationship.

Given this opening, the Senate Foreign Relations Committee held hearings on the topic in September 1984, and Congress passed Public Law 98–562, calling for energetic pursuit of a renewal of the 1972–1977 agreement and for "exploring further opportunities for cooperative East-West ventures in space." In February 1985 Senator Spark Matsunaga, the leading congressional proponent of renewed cooperation, introduced a joint resolution in support of U.S.-Soviet cooperation on Mars exploration missions, envisioned on an unmanned basis beginning in 1990 in the United States and in the Soviet Union even

Table 6.1
Potential U.S.–Soviet Collaborative Activities
(From OTA Workshop, May 1984)

Sun-Earth (Heliospheric):
- Joint meetings to develop space plasma theory
- Joint coordination and data exchange in solar terrestrial physics—specifically for International Solar-Terrestrial Program (U.S./ESA/Japan)
- Exchange of co-investigators
- Hosted instruments (detectors)
- Joint Starprobe mission to the Sun (very long range)

Astrophysics:
- Joint planning for:
  - Gamma-ray burst studies using Gamma Ray Observatory and other spacecraft
  - Very long baseline interferometry (complementary orbits of spacecraft)
- Data exchange regarding contamination of cooled surfaces (infrared telescopes) and plasma glow problems (ultraviolet telescopes)
- Co-investigators on Space Telescope, Gamma Ray Observatory, and Advanced Astronomical X-ray Facility
- Mounting of Spacelab experiments on Salyut for long-term exposure

Planetary:
Venus:
- Joint planning or joint missions as part of a sequence to investigate the properties of the atmosphere of Venus
- Joint planning/missions for "long-lived" Venus surface studies
Mars:
- Coordinated planning for Mars missions ca. 1990 (Phobos lander and Mars Geochemical Climatological Orbiter (MGCO))
- Joint planning/missions for Mars sample analysis or return

Note: ESA-European Space Agency

earlier. At the initiative of Senators Spark Matsunaga, Charles Mathias, and Claiborne Pell, the Congressional Office of Technological Assessment (OTA) used the tenth anniversary of the ASTP to review U.S.-Soviet cooperation in space, including sponsorship of a workshop on possible future directions of cooperative activity and inquiries among Soviet scientists about mutual priorities.[21]

Table 6.1 shows the range of collaborative activities advocated by the OTA workshop in May 1984. Participants included a group of 13

Table 6.1 (continued)

Moon:
- Lunar geochemical orbiters
- Continued lunar sample exchange

Comets:
- Soviet contribution to instrument design for U.S. mission to Comet Kopf (1990) [possibly a hosted experiment]
- Coordinated or joint cometary sample return missions

Outer Planets:
- Joint orbiter/probe missions to Saturn, Uranus, or Neptune [after the NASA/ESA Cassini mission to Saturn and Titan, Uranus is the next cooperative opportunity here]

Life Sciences:

Effects of long-duration spaceflight:
- Data exchange and joint or hosted flight experiments, especially on problems of (human) bone loss, radiation effects, life support, and countermeasures
- Joint ground-based simulations (e.g., long-duration bed rest)
- Joint (or hosted) biological experiments aboard Cosmos biosatellites and/or Spacelab, using various animal and plant species

Exobiology:
- Joint unmanned missions or data exchange to further investigate the question of life on Mars
- Joint meetings and/or data exchange regarding search for extraterrestrial intelligence (SETI)
- Joint collection and analysis of Antarctic meteorites

Global biology:
- Earth observations data exchange

Life support systems:
- Joint ground-based demonstration and flight testing of life support systems (including bioregenerative type)

Source: Nancy Lubin, *U.S.-Soviet Cooperation in Space*, OTA-TMSTI-27 (Washington, D.C.: U.S. Congress, Office of Technology Assessment, July 1985), p. 49.

U.S. scientists with experience in cooperative programs with the Soviet Union.

Following the May 1984 OTA workshop, the project director, Dr. Nancy Lubin, interviewed Soviet scientists in Moscow for reactions and views on the most promising areas for future cooperation in space science. She reported the following suggestions, which coincide strongly with the workshop list:

Planetary research:

—Study of asteroids, comets, and interplanetary dust

—Study of Mars, including sample return

—Continuation of Venus study

—Study of planetary moons and Saturn's rings

Life sciences:

—Human and animal responses to spaceflight factors

—Standardization of research methods and data collection techniques

—Further ground-based simulation studies

Solar-terrestrial physics/astrophysics:

—General interest in cooperating in these fields.[22]

In 1985 a warming of the Reagan administration's attitude toward selective cooperation with the Soviet Union appeared to be moving the countries slowly in the direction of resumed space collaboration, despite SDI as the major focus of bilateral conflict. Then the *Challenger* disaster in February 1986 threw NASA into protracted organizational disarray and obscured the cooperative momentum that had begun to show promise. A searching inquiry into the dynamics of the civilian space program brought a hiatus in U.S. manned programs whose resolution was still uncertain during the spring of 1988.

Meanwhile, the formal framework of renewed space cooperation was restored during Secretary of State Shultz's visit to Moscow in April 1987. Shultz and Soviet Foreign Minister Shevardnadze signed an agreement on April 15, reinstating the program that had gone unrenewed in 1982 because of U.S. protest over the declaration of martial law in Poland.[23]

The new agreement specified coordination of national projects in solar-system exploration, space astronomy and astrophysics, earth sciences, solar-terrestrial physics, space biology, and medicine. The principal short-term projects envisioned were coordinated unmanned missions to Mars and its moon Phobos.

In early 1988 an aggressive Soviet commercial bid for Western satellite launching business left many U.S. officials chagrined by the sudden shift of fortune and uncertain whether this new prospect represented threat or opportunity.[24] As negotiations proceeded toward an expanded scope for scientific exchanges in April 1988, one U.S. State Department official observed of that effort, "We are virtually at the level of activity we reached at the highest level of detente."[25]

THE PROMISES OF SPACE COOPERATION

To assess the promise of Soviet-U.S. space cooperation broadly, let us return to the text of the May 1972 agreement, particularly to the more abstract aspirations expressed in the Preamble and Article 4.

They go beyond short-run scientific and political rationales. The latter were clear-cut and, while not identical on each side, they overlapped substantially: Space exploration was too vast and expensive for one country to pursue independently. Duplication of effort was wasteful and inevitably retarded the progress that cooperation could offer. The two scientific communities had much to learn from sharing their complementary strengths. The initial challenge was to create the organizational base for scientific exchange or, rather, to discover whether that could be done despite deep-seated political estrangement. The political rationale stemmed from mutual recognition that coexistence was a requisite for survival, that neither political system was likely to collapse, and that neither could impose its values or institutions on the other. Limited cooperation, which did not yield political advantage unevenly, could reinforce the stability of a bilateral relationship, always vulnerable to dangerous oscillations, and could serve mutual self-interests.

Put another way, space cooperation, carefully delimited and regulated, would not damage the relative political positions of either party and would offer the prospect of positive nonpolitical payoffs. Beyond that minimum, other political aspirations hovered: the cultivation of third-party approval, the ratification of equal status for the Soviet Union, the reduction of uncertainty about rival scientific capabilities, and the promotion of greater openness toward the international community by the Soviet Union. These asymmetrical aspirations characterized the agendas of the respective parties.

Some of these aspirations, when projected into the future, fed the skepticism and caution of critics on both sides. Chief among them were military professionals, understandably anxious about the implied flow of technological expertise and loss of positive control over militarily significant information that could prove an intelligence bonanza to the adversary. Unlike such scientific fields as medicine, relatively distant from any direct impact on a perceived military balance, space science was inseparable substantively and organizationally from the advance of military technology and strategy in the two countries.

Set against the mutually felt political disadvantages of space science as an arena for exploring the potentials of cooperation were the visibility and popular appeal of a field that excites public imagination. The symbolic returns of cooperation in space promised a magnified political impact that virtually no other field could offer. If the Soviet Union and the United States could cooperate in space, there would be no mistaking the message anywhere; the implication would be that much more and varied cooperation would also be feasible.

What more really could be expected if the short-term projects worked out? That was the question addressed in the 1972 Preamble, where the high-mindedness of each side invoked universal aspirations of peace and well-being as a platform for specific commitments. Differences of philosophical premise, of readings of future possibilities, and of political temperament always allow such language to mean different things to different people.

There are a few things the collaborative experience allows us to say with confidence. There is a mutual scientific payoff to be realized by cooperation, and it is self-reinforcing. Joint scientific endeavors generate the appetite for more. Horizons broaden for both intensive and extensive expansion. When agreements have been concluded, and carefully elaborated and interpreted to remove misunderstanding, the Soviet side fulfills its commitments just as punctiliously as the U.S. side. Given the potentials of space research for improving human life on Earth—potentials already redeemed in some of the spin-offs from cooperation in the past 15 years—and given the capabilities of the respective scientific communities and the support structures of each government, it is hard to avoid the conclusion that human progress will be better served by cooperation than by the alternative of isolated parallel competition.

It has also been demonstrated that organizational and interpersonal ties provide the matrix in which cooperation can be fruitful across political barriers that divide the United States and the Soviet Union. The apparent regeneration of active collaboration in the latter 1980s, after years in which political obstacles nearly shut down earlier momentum, shows the useful legacy of earlier structures and understandings. The memories of collaboration are, on balance, memories of success.

We may also say with confidence that the fears of acute military or political disadvantage to one side or the other have proven not baseless but avoidable. It is highly probable that militarily exploitable discoveries will emerge from future cooperation, but there is little reason to think that advantages will be so unbalanced that they will constitute an unacceptable cost.

The political consequences of the collaborative process in space research justify hopes for modest indirect effects on the bilateral relationship. But they certainly disappoint the more far-reaching vision to make cooperation supplant conflict and provide a remedy for the enduring political estrangement of the two political orders. Space cooperation, like other modes of cooperation characteristic of the détente of the 1970s, showed no measurable capacity to moderate independently generated political conflict. The matrix of cooperation did not establish strong enough common purposes to withstand the divisive pressures of international politics, much less defuse them. Punitive decisions to withdraw cooperation stopped only cooperation, not offensive or hostile behavior.

Is there, then, in this experience any support for the old theory of functional spillover, the notion that cooperative practices can by example spill over to affect new dimensions of international interaction? There is nothing conclusive, but there is what we might call circumstantial evidence. Attitudes of principals involved in collaboration certainly change, and the record suggests that collaborators reinforce their commitments. Priorities also change, and vested interests result from protracted mutual commitment. Public attitudes change, too, and stereotyped images of intransigent malevolence yield to more complex realities. Insofar as public attitudes are politically relevant to conditioning the limits of maneuver for public officials, they may subtly affect the environment of international interaction. But the returns of such spillover are not likely to be dramatic; and they may not even be attributable in any specifically measurable sense. As the experience of conflict reinforces the probability of more and deeper conflict, however, the experience of cooperation tends the opposite way.

Four cautions also emerge from the story sketched here. First, when expectations are too high, disillusionment may jeopardize the process as well as the product. Unreasonable expectations are easy to create in so salient a public spectacle as space research and exploration. The temptation to oversell space collaboration should be resisted.

Second, the foundation of formal and detailed international legal agreements is basic to successful U.S.-Soviet cooperation. Without formal treaty instruments to legitimate collaboration, Soviet participation cannot be unleashed in a sustained way. It is part of recognizing our different institutional dynamics to pay full attention to this prerequisite, unlikely as it is for Americans to be patient with it.

Third, the temptation to make space cooperation serve short-term military needs, to become a cover for sophisticated espionage, demands constant resistance. The temptation will always be there on both sides, and there is no definitive remedy. Only prudent forbearance can avert this poison to cooperation.

Fourth, the lessons of "linkage politics" are important to Soviet-U.S. interaction in space science. Experience suggests that reprisals in the form of withdrawn cooperation are likely to be ineffectual for changing or deflecting, or even deterring, national policies associated with what are perceived to be vital self-interests. To use reprisals, intuitively appealing as the gambit may seem, is likely only to squander the positive values of cooperation. Recognizing that in U.S.-Soviet relations political crises will inevitably arise in the future as they have in the past, one should seek to maintain "bridges across political chasms" *especially* in times of conflict, so that infrastructures that work to obviate sources of future conflict may endure.

In July 1987 a meeting of U.S. scientists in Boulder, Colorado, conducted a four-hour satellite conference with Soviet counterparts in Moscow. The chief topics were Mars collaboration and Mars life prospects. Carl Sagan, the U.S. sponsor for the Planetary Society, called on the "two space-faring nations" to lead an international commitment that would concert scientific energies "for good not evil," and lead the way toward making the solar system habitable, to provide a stepping-stone for exploration of the universe beyond.

To return to the metaphor with which this chapter began, it is time to turn the telescope around again, to reach for the ennobling unity of humankind in a cooperative adventure, to reach out to challenge the horizons of present imagination, together.

NOTES

1. See D. Finley, "Soviet-U.S. Cooperation in Space and Medicine," in Nish Jamgotch, Jr. (ed.), *Sectors of Mutual Benefit in U.S.-Soviet Relations* (Durham, N.C.: Duke University Press, 1985), ch. 7.

2. Edward Ezell and Linda Ezell, *The Partnership: A History of the Apollo-Soyuz Test Project* (Washington, D.C.: NASA, 1978), pp. 22–23.

3. Finley, "Soviet-U.S. Cooperation," pp. 135–138; Congressional Research Society, *Soviet Space Programs, 1976–80* (Washington, D.C.: U.S. Government Printing Office, 1982), pp. 209, 351–357.

4. Jamgotch, *Sectors of Mutual Benefit*, app. J.

5. See J. F. Triska and R. M. Slusser, *The Theory, Law, and Policy of Soviet Treaties* (Stanford, Calif.: Stanford University Press, 1962), ch. 2.

6. Ezell and Ezell, *The Partnership*, pp. 24–25.

7. Quoted in ibid., p. 58.

8. Quoted in ibid., p. 2.

9. D. Finley, "Conflict, Cooperation and Retaliation in Soviet-U.S. Relations," paper presented to the annual meeting of the International Studies Association, Washington, D.C., April 15, 1987.

10. Ezell and Ezell, *The Partnership*, p. 187.

11. Quoted in ibid., p. 22.

12. See Henry Kissinger, *The White House Years* (Boston: Little, Brown, 1979), pp. 1124–1164.

13. See D. Finley, "Detente and Soviet-American Trade," *Studies in Comparative Communism*, Spring–Summer 1975, pp. 66–97.

14. Finley, "Soviet-U.S. Cooperation," p. 134.

15. Jamgotch, *Sectors of Mutual Benefit*, app. J.

16. Ibid.

17. Quoted in *U.S.-Soviet Cooperation in Space*, Nancy Lubin, project director, OTA-TMSTI–27 (Washington, D.C.: U.S. Congress, Office of Technology Assessment, July 1985), p. 27.

18. Finley, "Soviet-U.S. Cooperation," p. 138.

19. *U.S.-Soviet Cooperation in Space*, p. 32.

20. *Soviet Space Programs*, pp. 209, 264–265.

21. *U.S.-Soviet Cooperation in Space*, p. 36.

22. Ibid., p. 48.

23. Henry Kamm, "U.S. and Soviets Sign a Pact over Exploration in Space," *New York Times*, April 16, 1987, p. A–14.

24. See Kathy Sawyer, "Soviets Move Aggressively in Marketing Space Services," *Washington Post*, January 13, 1988, p. 1, 12.

25. Kim McDonald, "New U.S.-Soviet Pact on Basic Sciences Nears Completion," *Chronicle of Higher Education*, April 27, 1988, pp. 1, 44.

FOR FURTHER READING

Aviation Week and Space Technology, weekly.

Cooper, Henry S. F. "Explorers." *The New Yorker*, March 7, 1988, pp. 43–61.

East-West Cooperation in Outer Space. Senate Committee on Foreign Relations, Hearings, September 13, 1984. Washington, D.C.: U.S. Government Printing Office, 1984.

Ezell, Edward, and Linda Ezell. *The Partnership: A History of the Apollo-Soyuz Test Project*. Washington, D.C.: NASA, 1978.

Frutkin, Arnold W. *International Cooperation in Space*. Englewood Cliffs, N.J.: Prentice-Hall, 1965.

Harvey, Dodd L., and Linda C. Ciccoritti. *U.S.-Soviet Cooperation in Space*. Miami: Center for Advanced International Studies, University of Miami, 1974.

McDougall, Walter A. *The Heavens and the Earth: A Political History of the Space Age*. New York: Basic Books, 1985.

U.S.-Soviet Cooperation in Space. Nancy Lubin, project director. Washington, D.C.: U.S. Congress, Office of Technology Assessment, July 1985.

Whelan, Joseph G. "Soviet Attitude Toward International Cooperation in Space." In Congressional Research Service, *Soviet Space Programs, 1976–80*. Washington, D.C.: U.S. Government Printing Office, 1982.

7

U.S.-SOVIET COOPERATION IN MEDICINE AND HEALTH

Harold Sandler, M.D.

Medicine is a social science, and politics nothing but medicine on a grand scale.

Rudolf Ludwig Virchow, M.D., 1847

Cooperation between U.S. and Soviet physicians and investigators in various fields of medicine and medical research has not been the order of the day. For most of this century Soviet medical researchers existed in a politically and scientifically controlled vacuum caused by two world wars, a revolution, and the paranoia and random terror of Stalinism. Significant openings came only after the end of World War II. Since that time, any attempt to measure progress in scientific and medical interactions has continually needed to be balanced against strains in governmental relations as the United States and the Soviet Union have participated in an ever spiraling, unremitting nuclear arms race. Relations improved during periods of relaxed political relations and soured in direct proportion to events that increased tensions. It has always been hoped that cooperative medical and scientific programs would help promote better understanding, ease tensions, and avert formal confrontations. As official channels have fallen victim to Cold War rhetoric since the late 1970s, more and more actions to promote cooperation have been undertaken by private citizens and non-governmental groups.

The material in this chapter will review unique contributions that the medical profession and the physicians' movement have made to the field of U.S.-Soviet cooperation, particularly since 1980.

BACKGROUND

This century has seen the greatest progress in medicine in the history of mankind, most of it occurring since the 1930s. The major change has been due to beneficial applications of technological developments, the hallmark of our times. Advances have followed in rapid succession, and with them the development of new techniques, new equipment, and even new fields of study.

Progress has not been limited to a single group or nation. The language of physicians has been international. Like the eradication of disease, medical advances have been accomplished by crossing borders. In the 1950s and 1960s, exchanges of information, people, and techniques became not only natural but also mandatory for scientists in order to keep abreast of methods and share insights concerning various disease states. Medical advances included transplant and replacement surgery of heart, lungs, kidneys, liver, and portions of the eye; laser techniques, microsurgery, and the fitting of computerized prostheses; computer-controlled scanning for accurate diagnosis and treatment of disorders that affect internal body organs; and the creation of beneficial drugs and treatments.

As one change followed another, East and West found these medical grounds to be areas where they could come together free of concerns raised by ideologies or politics. They also realized, as Virchow had demonstrated almost a century and a half earlier, that a people's health is a matter of direct social concern, that social and economic conditions do have effects on diseases, and that any move to improve health must carry with it improvement in social conditions. Based on these scientific and humanitarian concerns, medical exchanges between the United States and the Soviet Union have never ceased over the past decades, even during the worst of the Cold War period.[1]

It is to the credit of close cooperative efforts of U.S. and Soviet teams that the most significant medical achievement of the twentieth century was made—the eradication of smallpox. In 1967, when smallpox was targeted for attention by the World Health Organization, there were 12–15 million people infected with the disease and 2 million dying annually. By 1977 the last case had been identified, and by 1979 an official advisory group could certify that global eradication had been accomplished.[2] The Soviet Union provided a large amount of the vaccine that was used. The project stands as a model of what can be done when both countries are not distracted by Cold War issues.

Only a handful of U.S. scholars worked in the Soviet Union prior to 1958, and that was in the period from 1924 to 1936. In 1958, the Lacy-Zarubin agreement was signed, allowing official interaction and exchange in the fields of medicine and health for the first time. Paralleling the 1972 SALT I agreement, the era of détente saw a substantial increase in interactive programs in all fields of science, including medicine and medical research. A formal agreement was signed in 1972 by Health, Education and Welfare Secretary Elliot Richardson and Soviet Minister of Health Boris Petrovsky to broaden the scope of ongoing work to include cancer, infectious diseases, eye diseases and environmental health. The Joint Committee for Health Cooperation in the Field of Medical Science and Public Health was created to facilitate these broader ranges of exchanges. President Nixon established other working groups to facilitate programs in space medicine and biology, and artificial heart development.

In the early 1980s, overall scientific relations in the area of medicine and health tended to follow official governmental leadership. Levels during this period were only 30–50 percent of peak activity during détente, but showed signs of marked improvement. Agreements signed at the November 1985 Geneva summit allowed previously established programs in heart disease, cancer, artificial heart development, and environmental protection to continue. An agreement to reinstitute cooperative programs in space medicine and research was signed by Secretary of State George Shultz and Foreign Minister Eduard Shevardnadze in April 1987, allowing for the possibility of a joint U.S.-Soviet manned Mars mission after the turn of the century.

Faced with a decade of uncertainty regarding official approval and funding, an increasing number of joint medical projects could not rely on formal government sanction and support, though they received unofficial approval. By 1981–1982 medical activities, plus other endeavors in science and the arts, become significant enough to be defined in official State Department terms as "track two" or "citizen" diplomacy.

Most citizen diplomats with medical backgrounds were personally motivated by the realization that medical concerns had broadened since the turn of the century. Concerns included appreciation of environmental, social, and economic factors that induce disease. As more and more became known about radiation and the deadly, destructive power of nuclear weapons, physicians in the United States and Soviet Union saw an unprecedented threat to the lives of their patients and a potential threat to all life on the planet. Goaded by an understanding of the preciousness of life, doctors began speaking out on the medical consequences of atomic warfare. Findings revealed that a nuclear war could never be won; it would result in death, disease, and environmental change on a global scale; effective medical treatment would be unavailable; and prevention was the only effective treatment, thus requiring education of the public and all responsible officials.

Faced with the possible destruction of billions of human lives, most felt that the nuclear threat posed new moral and ethical issues. Confronted with a history of distrust between the United States and Soviet Union that spanned almost seven decades, physicians understood that these issues were too important to be left to the generals and bureaucrats. Many on both sides—good, honest, and patriotic people—saw the danger created by these national policies and wished to put things right. Initial efforts focused on a need for increased dialogue and social contact. Subsequent interactions promoted presentations at national and international scientific meetings, articles, messages to the heads of government, and exchanges of physicians to provide factual information on what could be the "last epidemic" the world would ever know.

OFFICIAL EXCHANGE PROGRAMS

The modern era of Soviet-U.S. interactions in the field of medicine was initiated in 1972 through tasks approved by the Joint Committee for Health Cooperation in the Field of Medical Science and Public Health. Work was extended for five years in 1977 and renewed for five years in 1983. Though potentially covering most fields of medicine and health, the program had focused mainly on heart disease and cancer, diseases that cause 75–80 percent of all deaths in the developed countries of the world. Under this agreement the National Heart, Lung, and Blood Institute of the National Institutes of Health (NIH) has worked with the A. L. Myasnikov Institute of Cardiology in Moscow, later absorbed into the All-Union Cardiology Institute (headed by Y. I. Chazov, Soviet minister of health), and the National Cancer Institute of NIH, with the Institute of Experimental and Clinical Oncology, Moscow (now the All-Union Cancer Research Center, headed by Academician N. N. Blokhin).

In 1974, documents signed by Secretary of State Henry Kissinger and Foreign Minister Andrei Gromyko added work in the field of artificial heart research. This latter agreement has been extended twice for five-year periods. In all cases careful annual review of the various programs has shown them to be beneficial to both sides.[3] They will automatically be renewed for successive five-year periods, unless either party announces the intention to terminate six months prior to expiration. Programs have enabled activities in seven major areas of medicine and health: cardiovascular disease, cancer, artificial heart development, environmental health, arthritis, influenza and acute respiratory disease, and eye disease.[4]

Cardiovascular Disease

The area of greatest interaction and benefit has been cardiovascular disease, the leading cause of death in both countries. Mortality per 100,000 individuals continues to exceed its closest rival, cancer, by a factor of two to three. Since the late 1970s, and particularly since the mid–1980s, Soviet investigators have shared findings concerning risk of heart attack for normal and susceptible populations, and autopsy material on patients who have died. This has contributed substantially to epidemiological information on various risk factors. In addition, Soviet scientists have provided information on newly developed drugs for treating abnormal cardiac rhythms and on biobehavioral approaches to the control of hypertension.[5] U.S. scientists have been allowed access to a large primate center in Sukhumi (located in the republic of Georgia) to study appropriate animal models evidencing blood pressure control problems.

During 1986, activities included trips to the Soviet Union by 15 U.S. scientists and 2 delegations (including 11 scientists) for a total stay of 323 days, or 10.7 person-months. During that period 15 Soviet scientists and 1 delegation (9 scientists) visited the United States for a total of 701 days, or 23.3 person-months. Two symposia were held: the second Joint U.S./USSR Lipoprotein Symposium at Bethesda, Maryland (September 1986) and the sixth Joint U.S./USSR Symposium on Congenital Heart Disease at Moscow (May 1986). Joint heart disease projects have proceeded in seven areas.

Plaque Formation in Arteries (Atherosclerosis)

Atherosclerosis, leading to the sudden or gradual blockage of heart blood vessels, is responsible for more deaths in the United States and Soviet Union than any other disease. Of the numerous recognized risk factors, elevated blood content of fatty substances (lipids), specifically blood cholesterol, have been shown to be implicated. Low-density lipoproteins (LDL, fatty substances) are a major carrier of cholesterol and directly associated with increased risk. High-density lipoproteins (HDL) are protective. Data collected on these blood-borne factors have been shared by the Lipid Research Clinic's Program of the NIH and comparable clinics in Moscow and Leningrad. The first formal report of this interaction was made in 1981 and subsequent reports have been presented at national and international meetings, the last being the World Congress of Cardiology, Washington, D.C., September 15–20, 1986. Studies showed marked and unexpected cross-cultural differences in risk factors between U.S. and Soviet populations.[6] Soviet middle-aged men have significantly higher HDL levels than similarly aged Americans. In both countries avoidance of obesity and moderate alcohol intake correlate with increased HDL and good health. In the U.S. sample smoking correlated inversely with HDL cholesterol.

Management of Coronary Heart Disease

A total of 1,648 patients (one-fourth from the Soviet Union) have been studied to evaluate the success rates of three types of possible treatment of a heart attack: intense medical management (Soviet Union), coronary bypass surgery (United States), and conventional medical management (both countries). The cost of surgical treatment to handle heart vessel blockage (coronary bypass surgery) is one of the greatest financial burdens facing U.S. and Soviet populations. Ability to postpone surgery, or not employ it, has far-reaching medical and financial implications. Definitive information will not be available until the 1990s, yet benefits from vigorous medical treatment are already present in the Soviet series.[7] Early in the exchange program U.S. scientists learned that Soviets use nitrous oxide to quiet patients experiencing a heart attack. Follow-up studies have substantiated the effectiveness of this treatment, and it is now used in the United States.

Heart and Lung Metabolism

Work has focused on a better understanding of coronary heart disease development, better treatment, and earlier diagnosis. This has led to joint studies to uncover the manner in which heart muscle cells obtain energy, coordinate contractions, and respond to alterations in the environment. Soviet scientists have led in the development of methods that use cellular metabolic substances (liposomes) for labeling damaged areas of heart muscle and for binding medications to these substances for more rapid delivery to damaged areas. Because of pioneering work in understanding cardiac cell metabolism in the presence of atherosclerosis, new areas of medical investigation are being opened. These involve using blood samples drawn at the time of routine medical examinations and analyzed for blood fatty substance content, thus allowing for improved estimates of atherosclerotic plaque formation and the ability to screen patients earlier for impending heart attack episodes.

Since the 1970s, this program has produced significant scientific benefits that have included studies to measure the benefits of special chemical substances that can be injected into the bloodstream, such as hyaluronidase, to dissolve blood clots in coronary vessels of heart attack victims; improvements in electrocardiographic methods for assessing heart damage; assessment of the role of calcium ions and their transport from the blood to the interior of the working heart cell, as a means of limiting damage after an attack; and development of new methods to evaluate the manner of cholesterol deposit in the body (nature of the receptor binding sites in cells) and atherosclerotic damage to arterial walls.

Congenital Heart Disease

New methods have been explored by the Bukulev Institute for Cardiovascular Surgery, Moscow, and various centers in the United States for the diagnosis and treatment of congenital heart disease. One of the more interesting projects dealt with a joint study on aortopulmonary septal defect, an inborn cardiac abnormality causing volume overloading of the heart and cardiac failure at an early age. New methods for approaching this problem were developed and jointly published.[8]

Sudden Death

The sudden triggering of an abnormal heart rate (arrhythmia) continues to be a cause of a great number of deaths in both countries. Research on this problem has been one of the most fruitful areas of collaboration between the United States and the Soviet Union.[9] Soviet investigators have developed unique techniques for basic research on arrhythmias, including development of promising new drugs for their control. Certain of these, such as ethmozin, a phenothiazide, are now under investigation in the United States and under license for manufacture by Dupont Chemical Company. In a joint study, 54 percent of patients resistant to other therapies responded to ethmozin. A more recent drug, the diethylamine of ethmozin, promises to be an even more powerful antiarrhythmic agent because it can influence both fast and slow interior electric currents of the heart. Joint studies have also been conducted on other useful drugs for controlling heart rhythm, including mexatil, lidocaine, aprinidine, and aconitrane. Clinically, these latter drugs are now used routinely in both countries.

A particularly helpful basic research tool for U.S. scientists has been the fast ambulance service in Moscow and Leningrad. This has provided an excellent means of applying newer methods of treatment, as well as invaluable autopsy material to evaluate failures.

Three conferences on sudden cardiac death have been held. The most recent was part of the first International Conference on Preventive Cardiology held at Moscow in June 1985, attended by over 1,000 doctors and medical researchers from around the world. Seventy U.S. cardiologists agreed on a program for addressing the issue of preventive cardiology. In the words of the conference chairman, Academician Yevgeni Chazov, head of the USSR Cardiological Research Center in Moscow, "It was the first representative scientific convention that not only discussed what was to be done, but also considered all of the latest achievements and failures and analyzed the reasons."[10]

Blood Transfusion

Efforts have concentrated on the prevention of posttransfusion hepatitis and preservation of blood for surgery. In 1977 the two nations developed protocols for the study of hepatitis B markers in the sera of blood from both populations, leading to protocols that facilitated determination of its prevalence and the development of methods for avoidance.

Hypertension

Collaborations in basic and biobehavioral research have focused on the use of nonpharmacologic approaches to blood pressure control, such as biofeedback methods. Basic research efforts have been greatly enhanced through access to the Institute of Experimental Pathology and Therapy in Sukhumi. This institute (under the leadership of Academician B. Lapin) houses a primate center unique in its research studies of baboons that demonstrate the effects of stress in causing elevated blood pressure.

Cancer

Programs that in late 1981 consisted of activites in cancer treatment, tumor immunology, viral oncology, genetic aspects of neoplasia, epidemiology, cancer pathomorphology, cancer control measures, and the role of cancer education centers in training personnel and the public have been restructured to work in three fields: cancer treatment, carcinogenesis, and cancer prevention. Annual meetings of delegations have begun once again following agreements signed at Moscow in October 1986. During the period 1979–1986, 94 U.S. scientists traveled to work in the Soviet Union for a period of 35.8 man-months, and 72 Soviet physicians spent 66.7 man-months in the United States. In 1980 a jointly authored monograph was published that dealt with the experimental evaluation of various antitumor drugs.[11] Results from these studies increased the number of chemotherapeutic agents and confidence in their use. Both countries felt interactions to be quite beneficial in this most important health-related field.

Work on the Soviet side has helped to add new information on biological and chemical factors that induce tumors, the role of nutrition in the etiology and prevention of certain tumors, the relationship between smoking and cancer, and the effectiveness of various treatment regimens.

Artificial Heart

Cooperation has focused on the development and testing of biomaterials for use in circulatory assist devices.[12] Despite recent human testing using the Jarvik I device, no totally acceptable device is available in either country. Collaborative efforts seek answers, as donor-transplant programs evidence limitations due to costs and availability of donor hearts. The third Joint U.S./USSR Symposium on Mechanically Assisted Circulation and the Artificial Heart was held at Moscow in 1985. Papers from the symposium were accepted for publication as a supplement to the journal *Artificial Organs* in 1987.

Environmental Health

The joint environmental health program has been conducted by the U.S. National Institute of Environmental Health Sciences and the Soviet A. N. Sysin Institute of General and Communal Hygiene. Attention has focused on the effects of physical and chemical agents on human health, particularly changes caused by microwave radiation and static and low-frequency electromagnetic fields. Soviet investigators have reported chronic fatigue and emotional stress at lower doses than reported by U.S. investigators. As a result, allowable standards for exposure have been set considerably lower in the Soviet Union and are under further investigation in the United States.

Arthritis

Three epidemiological studies on juvenile rheumatoid arthritis have been conducted by the National Institute of Arthritis and Diabetes in the United States and the Institute of Rheumatism in Moscow. The first of these, initiated in 1974 and completed in 1979, included data from 15 U.S. centers and 5 Soviet institutes. Treatment efficacies of aspirin, d-penicillinamine and hydroxycloroquine, with placebo control, were compared and led to new findings about the effectiveness of aspirin treatment. Results were presented at the annual meeting of the American Rheumatism Society in 1980.[13] A study of orally administered gold compounds is being conducted by both sides.

Influenza and Acute Respiratory Disease

Administered by the Communicable Disease Center, Atlanta, this program was added under a general agreement signed in 1974. Since its inception, 125 scientist-exchange visits have taken place between U.S. and Soviet institutes, allowing for shared information on influenza viral strains, epidemiology, and control of influenza viruses and other infectious diseases.

Eye Disease

Programs between the All-Union Research Institute of Eye Disease in Moscow and the National Eye Institute in Bethesda, Maryland, have promoted the use of short-pulse lasers for treatment of anterior eye segment disease and research for earlier detection of optic nerve dysfunction in the presence of ocular hypertension and glaucoma. Glaucoma is the second leading cause of blindness in both countries. In 1985 Soviet scientists provided the National Eye Institute with technology to build the first Q-switch laser for treatment. This laser, the first to be built in the United States, has proved to be a better clinical tool than the argon laser pioneered by Americans.

In assessing the value of cooperative medical programs, it is to their credit and vitality that they functioned and progressed from 1980 to 1985, a period when political interactions between Americans and Soviets nearly ceased. They stand as a model of the willingness and ability of scientists to cooperate productively. On July 31, 1986, the House Foreign Affairs Committee held a formal hearing to assess benefits from U.S.-Soviet scientific exchanges. Not a single participating government agency or outside organization, particularly those representing the medical profession, failed to affirm benefits and support their continuation on both scientific and humanitarian grounds.

Still, the prevalent political climate in both countries has had an important indirect effect by decreasing the number of participating scientists and scholars. According to Senator Paul Simon (D., Ill.), quoted June 13, 1986, in the *Washington Post*:

In the 27 years of exchanges, we have managed to average only 600 Americans and 250 Soviet scholars exchanged each year. Contrast these numbers with an average of 14,000 per year with Japan; 5,500 with Britain; 3,600 with West Germany; 3,000 with France; and 14,000 with the People's Republic of China. Exchanges can be most valuable precisely when relations are strained. Relations grew worse between 1981 and 1985, and two-way exchanges suffered.

Strained relations have markedly affected both the quality and the magnitude of accomplishments. A need to increase the number of individuals participating in Soviet-U.S. exchange programs, as well as stabilization of funding and format, were strong recommendations by participants during House hearings.[14]

SPACE MEDICINE

Benefits that have accrued to both the United States and the Soviet Union through joint ventures in the space program have differed from those in general medicine and health. The 1972 agreement for cooperation in the exploration and use of outer space for peaceful purposes led to exchanges of personnel and information in all phases of manned and unmanned space activities. Hundreds of Americans and Soviets traveled to each other's country for joint planning and training exercises, the largest official exchange of personnel in the history of cooperative efforts between the two nations. There have been lasting benefits, as Soviet and U.S. crew members have continued to meet periodically, speaking of the need for cooperation and lobbying for a joint manned mission to Mars. Based on these efforts, the Explorer's Association was created in 1984, founded by Jim Hickman (Esalen Institute, San Francisco Bay area), Rusty Schweickart (U.S. astronaut), and the Apollo/Soyuz cosmonauts.[15] This group has included 45 of the 150 individuals who have flown in space at least once. They have attempted to affect public opinion by expanding on the cooperative Apollo/Soyuz experience. More important, they have been willing to share personal experiences of viewing earth from space. The image of global interrelatedness received from this unique perspective has become a model and goad for realigning U.S. and Soviet thinking: Whatever their differences, however emotional and intractable, they are insignificant compared with what is shared.

Three volumes entitled *Foundations of Space Medicine and Biology* were jointly published in 1975 by the National Aeronautics and Space Administration (NASA, in Washington) and Nauk Press (in Moscow). This work summarized the latest knowledge gathered from all aspects of space exploration. For example, identical human bed-rest studies took place in 1979 at the Institute of Biomedical Problems in Moscow and NASA's Ames Research Center in the San Francisco Bay area. During a five-month period, specialists from both sides visited each other's laboratories, compared techniques, and developed confidence in using ground-based weightlessness simulation. This interaction halted needless duplication of work and saved millions of dollars for both countries. (A typical seven-day bed-rest study of ten subjects costs $300,000–$600,000 in 1985 U.S. currency.) Collaboration on other bed-rest projects, particularly on bone calcium loss, was also useful.

Information exchange in space medicine and biology has also taken place through presentations at formal national and international scientific meetings, involving data from ground-based as well as flight studies. Most Soviet bed-rest studies have durations of 180 days or longer. (A one-year study was completed in the spring of 1987.) This infoormation is proving invaluable to Western scientists, as both sides move to support a long-term human space presence. Since 1981 a program has been in place between investigators at the medical school of the University of California, San Francisco, and the A. Ushakov Institute of Biomedical Problems, Moscow, to transfer information on bone loss, one of the most crippling consequences of long-term space flight. Data collected during bed rest (up to one year in duration) and spaceflight (up to eight months) have been analyzed using computer-assisted tomography techniques developed at the San Francisco Medical Center. Findings have shown a steady, small, and unremitting loss over the duration of measurement.

In 1988, information was shared from Soviet long-term human missions ranging from 6 months to 342 days, the latter completed by Yuri Romanenko in December 1987. Data indicated the successful maintenance of physiological well-being without health loss on return to Earth. The major cost was the need to perform at least six to eight hours of unremitting in-flight exercise each day. Additional special attention to the problems of increasing human productivity during weightlessness will be required. In all, findings supported the Soviet program for the permanent presence of humans in space aboard their Mir space station and plans to achieve a future manned mission to Mars.

Bilateral discussions have been held on other medically related projects, such as monitoring air pollution by satellite and providing for docking and crew exchange from Soviet space stations and the U.S. space shuttle. The latter would provide experience for rescuing stranded personnel and an additional basis for joint scientific and medical projects.

Despite expiration of formal agreements, certain forms of U.S.-Soviet medical cooperation in space have continued. There has been work related to animal in-flight studies, global search and rescue, and unmanned space research. (Work in the latter two areas is covered elsewhere in this volume.) In all cases projects were initiated prior to 1982 and were closely monitored by the NASA offices responsible for their conduct. Joint biological experiments using Soviet biosatellites were started in 1973 with Cosmos 782. Three pioneering flights allowed U.S. and Soviet scientists to determine the effects of weightlessness on rats, including their fetal development. Starting in 1983, emphasis shifted to the study of rhesus monkeys. Cosmos 1514 (1983, 5 days) contained 1 fetal rat and 3 monkey experiments; Cosmos 1667 (1985, 7 days), a single U.S. monkey experiment; and Cosmos 1887 (1987, 14 days), 14 U.S. rat experiments. Specific monkey studies have included measurement of bone calcium changes using X-ray and radioisotope methods, daily body temperature and heart rate changes, and measurements of left common carotid arterial pressure and flow.[16]

U.S. investigators were allowed to visit and work with Soviet scientists in their own laboratories, using Soviet equipment. Similar opportunities for Soviet investigators to work on the U.S. side were also provided. A singular benefit for U.S. scientists was the opportunity to obtain invaluable experience and information on weightlessness more than a decade in advance of research plans by NASA. For Soviet scientists there has been the opportunity to work with more current techniques, particularly for recording and analyzing data produced by around-the-clock monitoring of physiological variables. Also important has been the use of invasive methods in animal models to accelerate the process of uncovering potential harmful effects of weightlessness on humans.

CITIZEN DIPLOMACY

Dating from the 1960s, increased efforts by citizen diplomats can be traced to the ups and downs of political relations. Efforts were based on uncertainty about official approval and finances. Supported by industry, nonprofit organizations, and private individuals, scientific dialogue was maintained due to its nonmilitary character and attention to scientific needs.

The strongest motivation was supplied by the threat of nuclear war and its moral and social implications. Roots of physician involvement can be traced to the rapid growth of public health concerns, demonstrating that doctors cannot shy away from diverse social and political issues that have impacts on the health of their communities. Indeed, such medical activism in the United States has led to improved nutrition for the poor, removal of asbestos from insulation, removal of lead from paint, and even legislation requiring safety caps on household chemicals and medications to prevent children from being poisoned. Soviet physicians had participated in similar moves to improve the quality of drinking water and sanitation, and to provide more convenient and rapid medical assistance for patients.

Large numbers of U.S. physicians became involved in the nuclear issue in the early 1960s when fallout (particularly strontium) from above-ground nuclear testing was found increasingly in the teeth of children. Interest was again stimulated in 1979 following the Three Mile Island nuclear power plant accident and continued due to the rapid buildup of weapons by both powers. Much credit must be given to Dr. Helen Caldicott, an Australian pediatrician who came to the United States to practice at Harvard University. Her educational efforts did much to effect a rebirth in dormant physician organizations.

Under her leadership physicians and medical groups initiated and continued vitally needed dialogue. Physicians have been particularly effective in bringing the nuclear message to the public and to policymakers, due to their highly respected social and scientific positions, their dedication to preserving and improving health and living conditions, and their demonstration that prevention of nuclear war is nonpartisan.

International Physicians for the Prevention of Nuclear War

Started in the United States in 1962 as Physicians for Social Responsibility, this antinuclear war group expanded in 1980 to become the International Physicians for the Prevention of Nuclear War (IPPNW). It seemed fitting that professionals and scientists who dedicate their lives to saving and prolonging life should speak out on the risks of nuclear weapons. Physicians and physician groups have exerted a pioneering effort to provide the first detailed and systematic evaluations of medical circumstances that would follow a nuclear exchange. The program has clearly demonstrated the inadequacy of medical institutions and emergency plans. Faced with the unparalleled nuclear threat, superpower physicians enlisted other medical workers to speak out from all over the globe. Membership has exceeded 150,000 physicians living in more than 45 countries.

The international movement was spawned by two cardiologists, Yevgeni Chazov and Bernard Lown, whose personal friendship began with the 1972 U.S.-Soviet cooperative agreement to study sudden death. Asked about the motivation of the group, Lown once replied:

... What could doctors do?.... We and the Soviets must build an organization that will bring a dialogue to our colleagues in the first place and to our patients in the second place. We are dealing with a complex process and we have to develop a public constituency.... We must build a people's diplomacy and a people's dialogue to negotiate a deeper understanding of one another, thereby diminishing the fear and paranoia, and thereby undermining the process that supplies the petrol for this engine of death riding roughshod over all of our interests.[17]

Chazov, in an article published in *Pravda* on October 1, 1985, stated:

The preservation of life and the health of their fellow man has always been the responsibility of individuals in the field of medicine.... In the event of a nuclear war doctors will not be able to fulfill their role as healers.... Unless an anti-nuclear attitude becomes widespread, as soon as possible, as a progressive and liberal way of dealing with one another, then as many realize, the threat of nuclear war increases for every single person on the globe.... In the end this depends less on the people who participated in the bloodshed of World War II. Those psychological memories will not provide knowledge of the dangers and scale of this new type of war—nuclear war.

IPPNW physicians have been instrumental in educating the public as well as other physicians. A historic television program was taped June 24, 1982, and broadcast during prime time in Moscow two days later. Three U.S. physicians (Lown, John Pastore, and James Muller) and three Soviets (Chazov; Mikhail Kuzin, director of the Vishnevsky Institute; and Leonid Ilyin, head of the Soviet Radiological Commission) discussed the inability to survive a nuclear attack or provide medical assistance. The program, conducted openly and uncensored, was seen by over 100 million viewers and was shown months later on PBS in the United States. Also, in 1983 a drive was launched to collect physician signatures on a petition calling for an end to the nuclear arms race. More than 1 million signatures were collected from doctors in 83 countries, representing nearly 25 percent of the world's physicians. Delegates recommended adding to the Hippocratic Oath a statement on nuclear war prevention. (This was done in the Soviet Union, but not in the United States.) In 1984 a physicians' group was initiated to tour and lecture in both countries. Topics centered on the medical consequences of nuclear war, "nuclear winter," the uselessness of civil defense programs, human fallibility, and the effects of the threat of nuclear war on children. Audiences ranged from 10–20 individuals to 500–1,000. One hundred Soviet and U.S. physicians were involved in this program.

IPPNW influence in the Third World was confirmed by the organization's being awarded the 1984 UNESCO Peace Education Prize. In 1984 it received the prestigious Beyond War Award from Beyond War, a grass-roots educational group based in Palo Alto, California. A Space-bridge hookup, linking San Francisco and Moscow, was achieved for the first time. In 1985, IPPNW was awarded the Nobel Peace Prize. In the words of the Nobel Committee, the group had "performed a considerable service to mankind by spreading authoritative information and by creating an awareness of the catastrophic consequences of atomic warfare." Chairman Egil Aarvik added that one of the main reasons for the choice was that "their work is based on solid scientific evidence rather than emotion."

The ultimate goal of physician members is to see the disbanding of their organization, which will take place when nuclear weapons no longer pose a threat to human life on the planet.

Individuals and Small Groups

Many specific benefits to U.S. medicine can be traced to U.S.-Soviet collaboration. A good example is a stapling gun widely used in surgery. It was brought to the United States in 1981 by Mark Ravitch, professor of surgery at the University of Pittsburgh.[18] He found Soviet physicians using the device to repair lung tissue during one of his frequent visits to the Soviet Union. Buying the device in a surgical supply store in Leningrad, he had it copied and introduced into the United States, where it is used in its original or slightly modified form in open heart surgery, organ transplantation, and gastrointestinal surgery in most major hospitals.

A bone-lengthening procedure, developed by Soviet surgeon G. A. Ilizarov, was introduced into the United States in November 1986.[19] Used for several years by French and Italian orthopedists, the device can induce lengthening of human bones by as much as eight centimeters over three to four months. The procedure uses a metal frame external to the bone to be lengthened, to which are attached fine metal wires that are passed through the bone. The wires are tightened and pull on the outer part of the bone to induce the lengthening. The procedure has been used successfully since about 1980 in the Soviet Union. After successful use at Stanford University, it is being considered for application by leading orthopedists.

Improvement and more widespread use of radial keratotomy, a surgical method for treating nearsightedness, can be traced to cooperative projects with Soviet doctors. Originally developed by the Japanese in 1953, this procedure places multiple small linear incisions around the entire surface of the cornea to a depth of one to two cells. The technique must be done microscopically with precision instrumentation and under computer control. The procedure had mixed results until technological improvements were instituted in 1973 by Vyatoslav Fyodorov, head of the Moscow Institute of Eye Microsurgery.[20] Following successful use of the procedures, U.S. entrepreneurs convinced him in 1983 to help set up a plant in Pinellas County, Florida, that would manufacture the necessary precision tools and implements, including eye microscopes and special operating tables.

Since 1983 the Esalen Institute in San Francisco has sponsored the Health Promotion Project for U.S.-Soviet physician dialogue and reciprocal book exhibitions in the medical sciences.[21] In January 1985 over 1,000 books, accompanied by a U.S. team of physicians and psychologists headed by Harvard psychiatrist John Mack, were exhibited at the Moscow Library of Science and Technology and at the Novosibirsk National Library of Medicine as part of a biyearly book fair. In April a Soviet team headed by Aron Belkin, director of the Soviet

National Research Center on Psychoneuroendocrinology (study of hormones and their effects on psychological and physiological health), reciprocated. They brought 1,000 Soviet books on health that were displayed at the University of California at Los Angeles school of nursing and the Fort Mason Center in San Francisco. In February 1986 a long-term collaborative agreement was signed with the Soviet Ministry of Health to continue personnel and information exchange in the emerging fields of psychoneuroendocrinology and behavioral medicine, as well as health promotion, alcoholism, and drug addiction.

Other individuals with medical backgrounds have provided new insights and increasing people-to-people contacts. Cynthia Lazaroff and nurse Sharon Tennison have organized tours, many including medical and graduate students. In July 1983 Lazaroff was able to assist a team of psychiatrists consisting of Eric Chivian, John Mack, and Joseph Goodman in initial research on children in the nuclear age. Through videotaped interviews in the United States and Soviet Union, studies have shown that Soviet children, like U.S. children, have detailed, accurate information about the effects of nuclear weapons, learned at a young age from mass media, schools, and parents; that they express concerns about a nuclear war and believe there will be no survivors; that Soviet children are more optimistic that nuclear war can be prevented; and that knowledge of nuclear issues has affected the lives and psychological well-being of children in both countries.[22] This work has continued under the auspices of the American Psychiatric Association's Task Force on the Psychosocial Aspects of Nuclear Developments and the Committee on the Developmental and Clinical Aspects of the Nuclear Threat of the American Academy of Child Psychiatry.

Two surgeons, Ward Trueblood of California and Robert White of Ohio, are among the increasing number of physicians who travel regularly in the Soviet Union, conducting surgical or medical procedures, followed by exchanges with Soviets to the United States.[23] They work voluntarily, without governmental support. Their efforts have been directed at providing information on Soviet medical practices from the viewpoint of the practicing physician, rather than of the researcher or academician. Experiences and findings have indicated that outside of a few specialized institutions in Moscow or Leningrad, the high level of U.S. medical technology and pharmacology is not available to the Soviet physician. Soviet doctors order fewer tests and concentrate more on preventive medical procedures. Through centralized budgeting and directives, the Soviet Union spends about one-tenth of the funds expended for health care in the United States. For Soviet physicians, interactions have provided a much needed opportunity to learn and assess alternative, often newer and more technological, approaches. For Americans there has been contact with otherwise estranged colleagues and access to innovative techniques, allowing greater communication between countries.

Chernobyl

The explosion and fire at Chernobyl's nuclear power plant no. 4 on April 26, 1986, was a practical demonstration that we live in an interdependent world that is growing ever smaller due to technological developments. The accident began at 1:23 A.M. in a 1,000-megawatt graphite core reactor with a steam explosion that killed two persons. A second explosion with extremely high temperatures and a burning plume 1,500 feet high rapidly lifted radioactivity to high altitudes. Early fallout was detected thousands of miles away (Poland, Sweden, Finland, Germany) and eventually in the western and central United States. Low-level radiation in the immediate area delayed evacuations, but within 36 hours after the initial explosions, a caravan of approximately 1,100 buses evacuated the entire population from an 18-mile area in 3 hours. Included were some 100,000 people (25,000–30,000 children), all subsequently examined and treated.[24]

During the period following the accident, hundreds of thousands of people were exposed to increased radiation from air they breathed, the water they drank, and the food they ate. Five hundred Soviet citizens were hospitalized following the accident; 31 died, and the rest returned home. The low death toll can be attributed to the availability of modern medical technology, particularly the use of bone marrow transplantation. This was provided on humanitarian grounds by the West, funded by monies from Armand Hammer, chairman of Occidental Petroleum Corporation, himself a former physician and long-time citizen diplomat. As a result, the services of experts Robert Gale, M.D., of UCLA and Yair Resiner, M.D., of the Weisman Institute, Rehovot, Israel, were made available, along with support personnel and equipment. They worked closely with Angelina Guskova, M.D. (physician in charge of hematology and oncology) and Alexander Baranov, M.D. (hematologist with direct responsibility for patients' care) at Moscow's Hospital 6. Over 300 other physicians were involved and another 5,000 physicians and health care personnel enlisted to do medical examinations and care in the field. New information indicated that bone marrow failure induced by radiation could be treated successfully and that humans could recover from considerably higher doses of radiation than was previously believed.

Medical collaboration between Western and Soviet personnel brought them closer. To continue the tedious and critically needed medical follow-ups, a privately sponsored group, the Gale-Hammer Institute, was created. Through an agreement signed with Andrei Vorobiev, M.D., head of the Institute for Postgraduate Medical Education of the Soviet Ministry of Health, exposed individuals will be observed over the next three to five decades. These processes provide good prospects for providing information on the long-term medical effects of radiation exposure and yet another avenue for exchanges of personnel, ideas, and equipment.

Experts now agree that there will be long-term biomedical consequences. Over the next 50 years the radiation released at Chernobyl will result in 2,500 to 75,000 extra cancer deaths, up to 1,000 extra cases of severe mental retardation, and up to 5,000 extra cases of genetic disorders. Of greatest interest (and a surprise to many), 60 percent of projected cases are expected to occur outside the Soviet Union, predominantly in Europe but also in the United States and throughout the Northern Hemisphere. The lesson from Chernobyl is that territorial boundaries do not protect us from radiation.

The conclusions that can be reached from Chernobyl were summarized by Gale and Hammer in an article written on the first anniversary of the accident:

... Chernobyl suggests conclusions that affect our strategy for the remainder of this century and the next. We live in a technical age. Many of its technologies, such as space exploration and nuclear energy, are by definition international. In the context of these technologies, we live on a very small planet. An accident at a Soviet nuclear reactor 5,000 miles away affects the lives of Americans. An accident in space such as an unscheduled satellite re-entry can affect 5 billion inhabitants of the planet. These are international problems; they are also international opportunities. We must learn to work together to attack these important issues.... The tragedy of Chernobyl may lead to a new level of scientific collaboration between the Soviet Union and the United States and perhaps thereby to peace. It would be irresponsible for us to do less.[25]

EVALUATION

U.S.-Soviet relations have been the dominant issue in U.S. foreign policy since the end of World War II. With few exceptions since 1917, the U.S. mind-set has been that you cannot work with or trust the Soviets. Yet, U.S. and Soviet physicians eradicated smallpox from the face of the planet within a decade of undertaking the task. They have regularly exchanged medical findings and breakthroughs for over 30 years in an effort to improve the health and well-being of patients and citizens, and were awarded a Nobel Peace Prize in 1985 for educational efforts concerning the dangers of nuclear war. At the same time astronauts and cosmonauts have been able to link in orbit and exchange spacecraft, scientists in this field have been able to work productively and harmoniously on earth, providing invaluable information to allow humankind to establish a permanent manned presence in space.

Under Gorbachev's leadership, Soviet dogma has begun to change. Since March 1985, there have been moves to improve Soviet science and technology, to reach out for accords to halt the nuclear arms race, and to increase exchanges with the West. It is not only prudent but also vital that the West be prepared to react in a fashion other than the good guy/bad guy syndrome that has been so typical of the past.

Steps toward reconciliation will not be automatic, nor will they be easy. Differences in culture and ideology confound the problem. It is in these spheres that Soviet-U.S. exchanges in medicine and public health, and the work of the IPPNW can have their greatest effect. Efforts have already initiated much-needed bridge building between U.S. and Soviet citizens and between their leaders. Additional efforts that allow automatic renewal of official programs in medicine can provide scientific participants with the assurance of program continuation and administration support that was lacking in past years.

Important achievements also warrant emphasis. Work in cardiology and cardiovascular research has been particularly productive; since the 1970s there have been 29 joint symposia (the proceedings of the great majority have been published in both Russian and English) and more than 600 scientific papers. There is every indication that this level of productivity can continue. Intensive interaction in cancer research and education is also resuming. Documentation that cardiovascular disease and cancer continue to represent the overwhelming causes of mortality in both countries is reason enough to seek and maintain cooperative relations in these fields. Due to the success of these programs, work is spreading to other research areas, such as diabetes and the acquired immune deficiency syndrome (AIDS), particularly when it is transmitted through blood transfusions.[26]

The same concerns that motivated physicians to develop public health activities have come to bear on nuclear issues. During the last half of this century, health care professionals have repeatedly been confronted with the question: What good is the application of the latest technological advances to alleviate illness, if the patient is returned to a situation that fosters its presence? Rapid developments in public health and holistic medicine came as a response, and with them educational programs to inform individuals and communities about medical risks and prevention.

Today physicians have a much more serious challenge. The question is: What good is it to develop technology to save people from devastating illness, if all life on the planet may soon be destroyed by nuclear weapons? Motivated by the goal to preserve life, physicians have once again felt compelled to speak out as in the past, to educate and act against this unparalleled public health threat. The critical need was summarized by Arnold Relman, editor of the *New England Journal of Medicine*:

What we physicians urgently need to be telling our government and fellow citizens is that even 1 percent (or less) of the total destructive power now in the possession of the superpowers is enough to doom our two countries and inflict untold damage on the rest of the world.... We cannot expect our luck to hold out much longer if we do not halt the arms race now. This is why most physicians, although we have no special expertise in foreign policy or diplomacy, agree that our government ought to be exploring every possible initiative to achieve an agreement on the early reduction of nuclear stockpiles.[27]

In the uncertain world created by the nuclear arms race, one wants to be terribly sure that decision makers have at hand the most realistic risk assessment that can be made. This is another area in which the physicians' movement has made a contribution. Thanks to clear-cut findings related to the medical consequences following a nuclear explosion, no one hears military or civilian leaders speak any longer about surviving or winning a nuclear exchange.

The Chernobyl disaster has become a modern-day symbol of the consequences of nuclear destruction to Europe and the rest of the world. It dramatically pointed to the fallibility of technology and its limited effectiveness for rendering medical assistance. This was a "small" disaster compared with the explosion of even a single atomic bomb. Coping required mobilization and use of nearly the entire medical capability of the Soviet Union as well as significant help from outside experts. The same would have been true had the accident happened in the United States.

Many U.S. scientists have felt that exchange programs are a rip-off. From this perspective nothing much has been gained scientifically, particularly during the period of détente; espionage may have occurred; and there may even have been unintended transfers of technology detrimental to national security.

This chapter cannot support this point of view. If revisions in Soviet politics were the objective, they did not occur. This only points to a need for clearer thinking about the differences between scientific and political motivations when undertaking cooperative programs. That enmity has not changed very much may be traceable to the mind-sets of decision makers and publics on both sides, conditions not immediately affected by scientific exchanges.

Yet, as noted by scientists and spokespersons at House committee hearings, indirect benefits do occur, and extend beyond research projects, formal reports, and scientific articles. Intangible gains include long-lasting social contacts, personal friendships, and more humanistic attitudes. The process takes place during formal interactions or when living in the other culture. For Soviets and Americans alike, experiences of ordinary citizens having the same goals and aspirations begin a much-needed erosion of enemy status so long portrayed in the media of both sides. Individuals with previous contacts and experiences with the "other" side are coming into decision-making positions, not only in medicine but also in business, science, the arts, and government.

Last, what about funding and national priorities? Since 1977 the U.S. Public Health Service and NASA have spent $1 to $5 million each year to support collaborative research and medical exchanges with the Soviet Union. Soviet investments have probably been half these amounts. Contrast these outlays with superpower expenditures for arms, totaling over $500 billion for 1986 and increasing regularly for three decades. In 1988, this represented $57 million dollars an hour, or $1 million a minute, day in and day out. By comparison, yearly costs for exchange and research programs represented one to five minutes of the joint arms race.

The medical benefits that might accrue, if these monetary resources were directed at solving pressing medical problems at home or on the world scene, would be truly significant. The cost in U.S. dollars for the ten-year effort to eradicate smallpox represents the equivalent of two hours of U.S.-Soviet arms expenditures. In the Third World 2 billion people do not have dependable or sanitary water supplies, lack of which accounts for 80 percent of all documented illness. UNICEF has repeatedly documented that 40,000 children die each day (15 million each year) around the world from malnutrition and infection, with diseases preventable by immunization, one-third of these being children below the age of five. It is estimated that safe water, immunization, and basic drugs could be provided to the children of the Third World by a cooperative U.S.-Soviet effort for less than the cost of one month of the arms race.[28]

The lessons from decades of U.S.-Soviet medical relationships and research confirm that cooperation is not only possible but also demonstrable, and of mutual benefit to both countries. Yet more must be done. Close cooperation will be needed if we are to continue scientific programs for the conquest of cardiovascular illness and cancer, to end the nuclear arms race, and to move our planet to a position where war and violence are no longer used to solve differences.

Americans and Soviets are stuck with each other on a very small planet, in a situation demanding cooperation, not confrontation. For those who might despair, one need not note only joint accomplishments. Consider U.S. relations with Britain, Germany, and Japan. Each was once considered a mortal enemy. Today they are the closest U.S. allies.

The United States is in a similar process of change with the People's Republic of China, also once considered a threat due to its belief in Communism. There is no reason for not moving to a similar relationship with the Soviet Union. The proven record of U.S.-Soviet interchange in medicine should remove doubts in this regard. The only thing that stands in the way of moving forward into other productive endeavors is the will and resolve to do so.

NOTES

1. Leon Eisenberg, "Rudolf Ludwig Karl Virchow, Where Are You Now That We Need You?" *American Journal of Medicine* 77, no. 3 (September 1984): 524–532.

2. Global Commission for the Certification of Small Pox Eradication, *Final Report. The Global Eradication of Small Pox* (Geneva: World Health Organization, 1980).

3. *Report on International Activities: National Heart, Lung, and Blood Institute, October 1, 1985–September 30, 1986* (Bethesda, Md.: National Institutes of Health, 1986).

4. *United States-Soviet Scientific Exchanges*, Hearings before the Committee on Foreign Affairs, House of Representatives, July 31, 1986, Document no. 63–629 0 (Washington, D.C.: U.S. Government Printing Office, 1986), p. 167.

5. Ibid., pp. 35–41, 169–170.

6. Debora D. Ingram, Michael D. Thorn, Sandra S. Stinett, and Alexander D. Deev, "USSR and US Nutrient Intake, Plasma Lipids and Lipoproteins in Men Ages 40–59 Sampled from Their Lipid Research Clinics Populations," *Preventive Medicine* 14, no. 3 (March 1985): 264–271.

7. Anna Nikolayeva, "International Conference on Preventive Cardiology Held in Moscow," *Soviet Life*, February 1986, pp. 56–57.

8. V. S. Chekanov and M. A. Proina, "Sovetsko-Amerikanskoe sotrudnichestvo v oblasti lechenia vrozhdennykh porokov serdtsa" [Soviet-American Cooperation in the Field of Congenital Heart Defect Treatment], *Sovetskoe zdravookhranenie* 1, no. 9 (September 1979): 54–57.

9. Phil Gunby, "Sudden Death Brings East and West Together," *Journal of the American Medical Association* 243, no. 3 (January 18, 1980): 213–215.

10. Anna Nikolayeva, "International Conference on Preventive Cardiology," pp. 56–57.

11. *Experimental Evaluation of Antitumor Drugs in the USA and USSR and Clinical Correlations*, National Cancer Institute Monograph 55 (Bethesda, Md.: National Institutes of Health, 1980).

12. Valeriy Shumakov, "Soviet-American Collaboration on the Development of an Artificial Heart and Mechanical Circulatory Assistance," *Artificial Organs* 7, no. 1 (February 1983): 110–111.

13. John Baum, Lev S. Alekseev, Earl J. Brewer, Jr., Alexandra V. Dolgopolova, Govid S. Mudholkar, and Kartik Patel, "Juvenile Rheumatoid Ar-

thritis, a Comparison of Patients from the USSR and USA," *Arthritis and Rheumatism* 23, no. 9 (September 1980): 977–984.

14. *United States-Soviet Scientific Exchanges*, passim.

15. *First Plenary Congress, the Association of Space Explorers, Final Report* (San Francisco: Association of Space Explorers, 1985), pp. 1–18.

16. Richard C. Mains and Edward W. Gomersall, *Final Reports of the U.S. Monkey and Rat Experiments Flown on the Soviet Satellite Cosmos 1514*, NASA TM–88223 (Washington, D.C.: NASA, 1986).

17. Gale Warner and Michael Shuman, *Citizen Diplomats* (New York: Continuum Press, 1987), pp. 39–40.

18. William A. Knaus, *Inside Russian Medicine: An American Doctor's Firsthand Report* (New York: Everest House, 1981), p. 160.

19. Ron Goben, "Leg-Lengthening Procedure Receives Apparent First U.S. Trial," *Stanford Campus Report*, February 4, 1987, pp. 23–25.

20. S. N. Fedorov and A. L. Ivashina, "Achievements of Soviet Ophthalmology," in S. Burenkov, ed., *Medicine and Health Care in the USSR* (New York: International Universities Press, 1985), pp. 143–159.

21. *United States-Soviet Exchanges*, pp. 268–273.

22. Eric Chivian, John E. Mack, Jeremy Walestsky, Cynthia Lazaroff, Ronald Doctor, and John M. Goldenring, "Soviet Children and the Threat of Nuclear War: A Preliminary Study," *American Journal of Orthopsychiatry* 55, no. 4 (October 1985): 484–502.

23. Ward Trueblood, "Two Faces of the Enemy," *PSR Newsletter*, November–December 1986, pp. 1–2; and Robert J. White, "Three Faces of Health Care: Russian/Chinese/American," *Ohio State Medical Journal* 82, no. 10 (October 1986): 669–675.

24. H. Jack Geiger, "The Accident at Chernobyl and the Medical Response," *Journal of the American Medical Association* 256, no. 5 (August 1, 1986): 609–612.

25. Robert G. Gale and Armand Hammer, "Out of Tragedy, an Opportunity: Chernobyl's Lesson Is That All of Us Must Share This Planet," *Los Angeles Times*, April 26, 1987.

26. *United States-Soviet Scientific Exchanges*, pp. 82–84.

27. Arnold S. Relman, "The Physician's Role in Preventing Nuclear War," *New England Journal of Medicine* 315, no. 14 (October 2, 1986): 889–891.

28. Victor W. Sidel, "War or Peace: Smallpox and the Use and Abuse of Public Health," *American Journal of Public Health* 76, no. 10 (October 1986): 1189–1190.

FOR FURTHER READING

Chazov, Yevgeni I., Leonid A. Ilyin, and Angelina K. Guskova. *Nuclear War: The Medical and Biological Consequences, Soviet Physicians' Viewpoint.* Moscow: Novosti Press, 1984.

Chivian, Eric, Susanna Chivian, Robert J. Lifton, and John E. Mack. *Last Aid—The Medical Dimensions of Nuclear War.* Boston: W. H. Freeman, 1983.

Ezell, Edward C., and Linda N. Ezell. *The Partnership: A History of the Apollo-Soyuz Test Project.* NASA-SP 4209. Washington, D.C.: NASA, 1978.

Grant, James P. *The State of the World's Children 1987.* New York: Oxford University Press, 1987.

Gromyko, Anatoly A., and Martin E. Hellman, eds. *Breakthrough: Emerging New Thinking.* New York: Walker and Co., 1988.

Keen, Sam. *Faces of the Enemy: Reflections of the Hostile Imagination.* San Francisco: Harper & Row, 1986.

Leaf, Alexander. "New Perspectives on the Medical Consequences of Nuclear War." *New England Journal of Medicine* 315, no. 14 (October 2, 1986): 905–912.

Mathias, Charles McC., Jr. "Habitual Hatred—Unsound Policy." *Foreign Affairs* 61, no. 5 (Summer 1983): 1017–1030.

Warner, Gale, and Michael Shuman. *Citizen Diplomats.* New York: Continuum Press, 1987.

8

SECURITY COMMUNICATIONS: RISK REDUCTION AND CONFIDENCE BUILDING IN SUPERPOWER RELATIONS

Nish Jamgotch, Jr.

Much of this book stresses a broad range of U.S.-Soviet cooperation—trade, travel, study, ideas, negotiations, international projects—indeed, all the many things the peoples of two prominent and powerful nations naturally do. This chapter focuses on a very special type of communications, designed and executed to ensure that misperceptions, risks, and accidents are kept to a minimum or prevented altogether.

In a thermonuclear world that necessitates supersensitive safeguards, no one of goodwill can deny the importance of reliable security information about the intent of military deployments. Often called confidence-building measures, special security communications have been invented to confirm the absence of feared threats; or, stated another way, they have served to make military intentions more open, predictable, and explicit. Clarified by the U.S. State Department, confidence-building measures in U.S.-Soviet relations are designed specifically

...to reduce the possibility of conflict—especially nuclear conflict—through accident, miscalculations, or failure of communications...and to inhibit opportunities for surprise attack or political intimidation, thus reinforcing stability in time of calm as well as crisis.[1]

At first glance, it would seem that measures to facilitate U.S.-Soviet security communications and confidence building pose startling contraditions: Why should two powers so avowedly hostile and animated by residual Cold War rivalry orchestrate intricate arrangements that inevitably increase the well-being of the other side as well as one's own? How can we explain the evolution of a confrontational postwar relationship that began at a minimal level of formal, often sour, diplomacy to one that today is steadied by an extensive and versatile network of collaborative projects to cope with emergencies? In short, after all that has happened, why trust the enemy to cooperate in security agreements?

The answers lie in a well-established and eminently rational principle in international politics: because of their primeval urge for self-preservation and human survival, nations frequently must collaborate to protect themselves against each other. The two most awesome superpowers in history have devised unprecedented mechanisms for security communications, because even ideological and political enemies have a crucial stake in understanding each other's intentions. There is no plausible way that their individual needs can be satisfied without safeguards of equal value to each *and* to the more general imperative for human survival the world over. Unlike, say, academic and cultural exchange, or bilateral trade, about which the United States has sometimes contended that the Soviets get the better deal (and even valuable sophisticated technology for military applications besides), methods for speedy, reliable, accurate emergency communications at the highest levels of leadership cannot be more advantageous to one than to the other. Their benefits are mutual and equal; hence their incontrovertibility and the strong incentive to create, modernize, and expand them.

Available options for information exchange, observation of military activities, and operational constraints on movements of troops and weapons show a considerable range and variety of applications.[2]

Information Exchange	Observation/ Inspection	Operational Constraints
Disclosure of military budgets, major unit and command locations and organizations, force levels, doctrines	Observers at major maneuvers On-site inspection Sensors at ICBM silos	Ban on simulated attacks Designated troop entry/exit points
Notification of accidental, unauthorized, or unexplained nuclear incidents	Noninterference with national technical means of verification	Ban on forward basing of offensive weapons and support equipment

Notification of maneuvers and missile test launches	Nonconcealment undertakings	Ban on multiple missile launches
Communication links (hotline)	Enhanced conditions for military liaison, mission officers, and other accredited military personnel	Maneuver/ movement ceilings
Nuclear risk reduction centers		Ballistic missile submarine sanctuaries/ antisubmarine-warfare-free zones

According to John Borawski, the significance of information exchange is underscored by the recognition that many times in history, surprise was achieved not because of an absence of warning but because there was a gross misreading of an adversary's intentions in the presence of ample warning. The classic case is that of Stalin, who in early June 1941 refused to heed foreign intelligence data that a Nazi attack was imminent.

Observation and inspection have the obvious purpose of alleviating or confirming suspicions about an adversary's intentions, particularly by making it difficult to prepare for war without detection. Refusal of a nation to permit observation or inspection would, of course, invite suspicion of aggressive intentions.

Operational constraints are designed to increase warning time and also to avoid deployments in potentially threatening modes. For example, during the Cuban missile crisis, President Kennedy suspended routine U.S. flights in the direction of the Soviet Union and deactivated the warheads of U.S. Jupiter missiles in Turkey. During the 1968 Soviet incursion into Czechoslovakia, NATO reduced reconnaissance flights over West Germany and moved a troop exercise of 30,000 men farther west from the Czech border by 200 miles. At the time of the 1981 political tensions in Poland, NATO toned down its surveillance and intelligence gathering.[3] Each of these actions was a form of sophisticated communication, employed to reduce the risks of unwanted war and to enhance security and mutual confidence in superpower relations. They are parts of a greater story of bilateral security cooperation, not widely known or well understood.

What follows is a review of the most notable history of U.S.-Soviet security projects, including the 1963 hotline and its two modernizations for direct emergency communications; the 1971 Accident Measures Agreement to prevent the unauthorized or accidental use of nuclear weapons; the 1972 Incidents at Sea Agreement to prevent provocative naval acts; the 1973 Agreement on the Prevention of Nuclear War, requiring that the superpowers avoid moves against each other or third powers that could precipitate military confrontations; and the 1987 Agreement on the Establishment of Nuclear Risk Reduction Centers in both superpower capitals. In addition, valuable multilateral agreements include the joint COSPAS/SARSAT satellite-aided search and rescue system. (The Soviet COSPAS stands for Space System for the Search of Vessels in Distress; the U.S. SARSAT stands for Search and Rescue Satellite-Aided Tracking.) There is also the 1985 agreement among the Anchorage Area Control Center, the Tokyo Area Control Center, and the Khabarovsk Area Control Center for the enhancement of safety over the North Pacific; and the 1986 Stockholm Agreement on Confidence- and Security-Building Measures and Disarmament in Europe.

DIRECT COMMUNICATIONS LINK OR HOTLINE

The 1963 hotline agreement arose from the Cuban missile crisis, the most dangerous U.S.-Soviet military confrontation since World War II, and from the belief that the unpredictable emergency and its resolution had demonstrated the value of rapid, reliable transmission of security information between the heads of government. True to the notion that crisis begets invention, an accord was achieved for a direct link to reduce the risks of misperception, surprise attack, and accidental war. Driven by public pressure from academicians and journalists, plus the work of the Eighteen-Nation Disarmament Conference of the United Nations, U.S. and Soviet negotiators forged an agreement on June 23, 1963. On August 30, the innovative system became operational.[4]

Contrary to the popular view of a red phone (perhaps attributable to Henry Fonda's stirring role as president in the movie *Failsafe*), the hookup allowed only for printed messages. Two full-time duplex telegraph circuits connected the Pentagon and the Kremlin, one a land and undersea cable (Washington-London-Copenhagen-Stockholm-Helsinki-Moscow) and the other a backup radio circuit (Washington-Tangier-Moscow). Emergency messages, the precise number of which remains undisclosed by mutual agreement, are transmitted in the native language of the sender and translated at the other end.

Accelerated arms control negotiations in 1969 produced momentum to upgrade the system with advanced satellite technology of the 1970s. Generally the system had worked quite well, notwithstanding a few hitches such as a power outage caused by a Finnish farmer accidentally cutting a cable while plowing, a manhole fire near Baltimore that deactivated the primary circuit, U.S. telephone workers inadvertently severing both cables, and power outages caused by commercial cable service interruptions.[5]

The September 30, 1971, agreement on measures to improve the U.S.-Soviet direct communications link established two satellite circuits for transmitting printed messages: the United States used INTELSAT (a single satellite in geostationary orbit, 22,500 miles over the equator); the Soviets employed their MOLNIYA (a system of four satellites in elliptical inclined orbits around the Earth). Multiple terminals were outfitted in each country. After tedious technical and procedural arrangements, the upgraded hookup became operational by 1978; the old radio circuit was terminated; and the original cable was retained as a backup for the new satellite circuits. Although the original capability of 66 words per minute was maintained, the new system was a welcome achievement in high-quality transmission, versatile multiple terminals, and, especially, nearly 100 percent technical reliability. It is generally understood that the upgraded link was imployed for urgent communications during the 1973 Arab-Israeli war, the 1974 Turkish invasion of Cyprus, and the 1979 Soviet incursion into Afghanistan.

More sophistication was provided for the hotline as a result of recommendations by Secretary of Defense Caspar Weinberger in his *Report on Direct Communications Links and Other Measures to Enhance Stability*, submitted to the U.S. Congress on April 11, 1983. Responding to a special congressional request in 1982, Weinberger identified four measures for coping with international crises and military incidents: (1) facsimile capability—transmission of charts, maps, and graphs by the hotline; (2) a joint military communications link; (3) a special hookup between each nation and its embassy in the other's capital; and (4) an agreement to consult in the event of nuclear incidents involving third parties. Based on negotiations held alternately in Moscow and Washington from August 9, 1983, to July 17, 1984, the emergency system was modernized with high-speed facsimile capability enabling the two sides to transmit highly complex data. Both sides decided against voice transmission—more difficult than written material to translate and far more subject to misunderstanding—believing that printed communications are more private, precise, and dependable. The joint military communications link and the improved embassy-capital communications were rejected by the Soviets. A new agreement to consult during incidents involving third parties was held in abeyance.

The July 1984 accord provided for three transmission links: two satellite systems and the old wire telegraph circuit as a backup. The system placed into service in September 1986 consisted of

- Two INTELSAT (U.S.) satellite circuits
- Two STATSIONAR (Soviet) satellite circuits

- Two cable (underwater/land) circuits
- INTELSAT and STATSIONAR Earth stations in each country
- Terminals in each country equipped for teletype and facsimile transmissions

Reinforcing security through communications of the most urgent sort, the genesis, development, and value of hotline operations have been incontrovertible, even though there has been scant commensurable recognition in popular, academic, or official literature. Without fanfare, criticism, or obstructions since its inception, the system has been available as a superpower safety net and check on tindery relations. In July 1985, it was agreed that it would be used if there were signs that third parties or terrorists might employ nuclear weapons. It should be stressed that when the hookup was invented, neither terrorism nor third-party interventions appeared to be realistic catalysts for World War III. Today, they provide frightening scenarios for security planners in both Washington and Moscow.

As both an engineering and a diplomatic achievement, facsimile capability constitutes a particularly impressive breakthrough: it can transmit text three times as fast as teletype; the clarity of graphic information requires practically no translation; and operator error is reduced substantially by minimizing or eliminating keyboarding.

Joint technical collaboration of the highest order has also been exemplary. The need to maintain a high level of technical sophistication and dependability has necessitated continuous consultations between the parties. This led, for example, to an additional agreement in January 1988 to dispense with the original cable (underwater/land) circuits and teletype that for many years had been reserved as a backup. Reportedly impressed by the system's trouble-free performance, the British and some of the Soviet Union's most proximate NATO neighbors have shown interest in direct hookups of their own.

ACCIDENT MEASURES

As early as 1967–1968, well before the first SALT negotiations were concluded in 1972, the Soviet Union proposed that the superpowers undertake confidence-building measures as part of a concerted effort to lessen chances of miscalculation that might generate a nuclear catastrophe. Both Foreign Minister Andrei Gromyko and General Secretary Leonid Brezhnev went on record in 1969 and 1971 in support of measures to reduce the possibility of accidental war or the enlargement of military crises that could lead to unintended consequences.

Parallel with the SALT negotiations for limiting strategic armaments and antiballistic (ABM) systems, talks progressed, expectably reflecting common interests as well as dissenting views, and eventually led to an agreement on September 30, 1971.⁶ Major provisions covered safe and secure organizational and technical procedures for the control and use of nuclear weapons. U.S. officials were particularly forthcoming about information to their Soviet counterparts. Efforts were made to convey detailed safety and security precautions, including programs for securing reliable personnel and the prevention of unauthorized access and technical mistakes, as well as weapons design features to prevent accidental detonation—all steps unreciprocated by the Soviet side.

Soviet negotiators stressed the need to restrict flights of bombers with nuclear weapons to home territory (obviously aimed at U.S. Strategic Air Command [SAC] operations). They also desired the elimination of forward-based aircraft in Europe and limits on ocean areas where nuclear-armed aircraft carriers and missile-launching submarines could patrol. The United States predictably rejected these proposals because of their patent negative implications for U.S. policy.

What was agreed to was nevertheless significant. Concerning the firing of weapons beyond national frontiers, each party undertook to give advance notice of launches extending beyond national territory in the direction of the other. On the matter of crisis communications, each signatory pledged to notify the other immediately in the event of an accidental, an unauthorized, or any other form of nuclear explosion that could risk the outbreak of nuclear war. In such cases, it was agreed that the party whose nuclear weapon was involved would move to render it harmless or to destroy the weapon without its causing damage. The parties also consented to notify each other "in the event of detection by missile warning systems of unidentified objects, or in the event of signs of interference with these systems or with related communications facilities, if such occurrences could create a risk of outbreak of nuclear war between the two countries." Joint deliberations produced another provision in Article 5, not originally advanced by either side:

Each party, in other situations involving unexplained nuclear incidents, undertakes to act in such a manner as to reduce the possibility of its actions being misinterpreted by the other party. In any such situation, each party may inform the other party or request information when in its view, this is warranted by the interests of averting the risk of outbreak of nuclear war.

It was understood that for the most urgent communications requiring prompt clarifications, the hotline would be used. Less pressing issues and routine requests for information could be serviced by appropriate diplomatic channels.

Regarding its NATO allies, the United States kept them quietly but fully informed as accident measures negotiations evolved. The Soviet Union concluded similar agreements with France on July 16, 1976, and with Great Britain on October 10, 1977.

During the early years of the Reagan administration, security and confidence-building proposals were offered under the START (Strategic Arms Reduction Talks) formula, including prior notification of all launches of ICBMs and SLBMs, greater exchange of military data on strategic nuclear weapons, and advance notification of major military exercises with strategic forces. There were additional recommendations concerning intermediate-range nuclear forces and launches of ballistic missiles (SS–20s and Pershing IIs) under negotiation in Europe, as well as the need for high-level contacts between U.S. and Soviet military leaders and even exchanges of information on defense budgets and plans. In July 1985, U.S. initiatives met with some success when the two sides signed an additional Common Understanding to the Accident Measures Agreement that clarified obligations to consult in the event of a nuclear incident involving third parties or terrorists.

INCIDENTS AT SEA

There were compelling reasons for mutual understandings and agreements concerning rules of the sea as the Soviet Union became a bona fide global military power with a world-class blue-water navy. Soviet motives for an aggressive and even confrontational posture at sea stemmed mainly from their decision to try and restrict the naval freedom and preeminence historically enjoyed by the United States. Selective harassment in particular was a means of demonstrating displeasure over intrusive U.S. maneuvers in the Black Sea and the Sea of Japan—Soviet home waters of special security sensitivity. U.S. inclinations to threaten and harass were not significantly different. The Cold War arms spiral obviously accentuated superpower military rivalry over naval power and operational effectiveness. On both sides, there was the added dimension of reconnoitering and provoking each other's ships suspected of snooping and gathering intelligence information.

Notwithstanding the generally cautious and low-risk behavior of both powers, dangerous incidents took place. Beginning especially in the late 1960s and early 1970s, hundreds of episodes pointed to an extraordinary need for superpower accident prevention. These included buzzing (high-speed reconnaissance of vessels by planes); the dropping of sonobuoys from the air to track submarines; simulated attacks on ships; accidental firing on ships during naval exercises; collisions; and shining searchlights on the bridges of vessels. After the North Korean seizure of the *Pueblo* in January 1968, the Soviets engaged in harassment of U.S. warships involving numerous violations of nautical rules of the road. Similarly, following the alert of U.S. forces during the October 1973 Arab-Israeli war, they undertook an intense campaign of anti-carrier maneuvers, using U.S. ships as targets. During the Cuban missile crisis, U.S. ships were known to follow, harass, and force Soviet submarines to surface, a matter that caused President Kennedy to consider more reliable means to control local naval commanders.[7]

As early as 1967, the dangers and frequency of naval incidents caused the United States to propose negotiations on the contentious issues of how to clarify and expand navigational regulations. The primary worry was that some relatively minor incident involving warships or aircraft could, through misunderstanding, be escalated into actual combat by local commanders.

The resultant May 25, 1972, Agreement on the Prevention of Incidents at Sea had three overriding purposes: (1) prohibition of provocative and dangerous maneuvers and various forms of harassment; (2) increased direct security communications at sea; and (3) annual bilateral naval consultations and regular exchanges of information.[8] Specifically, in a joint reaffirmation of the rules of the road, commanders must keep their ships well clear of each other and demonstrate the greatest vigilance and prudence in approaching vessels either launching or landing aircraft. Simulated attacks, searchlights to illuminate bridges, and the dropping of aerial objects hazardous to ships and navigation are prohibited. Internationally recognized signals at sea, including those for flight operations, and the display of navigational lights on overhead aircraft, as well as signals indicating intentions of ships in close proximity, are mandatory. Three to five days' advance notice is required for all naval exercises posing hazards to the navigation or flight of others. Especially important is the designation of U.S. and Soviet naval attachés in each other's capitals as primary communications channels regarding all collisions and other incidents at sea, thus making the agreement a naval responsibility. Additional provisions allow for annual reviews and a reconsideration of fixed distances to be observed between ships, between aircraft, and between ships and aircraft. The controversial issue of fixed distances was left in abeyance; however, a subsequent protocol, dated May 22, 1973, extended the above regulations by prohibiting simulated attacks on nonmilitary ships and the dropping of hazardous objects near them.

As a follow-up to the 1972 agreement, U.S. and Soviet naval operations became more circumspect and incident-free, particularly during the October 1973 Arab-Israeli conflict, when acute tensions and dozens of hostile ships in close proximity in the Mediterranean constituted a dangerous scenario for military conflict.

On the other hand, the record also bore reminders of lingering problems. After the shooting down of KAL flight 007, U.S. salvage operations in the Sea of Japan were brazenly intimidated by Soviet vessels. In November 1983, a Soviet frigate was reportedly interfering with flights from the U.S. carrier *Ranger* before colliding with the U.S. frigate *Fife*. A Soviet submarine operating without lights inadvertently collided with the U.S. carrier *Kitty Hawk* in the Sea of Japan in March 1984. In the same month, eight flares were fired at the U.S. frigate *Harold E. Holt* by the Soviet carrier *Minsk* in a confused and highly controversial incident involving the *Holt*'s signals to pass the *Minsk* on the starboard side.

Despite these alarming incidents, neither side expressed any desire to abrogate or modify the cooperative agreement. Both sides have acknowledged its value; they want it to continue. As part of the only official military-to-military program, unannounced and unpublicized meetings of top naval officers from both sides, alternating annually in the national capitals, provide rare opportunities for useful dialogue and problem solving. Discussions have ensued over whether flaws in the agreement are due more to unpredictable human errors or to technological deficiencies—certainly a vital concern the world over. Violations are carefully reviewed, based on evidence collected and transmitted from the past year. Complaints are accompanied by aerial photos, detailed maps, and records of signals passed—both flag and light. Commanders of ships found guilty of incidents are held strictly accountable and reportedly have been reprimanded by their own leaders on both sides.[9] Joint meetings have also produced improvements in alert procedures, including the use of radio communications as signals during conditions of reduced visibility at sea.

That the agreement establishes only security communications and rules, but no ceilings or limits on weapons, is both a weakness and a strength: a weakness, because cuts in sea weapons would be preferable to increases; a strength, because avoiding incidents at sea is obviously noncontroversial and readily escapes volatile domestic politics and a watchful, hypersensitive press. The agreement's very low profile has very likely enhanced its success. At the same time, the lack of public knowledge has taken its toll by producing only a partial and fragmented view of superpower projects for risk reduction and accident prevention over vast areas of the world.

Positive incidents at sea hardly fit the image of the two superpower navies, but examples show that common interests can on occasion prevail. As stated in the *Christian Science Monitor* (March 18, 1987), President Reagan was conspicuous in his praise of the U.S. Coast Guard helicopter rescue (March 14, 1987) of 37 Soviet sailors from their sinking freighter *Komsomolets Kirghizy*. It was an example, he said, that should be followed by world leaders. Also, quite unexpected in U.S.-

Soviet naval relations in the Persian Gulf, the two forces coordinated tactics, including U.S. helicopters and a battle cruiser, and a Soviet radio message and minesweepers, in order to blow up a mine in January 1988, during the Iran-Iraq war. Although limited, the episode was reported in the *Washington Post* (January 14, 1988) as the first involving a joint military operation.

The primary issue, however, is that the agreement has successfully reduced inadvertent provocations and conflicts at sea: reported incidents, exceeding 100 a year in the late 1960s, were down to 40 in 1982–1983 and to only 1 in 1986–1987. This is a remarkable achievement when one considers the size and complexity of superpower navies.

The 1987–1988 record, slated for review at the June 1988 Moscow naval meeting, was expected to be as good, notwithstanding the widely publicized February incident involving the bumping of an American destroyer and cruiser by two Soviet frigates in the Black Sea. U.S. State Department officials took the position that because the incident took place inside the 12-mile limit claimed by the Soviets as territorial waters, the Incidents at Sea Agreement did not apply. Both prudence and quiet diplomacy, it seemed, deflated the issue quickly in order to keep more important matters, such as arms control and the May summit between Reagan and Gorbachev, on schedule.

PREVENTION OF NUCLEAR WAR

The overwhelming imperative in the postwar thermonuclear age has been for explicit precautionary guidelines to avoid the most awesome catastrophe ever conceived and planned. Negotiations for the prevention of nuclear war were initiated in the atmosphere of détente and peaceful cooperation during the last session of the Moscow summit between President Nixon and General Secretary Brezhnev in May 1972. A formal agreement was concluded during Brezhnev's visit to Washington that June, committing the superpowers to policies "that remove the danger of nuclear war and of the use of nuclear weapons."[10]

Accordingly, the parties agreed to prevent a dangerous exacerbation of their relations, to avoid military confrontations, to refrain from the threat or use of force against each other or their allies, and to exclude nuclear war between themselves or between either of them and third countries. Urgent bilateral consultations are called for if at any time international relations between the superpowers or any other countries indicate the risk of nuclear conflict. The parties, in addition, are free to inform their allies, the United Nations, and other powers about the progress and outcome of bilateral consultations.

From the beginning of these negotiations, there was a clear intent to extend the principles of caution and restraint from the technical realm to the political: to expand safeguards against accidental or unauthorized use of nuclear weapons (the 1971 Accident Measures Agreement) to a formal enunciation of principles against miscalculation and escalation. The Soviets concentrated more on seeking a bilateral accord against first use, while the United States, reserving the right of first use as part of a deterrent strategy, instead conceded that nuclear war is unwinnable and supported the above pledge to consult in order to prevent it.

Since 1973, the agreement has lacked any apparent operational significance and has functioned primarily as a cooperative expression of international ethics, morality, and resolve in support of the most fundamental requirements for human survival and planetary preservation.

COSPAS/SARSAT

Although not the same as security communications to avert military hostilities or nuclear mishaps, the COSPAS/SARSAT satellite-aided search-and-rescue system has been a remarkable multilateral venture in advanced satellite technology—call it extraterrestrial aid—designed to save lives through international cooperation. Superpower leadership made it happen.

The complex project reportedly grew out of the spectacular U.S.-Soviet Apollo-Soyuz space docking in 1975. In the spirit of "now, what else can we do?" the Soviets approached the U.S. National Aeronautics and Space Administration (NASA), reviewed a list of plausible programs, and selected satellite rescue. The decision was formalized in a joint memorandum of understanding on November 23, 1979, by the two superpowers, plus Canada and France; and ever since it has functioned as a four-power satellite system to locate emergency beacon transmissions from downed aircraft and ships in distress from 600 miles away—straight up!

The basic concept of the program employs Earth satellites equipped with receivers set to international distress frequencies that detect and relay emergency transmissions from aircraft and ships to ground stations. Four satellites (two U.S. and two Soviet) simultaneously operate from low, near-polar orbits. The complete spacecraft constellation ensures global coverage in under three hours, a vital capability when one considers that the probability of saving survivors is over 50 percent if help arrives within eight hours. There are ten operational local user terminals and six mission control centers, with more slated for the future. Local user terminals receive and process emergency information from the satellites and forward location data to their respective mission control centers. When alerted, a center relays a call for help to the appropriate rescue coordination center.

Operations have confirmed one of the many impressive technological breakthroughs of our satellite age. The ability of a satellite several hundred miles above the earth to pick up beeps of small planes and ships in distress has made possible a remarkable expansion of search-and-rescue techniques. In March 1988, the American National Oceanic and Atmospheric Administration (U.S. Department of Commerce) confirmed that 1,121 lives have been saved since the inauguration of the system.

Ever since the first successful rescue in 1982, plans have advanced to reduce the incidence of false alarms, to upgrade the system's reliability, to generalize the use of uniform beacons for signal transmission, and to provide enhanced data handling for speedier lifesaving. It is expected that a new global system operating on 406 MHz (1 million cycles per second) will be fully operational in the 1990s, with improved frequency signals for more accurate location of distress incidents and more classes of users. Active rescue system participants already include, in addition to the four original partners, Bulgaria, Denmark, Norway, Great Britain, Brazil, India, Japan, Sweden, Switzerland, and Chile. To assure the program's future, the four founding partners are considering a new intergovernmental agreement, akin to a treaty, committing the parties to a permanent program and a fully international search-and-rescue system. A 1987 COSPAS/SARSAT steering committee report envisioned a truly global and long-term humanitarian service:

... the System should be available for use by all nations on a nondiscriminatory basis and free of charge to the end user. All such nations should be provided with opportunity for coordination of activities, and exchange of information on the system.[11]

Multilateral ventures motivated by U.S.-Soviet leadership obviously bear inherent advantages and momentum. Cooperation to save lives rather than take lives sets a dramatic example. One additional inconspicuous strength of the COSPAS/SARSAT program is that it escapes controversy because of an absence of technology transfer or intelligence leaks threatening to national security sensitivities. As long as successful rescues continue and lives are saved, more nations will want to participate in the obvious benefits. There is good reason to hope that what began as a memorandum of understanding for a pilot project will become a permanent international institution. Meanwhile, the program will continue to perform lifesaving functions during a transitional phase planned to extend through the 1980s.

ANCHORAGE-TOKYO-KHABAROVSK AIR TRAFFIC CONTROL

So often, learning requires profound tragedy. The September 1, 1983, shooting down of KAL 007 was very likely caused by the plane's mis-programmed flight instruments and by Soviet incompetence in detecting, locating, and identifying an errant commercial airliner over Kamchatka and the Sea of Okhotsk. The aftermath produced a tense atmosphere of mutual accusations as well as quiet moves to avoid another incident.

Beginning in February 1985 and into late July, trilateral conferences of U.S., Japanese, and Soviet delegations explored, in principle, measures for enhancing the safety of flights over the North Pacific. An implementing agreement signed on November 19, 1985, provided that an extraordinary air traffic control system would be established and maintained around the clock, using the English language, to assist civil aircraft in emergencies: Anchorage and Tokyo-area control centers would supply all vital information on aircraft inadvertently entering the Soviet Union, and the Soviet Khabarovsk-area control center would communicate with Anchorage and Tokyo concerning unidentified aircraft appearing in Soviet airspace.

Information to be exchanged includes type of aircraft; radio call sign; transponder code; nationality; operator; location, altitude, and speed; time and nature of the event; pilot's intentions, if known; assistance requested and actions taken; and information relevant to responsible search-and-rescue agencies.

The agreement provides for a new direct-speech circuit between Tokyo and Khabarovsk, employing an existing telephone cable. This is backed up by a high-frequency speech circuit between Khabarovsk and Sapporo (with connection to Tokyo) using a domestic telephone channel. Potential emergencies covered by the agreement include technical failures requiring immediate landing; unlawful seizures of aircraft; loss of communication; procedures for reporting unidentified aircraft; and measures for guiding off-course aircraft out of the Soviet Union.[12]

The Soviets are the key to whether these emergency measures will be implemented. Their historic sensitivities to violations of their airspace and the wish to avoid a public relations disaster from another Korean Airlines tragedy are the principal guarantees that the special telephone hookup, a mini-hotline, will be used. The speed and efficiency with which they act to prevent a recurrence will be an important test of goodwill as well as of self-interest on the part of the Gorbachev leadership.

SECURITY AND CONFIDENCE BUILDING IN EUROPE

The Stockholm Conference on Confidence- and Security-Building Measures and Disarmament in Europe (CDE), convened on January 17, 1984, has by all accounts produced the most impressive achievement in East-West security agreements in many years. Comprised of 35 nations, including NATO and the Warsaw Pact, its purpose from the beginning was the establishment of a military confidence-building regime to reduce the risk of war in Europe. In contrast with the largely political outcomes of the 1975 Helsinki Final Act, the Stockholm Agreement, signed September 19, 1986, pledged 35 signatories to mandatory observation, aerial inspection, and advance notice of major military activities all across Europe, from the North Atlantic to European Russia. Culminating almost three years of tough bargaining, the accord allows each alliance to increase its security by openly learning a great deal about the military capabilities of the other. On September 22, 1986, President Reagan acknowledged the risks of war in Europe, site of the greatest concentration of military forces of both East and West. The accord, he announced, was a powerful force for peace, and evidence that seriousness of purpose and hard work can establish common ground for a more secure future.[13]

The agreement's principal provisions provide that participating states will refrain from the threat or use of force. Both NATO and the Warsaw Pact are required to exchange detailed information 42 days or more in advance of all troop concentrations and military exercises of at least 13,000 soldiers or 300 battle tanks. If 17,000 troops are used, or 5,000 in amphibious or parachute exercises, all other signatory countries must be invited to send observers. Annual calendars of military activities subject to prior notification must be exchanged with all participating states by November 15 of each year for the upcoming year's exercises and maneuvers, and must include their precise type, purpose, characteristics, area, and troop numbers. Naval activities are subject to notification only when connected with amphibious maneuvers for land exercises.

Under the category of "constraining provisions," if more than 40,000 troops are planned for, two-year notice must be provided. Military activities involving more than 75,000 troops are specifically prohibited in the absence of a two-year notice, as are movements of more than 40,000 troops unless they are included in the annual calendar not later than November 15.

Stringent compliance and verification requirements provide for three on-site inspections per year of any state engaged in notifiable military activity. Inspection, limited to a team of four, may take place on the ground, in the air, or both, beginning within 36 hours of a request, and must terminate within 48 hours after initiation. Provisions allow for inspection teams to carry their own observation and recording equipment.[14]

As a major concession, the Soviets must allow inspection of the Warsaw Pact's territory as far east as the Ural Mountains, the first time in any East-West accord that they have agreed to inspection of any military activities on home ground. The United States softened its initial negotiating position, finally agreeing that host nations being inspected, instead of neutral nations, will provide planes, helicopters, and pilots to carry officials from the other side.

There is much to commend the Stockholm agreement as a historic breakthrough heightening the predictability and transparency of military activities and undercutting opportunities for planned aggression. Signatories are pledged to initiate no significant military activities without both prior announcement and formal, detailed explanation. That nations must publish schedules of military activities far in advance will inhibit, though not prevent, surprise deployments and the use of force for political purposes. Inspection and observation can magnify the intent behind sudden, large-scale maneuvers, thereby reducing the probability of intimidation. There is no eliminating such possibilities in the future; but the price would be raised substantially for any nation so inclined, thus offering a modicum of deterrence.[15]

Implementation of the agreement in 1987–1988 has confirmed the expectations of its 35 members. Every nation anticipating notifiable military maneuvers has submitted advance calendars. As of mid–1988, ten on-site inspections had been completed, five by each side, including the first U.S. observations in the Soviet Union's Belorussian Republic in August 1987.

The Stockholm conference can also be valued as an ongoing process of incremental confidence-building projects that are envisioned as steps toward significant arms reductions. For example, Soviet negotiators have stressed the June 11, 1986, Warsaw Pact communiqué (also called the Budapest appeal) proposing a 25 percent cut in NATO and Warsaw Pact conventional forces and tactical nuclear forces (less than 600-mile range) in all of Europe from the North Atlantic to the Urals. Indeed, a quite persuasive case can be made that the momentum of the Stockholm provisions actually rendered the Vienna conference on mutual and balanced force reductions in Europe a dead letter, creating more promising opportunities for arms reduction. New discussions involving Stockholm signatories, all 35—NATO, Warsaw Pact, and the others— include all European forces. Two separate negotiations have been under way: one to extend and strengthen security and confidence building in Europe; the other, as a mandate for conventional arms reductions leading to symmetrical balances between subcategories of NATO and Warsaw Pact forces.

Even broader concerns have been expressed. Throughout the Stockholm process, the United States underscored information exchange; the Soviets emphasized arms reduction. U.S. policy sought a fuller implementation of the Helsinki Conference on Security and Cooperation in Europe (CDE's parent body), in order that security concerns, vital as they are, not crowd out the many other international commitments of the Helsinki Final Act. U.S. chief negotiator Ambassador Robert L. Barry echoed these wider interests when he quoted President Reagan (January 21, 1986):

...The Stockholm Conference can contribute to security in the larger sense, that which encompasses political, economic, cultural, and humanitarian human rights—as well as strictly military matters. The attainment of this broader concept of security is the fundamental objective of the United States.[16]

It is easy to be enthusiastic about Ambassador Barry's assessment that the successful outcome of the Stockholm provisions "should supply a positive political impulse to other arms control and security negotiations and to the East-West relationship as a whole." By reducing markedly the feasibility of surprise attack with conventional weapons from Eastern Europe, the Stockholm provisions have effectively deflated NATO's rationale for the first use of nuclear weapons, a principal part of U.S. military doctrine since the 1950s.

In their 1983 analysis of the nuclear predicament, Harvard University's Nuclear Study Group confronted the grisly question of how a nuclear confrontation might begin. After postulating five plausible scenarios, they analyzed the most frightening prospect—all-out nuclear exchange—and its probability. They predicted that nuclear war occurring through the escalation of conventional conflict appears more probable. Avoiding conventional war is thus, in their view, one of the most important ways of avoiding nuclear war.[17]

Could U.S.-Soviet attitudes change as much as the French-German relationship has changed since World War II and evolve into a bona fide security community? Probably not. But if the Harvard group is correct about escalation dynamics, the future is a little more secure because of the willingness of the United States and the Soviet Union to adopt practical approaches for reducing secretiveness and misperceptions that could explode into military confrontation. Incentives for conventional aggression in Europe have been markedly weakened by the successful implementation of the Stockholm provisions.

NUCLEAR RISK REDUCTION CENTERS

Even more could be attained for superpower security by the steady implementation of the agreement for nuclear risk reduction centers (NRRCs) in each capital city. The notion probably goes back to Henry Kissinger's professorial days at Harvard, where he urged in 1960 that there be binational teams in Moscow and Washington for 24-hour-a-day conflict resolution.[18]

The novel idea was taken up in 1981 in the Senate Armed Services Committee by Senator Sam Nunn, widely esteemed in arms control matters and a strong proponent of the view that the most likely cause of a general nuclear war would be misunderstanding, miscalculation, or uncertainty following a terrorist detonation of a nuclear bomb. With substantial support from several prestigious academic think tanks, plus the U.S. Senate, Senators Sam Nunn and John Warner made a personal appeal to General Secretary Gorbachev during their visit to Moscow in September 1985. This was followed by President Reagan's summit endorsement on November 21, 1985, which supplied essential momentum to invigorate the idea. At their October 1986 Reykjavik summit, the president and general secretary affirmed the progress made by U.S. and Soviet experts. Formal negotiations in Geneva in January and May 1987 produced an accord in principle, followed by an announcement on September 15 that the parties agreed to establish NRRCs in Washington and Moscow.

Senators Nunn and Warner, prime movers for the project, welcomed the agreement, which had been five years in the making. Said Warner:

... the establishment of nuclear risk reduction centers in both Washington, D.C. and Moscow will significantly reduce the chances of an accidental nuclear incident. All mankind benefits from the increased safety such an agreement provides.

Nunn added:

... This agreement demonstrates that the two superpowers can act together to advance their mutual interests in enhancing stability and reducing the risks of nuclear war.... It is clearly in our mutual interest to avoid stumbling into a nuclear war through miscalculation or misunderstanding.[19]

Warner, who had been the chief negotiator for the Incidents at Sea Agreement of 1972, stressed the value of precedent in superpower security safeguards:

The Incidents at Sea Agreement, which in several ways was used as a model, a precedent, for the agreement on Nuclear Risk Reduction Centers, has proven extremely successful in preventing or resolving disputes between the U.S. and Soviet Navies. It's my hope that nuclear risk reduction centers will provide an equally important means of exchanging critical information, thereby lessening tension and avoiding unintentional military confrontation. . . . [20]

Stating President Reagan's conviction that "a nuclear war cannot be won and must never be fought," the 1987 agreement institutionalized a new framework and mechanisms for consultations to protect against unintended military confrontations and accidental nuclear war. The centers are equipped to communicate directly at the government-to-government level, using satellite links similar to, but separate from, the hotline reserved for heads of government. Without supplanting or duplicating existing crisis management channels, the centers have multiplied valuable communications options below the head-of-state level. The result is greater versatility, in addition to state-of-the-art communications technology (equivalent to the hotline upgrade), for rapid and reliable transmission of emergency data, texts, and graphics. The agreement's roomy framework and agreeable principles are sufficiently flexible to allow for new functions yet to be devised in the course of implementation.

Going beyond the hotline, a channel for information on crises in progress or about to occur, or the SALT agreement's Standing Consultative Commission, which meets only periodically or on specific questions of treaty compliance, NRRCs engage staffs of specialists around the clock. Contrary to earlier ideas about binational staffs, resisted by the U.S. Department of Defense, each nation uses its own experts.

The major advantage over previous security arrangements is that, in addition to customary diplomatic channels, the centers could accommodate new forums for joint discussions on military doctrine and planning; they could serve as important conduits for the exchange of accident notifications (such as the discharge of missiles in either direction); they could continuously review ways to make exchanges of security information under existing agreements more efficient and reliable; and they could be used to contain the escalation of hostilities and to maintain a continuous dialogue and watch on terrorism and other situations that could precipitate a nuclear confrontation.

Inauguration of the first NRRC in Washington, D.C., on March 22, 1988, provided clues of immediate responsibilities.[21] Assistant Secretary of State for Political-Military Affairs H. Allen Holmes was designated to direct the first 24-hour-a-day staff of Russian-speaking State Department officers and specially trained communications personnel. As expected, their chief purpose is to reduce risks of nuclear conflict by providing high-speed, direct transmission of information and notifications in accordance with security measures to prevent nuclear war

(1971) and incidents at sea (1972). A central role will be played in the implementation of the 1987 Intermediate Nuclear Forces Treaty by providing stipulated inspection and compliance notifications. The NRRCs are expected to perform the vital and demanding tasks of information exchange for the verification of many existing and future arms control agreements.

THE FUTURE: MORE PRECARIOUS OR MORE SECURE?

Looking to the future, three questions must be addressed in evaluating superpower security communications: (1) What are their primary values and what causes them to work? (2) How has high technology affected both bilateral and international security? (3) Aside from expected improvements in technical reliability and performance, what special dynamics and potentials are revealed by U.S.-Soviet cooperation?

First, let us recognize that the extraordinary measures reviewed in this chapter cannot resolve fundamental geopolitical and ideological rivalry that fuels so much of U.S.-Soviet hostility. Many of the measures are precautionary and have never been tested under crisis conditions, a fact that may be due to both phenomenal good luck and purposeful planning. Nevertheless, elaborate bilateral negotiations, most of them moving ponderously and quietly over a number of years, testify to the recognition of a common military threat to humanity and the willingness to address it jointly.

The need is compelling to constrain crises that may escalate out of control because of miscalculation, miscommunication, or accident. When contemplating the worst relations between the United States and the Soviet Union, and scenarios showing them inching toward the brink of nuclear war, the first picture that springs to mind is the 1962 Cuban missile crisis. Not much is remembered about the ominous state of affairs during the June 1967 Arab-Israeli war, when for more than an hour, President Johnson had no idea who had attacked the U.S.S. *Liberty*, a communications ship off the Sinai Peninsula.[22] The president used the hotline to communicate to Moscow that the United States had no intention to intervene in the war; and later, when the Israelis admitted their mistaken attack, that, too, was relayed via the hotline to the Soviets.

Mind-boggling scenarios for nuclear conflict have long dominated research on superpower accident prevention. In their pioneering study, William Ury and Richard Smoke comprehensively surveyed the dangers of an unintended war, made all the more possible in our time because of political hot spots all over the world, nuclear proliferation, and the risks of nuclear terrorism. U.S.-Soviet responsibility was the pivotal issue in six recommended measures to stabilize and even prevent a massive crisis:

1. Technical procedures to defuse "crisis triggers"

2. Joint binational facilities in Washington and Moscow connected by instant teleconferencing

3. A declared policy of reflection and consultation to ascertain the origins and intentions of nuclear detonations before making a retaliatory strike

4. Semiannual meetings between the U.S. secretaries of state and defense and their Soviet counterparts to enhance crisis management

5. Briefing exercises for the U.S. president and top advisers at which specialists and participants in previous crises would pass on their expertise

6. The use of third parties to mediate and defuse regional conflicts.[23]

All these measures for ensuring high-quality decision making accentuate the values of speedy, accurate information transmission when it counts most.

All along, the underlying philosophy has been that precise, accurate communications need not be frustrated by sharp political and ideological differences. During especially troublesome relations, even modest progress in multiplying lines of expert information is undeniably positive. Fortunately, reciprocal allegations that the sides have reneged on arms control agreements have so far spared the field of security communications; obviously, their highly sensitive and classified nature makes a definitive and comprehensive analysis in the public realm impossible. Yet this much can be ventured: the marked absence of official recriminations and accusations of violations indicates that established lines of security information are beneficial, relatively trouble-free, and functioning quietly, at least up to expectations. These are powerful inducements that supply momentum and cause them to work. The aphorism "No news is good news" applies.

Viewed years from now, complex bilateral as well as multilateral measures for security communications will have justified themselves fully if, in addition to risk reduction, accident prevention, and confidence building (intrinsically valuable in and of themselves), they also succeed in nudging the superpowers toward a build-down of weapons. However heartening the measures enumerated in these pages, they must be considered supports, not substitutes, for quintessential strategic arms control that reduces delivery systems and warheads, and above all avoids an improvident arms spiral into space.

Second, imagine for a moment that agreements such as the hotline and Incidents at Sea are buried in a time capsule and unearthed a century from now. It is highly plausible that citizens of the future will question amazedly how the superpowers ever got along without them and why sophisticated bilateral security communications were not commonplace much earlier. The obvious answers are that strategic nuclear weapons, joined by an explosion in delivery systems and hi-tech communications capabilities, were unforeseen or only remote possibilities when the United States and Soviet Union took off on their arms race after World War II.

Today, in devising technical measures to prevent and resolve crises, Americans and Soviets have gone beyond mere symbolic gestures of goodwill and conference negotiations: high technology employed in frenetic preparations for destruction in the name of national security is also proving its worth in making humanity's survival more likely. President Reagan's 1987 Washington summit warning, *doveryai, no proveryai* ("Trust, but verify," a Russian saying), was followed by a responsive quip from General Secretary Gorbachev. That it has been repeated many times is a reminder that a true and persuasive verification regime can be a reality in our time only because of the wealth of modern communications technology.

We should also note, however, that crisis management and human survival depend on considerably more than complex advanced technology and risk-reduction agreements. The Soviet 1983 shooting down of KAL 007, the 1987 Iraqi attack on the U.S.S. *Stark*, and Mathias Rust's spectacular, uninvited 1987 landing of a Cessna in Moscow's Red Square speak volumes about human fallibilities and the unexpected vulnerabilities of even the most sophisticated defense systems, however elaborate our precautions. Multiplying the modes, versatility, and reliability of crisis communications—even risking felicitous redundancy—may be a way of narrowing prospects for human error, granted that these may never be ruled out entirely.

Third, the United States and the Soviet Union appear satisfied enough with security communications so that instead of retaliatory lapses, curtailments, or suspensions, there seem to be very strong incentives to maintain their continuity and more. In some cases, dissatisfaction over inadequate performance has prompted extensive expansion, upgrading, and refinement of existing accords. Such is clearly the case with the hotline, which began in 1963 as a simple teletype system sustained by oceanic and overland cable, and then was progressively improved in 1971 and 1984 with ultramodern equipment, including the capacity for facsimile transmission. Yet another example is that insufficient safeguards for commercial aviation, dramatized by the downing of KAL flight 007, were improved and reinforced by an Anchorage-Tokyo-Khabarovsk mini-hotline over the North Pacific.

In several risk-reduction and security agreements, this functionalist dynamic has been at work. In his book *A Working Peace System* (1943),

David Mitrany posited that nation-states increasingly vulnerable in a dangerous and complicated world would be forced to cooperate. In his view, problems worldwide in scope would require a more and more concerted attack by members of the international system. Resultant habits of cooperation (or, in the context of this chapter, confidence building) would lead to more benign mutual perceptions and an extension and refinement of existing collaboration. There would be greater consensus on additional areas of needed activity (spillover, he called this), leading to higher, more valuable levels of interaction.

Verifying permissible levels of nuclear testing offered one such exceptional example of expanded collaborative activity, which was motivated by treaties in 1974 and 1976 to impose bans on underground nuclear explosions with yields of over 150 kilotons. In January 1988, 20 U.S. experts calibrated seismic instruments, measured underground chemical explosions, and undertook geological tests in the vicinity of Semipalatinsk in the Soviet Union. Soon after, 20 Soviet experts reciprocated by conducting their own experiments at a U.S. nuclear test site in Nevada. Such exercises to improve verification measures—even to make them foolproof, if possible—are prime attempts to break through to better and better forms of highly specialized security communications.

Several U.S.-Soviet accords offer other functionalist possibilities. Standing agreements could be extended to additional problem areas and fine-tuned to fulfill the expanding expectations of the parties. For instance, under the hotline and Accident Measures agreements, there could be advance notice of *all* missile launches. As an extension of the Incidents at Sea Agreement, there could be mandatory notification of *all* naval exercises. Procedures applicable to U.S. and Soviet navies could be applied to aerial incidents (rules of the air, as it were) or to outer space, where there are bound to be steady increases in the frequency and numbers of reconnaissance satellites, space platforms for research, and even tests involving strategic missile launches and antisatellite systems. NRRCs could eventually include discussions and analyses of all military exercises that might appear provocative (for example, the Soviet test missile that flew close to Hawaii in the summer of 1987). As in the case of the Stockholm Agreement on Confidence- and Security-Building in Europe, the purpose would be to deflate suspicions and enlarge areas where military activities would be transparent and predictable.

The success of superpower collaboration on security communications, risk reduction, and accident prevention is tied to one of the colossal paradoxes of our time: never in the human story have two powers mounted such massive arsenals against each other and at the same time so ingeniously invented a nexus of safety measures to prevent their possible consequences. The vitality and momentum of U.S.-Soviet safeguards tell an eloquent story, recognizing that human survival is the key to everything and that national self-interest cannot endure apart from the general interest. Years of contentious negotiations and pages of tedious verbatim commitments in legalistic language weigh far less than the recognition that in a nuclearized world, there is no rational alternative to security that is joint.

NOTES

1. "Arms Control: Confidence-Building Measures," *GIST* (U.S. Department of State), November 1985.

2. These categories of security communications are drawn from John Borawski, ed., *Avoiding War in the Nuclear Age* (Boulder, Colo.: Westview Press, 1986), pp. 11–13. (The term "confidence-building measure" reportedly first appeared in a U.N. General Assembly resolution, December 16, 1955, p. 5.)

3. Ibid., p. 13.

4. "Memorandum of Understanding Between the United States of America and the Union of Soviet Socialist Republics Regarding the Establishment of a Direct Communications Link," in *Arms Control and Disarmament Agreements* (Washington, D.C.: Arms Control and Disarmament Agency, 1982), pp. 31–33.

5. Sally K. Horn, "The Hotline," in Borawski, *Avoiding War*, p. 46.

6. For an account of this background and the ensuing negotiations, see Raymond L. Garthoff (member of the SALT I delegation), "The Accident Measures Agreement," in Borawski, *Avoiding War*, pp. 58–65. A full text of the Agreement on Measures to Reduce the Risk of Outbreak of Nuclear War Between the United States of America and the Union of Soviet Socialist Republics is in *Arms Control and Disarmament Agreements*, pp. 111–112.

7. These and other incidents are recounted in Rick Atkinson, "U.S., Soviet Navies in Civil Contact About Abrasive Encounters at Sea," *Washington Post*, June 24, 1984; and Sean M. Lynn Jones, "Avoiding Incidents At Sea," in Borawski, *Avoiding War*, pp. 72–86.

8. For a text of the Agreement Between the Government of the United States of America and the Government of the Union of Soviet Socialist Republics on the Prevention of Incidents on and over the High Seas, May 25, 1972, see *Department of State Bulletin* 61, no. 1722 (June 26, 1972), pp. 926–927.

9. Based on personal discussions with the Office of Soviet Union Affairs, U.S. Department of State, June 1987 and May 1988.

10. *Arms Control and Disarmament Agreements*, pp. 158–160.

11. Unpublished report, "Summary of Discussions, Third Meeting, COSPAS/SARSAT Steering Committee" (Quebec, Canada, February 9–20, 1987), p. 7; also COSPAS/SARSAT Secretariat, *Information Bulletin* no. 2, December 1987 (available from National Oceanic and Atmospheric Administration, Washington, D.C.).

12. Agreement Among Anchorage Area Control Center, Tokyo Area Control

Center, and Khabarovsk Area Control Center, July 29, 1985, unpublished document from the U.S. Federal Aviation Administration; *Department of State Bulletin* 85, no. 2103 (October 1985): 61. See also U.S. Department of Transportation, *News*, August 8, 1986.

13. "President's Statement," *Department of State Bulletin* 86, no. 2116 (November 1986): 25.

14. Ibid. See pp. 20–25 for a full text of the September 19, 1986, agreement.

15. Robert L. Barry (ambassador and head of the U.S. delegation), "Address to the Stockholm Conference on Confidence- and Security-Building Measures and Disarmament in Europe," *Current Policy* (U.S. Department of State, Bureau of Public Affairs), no. 793 (February 4, 1986).

16. *Department of State Bulletin* 86, no. 2116 (November 1986): 26.

17. Albert Carnesale et al., *Living with Nuclear Weapons* (New York: Bantam Books, 1983), p. 67.

18. R. Jeffrey Smith, "A Risk Reduction Center Gains U.S. Support," *Science* 231 (January 10, 1986): 107.

19. "Agreement Signed on Risk Reduction Centers," press release, U.S. Senate Committee on Armed Services, September 15, 1987. The press release included an unpublished copy of the agreement and two protocols.

20. Ibid.

21. David Shipler, "Talks by Shultz and Shevardnadze," *New York Times*, March 23, 1988, p. A7.

22. William Ury and Richard Smoke, "Beyond the Hotline: Controlling a Nuclear Crisis," in Borawski, *Avoiding War*, p. 133.

23. William Ury and Richard Smoke, *Beyond the Hotline: Controlling a Nuclear Crisis* (Cambridge, Mass.: Nuclear Negotiation Project, Harvard Law School, 1984), pp. iii–viii.

FOR FURTHER READING

Berg, Rolf, and Adam-Daniel Rotfeld. *Building Security in Europe*. New York: Institute for East-West Security Studies, 1986.

Blechman, Barry M. (ed.). *Preventing Nuclear War: A Realistic Approach*. Bloomington: Indiana University Press, 1985.

———. "A Minimal Reduction of a Major Risk." *Bulletin of the Atomic Scientists*, April 1988, pp. 44–46.

Byers, R. B., F. Stephen Larrabee, and Allen Lynch, (eds.). *Confidence-Building Measures and International Security*. New York: Institute for East-West Security Studies, 1987.

George, Alexander L., Philip J. Farley, and Alexander Dallin, (eds.). *U.S.-Soviet Security Cooperation: Achievements, Failures, Lessons*. New York: Oxford University Press, 1988.

Larrabee, F. Stephen, and Allen Lynch. *Confidence-Building Measures and U.S.-Soviet Relations*. Occasional Paper Series no. 1. New York: Institute for East-West Security Studies, 1986.

Lewis, John W., and Coit D. Blacker. *Next Steps in the Creation of an Accidental*

Nuclear War Prevention Center. Stanford, Calif.: Center for International Security and Arms Control, 1983.

Nye, Joseph S., Jr. (ed.). *The Making of America's Soviet Policy.* New Haven: Yale University Press, 1984.

9

SUPERPOWER COOPERATION: THE WAY AHEAD

Nish Jamgotch, Jr.

This volume began with a demanding rhetorical question about the two most powerful competitors in the history of international relations: Why cooperate? It remains to address three essential issues: (1) What are the salient conclusions of the preceding seven case studies? (2) What types of mutual benefits ensue from cooperative agreements and projects, and how can one best understand and appreciate them from a neofunctionalist perspective? (3) What policy revisions would facilitate a more promising new future in U.S.-Soviet relations?

SEVEN CASE STUDIES

In Chapter 2, Yale Richmond's summation underscores the great significance of academic and cultural exchanges, even if their values are difficult to quantify and tally precisely. The record shows that Winston Churchill's inimitable 1939 characterization ("Russia is a riddle, wrapped in a mystery, inside an enigma") has been superseded by enlightenment and expertise derived from more than 30 years of concerted academic and cultural programs. Firsthand experience on both sides has provided a basis, although little guarantee, for more informed policy decisions. Indeed, long before Gorbachev became general secretary, he did the unusual; he benefited from unescorted automobile travel in France, an episode that was bound to enrich his perspective on world affairs. The policy statements of President Eisenhower, who initiated exchanges in 1958, and of President Reagan, who accelerated them after the 1985 Geneva summit, are strong reminders that citizens on both sides can leap governments, communicate, and collaborate for mutual understanding and a more reasoned appreciation for deep political differences.

The thesis of Chapter 3, by Christopher C. Joyner, is that the 1959 Antarctic treaty was a pioneering preclusive agreement and model for the future: one-tenth of the globe was rendered off limits to weapons of mass destruction. Treaty provisions provided for confidence building based on both scientific and military cooperation, a specific demilitarized zone, free access and unique on-site inspection of governmental facilities, and special mechanisms for the settlement of disputes. Despite the markedly divergent political and ideological systems, U.S.-Soviet diplomacy concerning the South Pole largely avoided the harsh polemics and antagonisms that animated so many of their other relationships. Scientific collaboration, too, produced significant joint studies on the physiological adaptation to isolation and climate, oceanography, atmospheric physics, marine biology, petrology, glaciology, geological mapping, hydrology of freshwater lakes, and investigations of the ozone hole in the atmosphere above the pole. As a basis for advancing the parties from science, arms control, and environmental management to resource exploration, the treaty has exemplified valuable elasticity and vitality.

Chapter 4, by Gary K. Bertsch, presents a mixed picture of trade relations, ranging from early hopes during the first Nixon administration to the economic warfare mentality of the early 1980s, when U.S. leaders sought to employ commerce as a political weapon against Soviet bad behavior. Due to pragmatic economic interests and pressure from grain growers, the record was more positive in agriculture; the U.S. grain embargo was dropped in 1981 and a new long-term agreement was concluded in 1983. The thaw in bilateral relations in 1985 included steps toward a more favorable business climate and greater encouragement of U.S. pro-trade forces by the Reagan administration. The spring 1988 trip to Moscow by Secretary of Commerce William Verity and over 500 U.S. business executives appeared to sound even stronger signals of U.S. commercial interests, including the formation of a new trade consortium for joint economic ventures. Professor Bertsch is not sanguine about prospects for fully normalized economic relations in the next half-decade. Primary commercial requirements for the Soviets continue where they have always been: they seek most-favored-nation tariff treatment, U.S. government credits, and a major relaxation of export controls. Implied political preconditions also abound, connected to festering differences over arms control, regional disputes, and human rights.

Chapter 5 by Donald R. Kelley, shows that U.S.-Soviet cooperation in environmental protection and conservation has been one of the most durable aspects of superpower relations. Cooperative projects have focused on many areas of pollution abatement in air and water, and on studies of agricultural, biological, and genetic consequences of pollution. Important work also has taken place in the fields of urban and marine environments, nature preserves, environmental changes in climate, arctic and subarctic ecology, and earthquake and tidal wave forecasting. Especially in some of the most successful showcase projects, achievements have stimulated a heightened sense of community and mission, so fundamental to productive collaboration in good times and to all-important informal communications during periods of exceptional political tension. U.S. presidents have used the 1972 environmental agreement both to indicate displeasure with Soviet actions and to warm relations during troubled times. Although the agreement is among the least known by the general public, it has alerted the superpowers to the vital commonly felt issues of environmental quality, highlighting the link between science and politics and an especially rich field for even more fruitful cooperation in the future.

In Chapter 6's analysis of the record in space, David D. Finley stresses that a changed macropolitical environment enabled new prospects for cooperation in the 1980s and 1990s. Valuable scientific payoffs have become more apparent to both scientific communities. A May 1984 workshop sponsored by the Office of Technology Assessment produced an impressive array of potential collaborative activities, including work on space plasma theory; solar terrestrial physics; studies of Venus, Mars, the moon, comets, and outer planets; the effects of long-term spaceflights; and exobiology (unmanned missions to investigate extraterrestrial life and intelligence). A marked boost in the coordination of space research was given by Secretary of State Shultz's April 1987 visit to Moscow. While cautioning about expectations that joint practices can by example effect new dimensions of interaction, Finley nonetheless reminds us that the regeneration of superpower collaboration since the mid–1980s, after years of neglect and stagnation, demonstrates the soundness of earlier understandings and organizational arrangements. On his balance sheet, memories of joint projects are memories of success. The key is the recognition that space research is too vast and costly for one nation, and that cooperation that avoids uneven political and military advantages bears the greatest prospect of success.

In Chapter 7 the comprehensive review and analysis of medical cooperation by Dr. Harold Sandler reiterates an indomitable message: since illness knows no national frontiers, the language and treatments of medicine are naturally global. Ranging from the cooperative eradication of smallpox to joint programs on cardiovascular disease, cancer, artificial heart development, environmental health, arthritis, influenza, and acute respiratory disease, eye disease, and space medicine, Sandler sets forth an extensive array of humanitarian achievements by physicians motivated both by the universal values of scientific dialogue and by the moral and social implications of the threat of nuclear war. The foundation of medical activism and the U.S.-Soviet physicians' movement is the recognition that doctors cannot avoid great international social and political issues that so directly challenge the health of their communities. Decades of U.S.-Soviet medical collaboration and research confirm the benefits to both nations. He concludes that the longevity of relationships, stability of personnel, and universal humanitarian goals have all reinforced the credibility of bilateral programs and provided long-awaited evidence of changing attitudes.

Chapter 8, by the present author, bears the message that a vast and dangerous arms race in the nuclear age has necessitated extraordinary measures to minimize the risks of misperceptions and accidents in superpower relations. In collaborating to make their military intentions more open, predictable, and explicit, Americans and Soviets have orchestrated creative, even ingenious, safeguards against the very war for which they have been preparing for some 45 years. Security communications, whose benefits show no favoritism, bear incomparable incentives for compliance by both sides. If they are curtailed, the curtailer suffers as much as the intended victim. This, of course, is only one of many illustrations of true interdependence.

A TYPOLOGY OF MUTUAL BENEFITS

Let us be unmistakably clear that U.S.-Soviet cooperative projects cannot be exercises in fundamentals—that is, the transformation of inexorable national differences, rivalry, and enmity. But joint enterprises that have heightened the dependability of both sides to maintain the status quo and a stable peace have proved indispensable. They should be strengthened and expanded. Most productive have been projects with outcomes that neither side can afford to squander. Included are benefits in perceptions, ecological management, functionalism, culture and education, commerce, and security.

Perceptual Benefits

A persistent and poorly understood aspect of U.S.-Soviet relations is that psychological factors distort mutual perceptions and create irrational responses in both directions. Much has been said about anxiety and defense mechanisms in order to explain the tendency of the United States and the Soviet Union to idealize their own group and denigrate the opponent.[1] Certainly one consequence is that a hostile stereotyping and dehumanization of the enemy makes it exceedingly difficult to justify enterprises of obvious common interest. Over the years, distortions that exaggerate Soviet capabilities, accomplishments, and malicious intentions have become so embedded in the U.S. public mind that nothing short of the boldest leadership and public enlightenment can ease perceptions toward more sophisticated understanding.

The Soviets, too, make it exceedingly problematical to comprehend the important refinements of U.S. society. There are several contributing factors, including the baleful influence of Marxist-Leninist ideology, a historic fear and suspicion of foreigners, a Spartan system of managed public information, and even the gloomy reporting of Soviet correspondents.[2]

Reciprocal dehumanization is especially dangerous in the thermonuclear age. Outmoded Cold War vocabularies and images that relegate the superpowers to a perceptual cul-de-sac are not likely to generate the fresh, creative insights so vital in even adversarial relations. In public policy, it is exceedingly important to elicit the mutual respect and mood for concessions and compromise that are so essential to successful diplomacy.

As stated by Marshall Shulman, a long-time observer of U.S.-Soviet relations, what we face is a compelling need to submit the pictures in our heads to the process of reality testing:

The human mind needs its stereotypes, to make more manageable the reception of complex data and stimuli, from such sources as each morning's newspaper. But we can seek continuously to refine our stereotypes and to make them more differentiated, so that they come closer to a reflection of reality. This will in turn make possible a mobilization of the intellect, helping us to act with greater rationality on the bases of a more objective understanding of the nature of the problems we face.[3]

It must be stressed that superpower conflict is not rooted in misperceptions—rather, in fundamental differences in history, national interests, capabilities, and intentions. But these differences (and potentially valuable problem solving) are aggravated by misperceptions that can be ameliorated by cooperative programs.

Cooperation, plus a fuller comprehension of its consequences, *can* create a more balanced picture in the interest of undoing some of the malevolent images and malignant social processes that have bedeviled relations for so long.[4] Tangible achievements and mutual benefits, such as those set forth in these pages, can help to attract official and public perceptions on both sides away from a Manichean dichotomy in world affairs and away from images that are anachronistic and unproductive.

Benefits cannot be quantified—as when Soviet gold bullion is exchanged for metric tons of Kansas wheat and Iowa corn. Perceptions do, however, benefit from the knowledge that, even with antithetical belief systems, both U.S. and Soviet citizens can pledge themselves to humanitarian purposes.

Picture, for example, the International Physicians for the Prevention of Nuclear War, which represents over 75,000 physicians worldwide. Founded in 1980 by Americans and Soviets, the organization was awarded the Nobel Peace Prize for 1985. Apart from the merit of peace efforts by doctors, what must not be lost is the significance of fresh contemporary images when Soviet physicians and scholars work to change official thinking about military doctrine in their country, while Americans do the same in theirs.

Similarly, as people-to-people exchanges have become a hot growth industry since the 1985 Geneva summit, U.S. and Soviet cardiologists have participated in live satellite conferences on the prevention and treatment of heart disease. The project was one of ten satellite medical conferences organized for 1986 by the U.S. Information Agency (USIA). Both USIA and private citizens' groups witnessed an outpouring of interest by Americans eager to erode barriers between East and West by volunteering for creative programs devised by both sides. Also included in 1986 was an effort to enlist youth through a swap of 20 "young astronauts" and "young cosmonauts," ages 6 to 17, for 10-day stints at U.S. and Soviet space facilities and museums.[5]

In the more popular realm of athletics, no one can know precisely how much reality testing results from widely televised sports contests. Yet one must acknowledge that the growth in sports broadcasting provides excellent opportunities to see slices of life that are appealing to all ages. The opening ceremony of the Goodwill Games in Moscow, televised by Turner Broadcasting in July 1987, was especially memorable for its virtuoso performance by the Soviet card section, undulating and flashing humane messages, canceling a nuclear cloud with words that peace and goodwill can overcome implements of death and destruction. Scholastic Sports America, broadcasting in September 1987, showed telecasts of Americans and Soviets competing in basketball, gymnastics, swimming, and even skateboarding. Interviews with young Soviet athletes were included, complete with candid conversations and glimpses of family life. Revealing these human dimensions, plus the conspicuous skill, sportsmanship, and decorum on both sides, assuredly posed a stark contrast to images of Rocky vs. Drago and a life-or-death struggle that have long soured bilateral relations.

Likewise, especially at the time of the Chernobyl nuclear accident, of the Daniloff affair, and during critical phases of arms control negotiations, regular appearances of Soviet diplomatic and press officials on U.S. news programs have undoubtedly had an eye-opening impact. Young, sophisticated, knowledgeable, and very professional, their adroit parrying of questions in remarkably polished English has conveyed pictures of candor, level-headedness, and respectability very foreign to the ingrained beliefs of many Americans.

At the highest levels of politics, U.S. and Soviet leaders, locked in negotiations—notably the 1987 Washington summit—have also produced a deep impact on public perceptions. Showing shrewdness and careful forethought, Mikhail and Raisa Gorbachev descended upon the U.S. diplomatic stage and tapped the political sensitivities of Americans, average citizens and seasoned pundits alike. By executing a dazzling media blitz—a virtual tour de force—the Gorbachevs provided masterful lessons in public relations, even challenging U.S. leaders on their own turf. At the same time, a fresh positive image of the new Soviet leadership was reinforced.

Perceptual benefits accrue ever so slowly—indeed, imperceptibly—until major media events such as the 1987 Washington summit transform them into big jumps in more facilitative images and concrete understandings. American polls in 1987 clearly showed not only deep residual distrust of the Soviet Union but also a strong desire to reduce tensions and lessen the chances of war. Americans are expecting more and better efforts to reconcile historical and political differences.[6]

Ecological Benefits

As used by Thomas Kuhn in his work on scientific revolutions, the term "paradigm" has entered our vocabulary to describe shared understandings of facts, standards, and rules of scientific inquiry. Ours is a world in which a dominant social paradigm has exerted a profound effect on the ways nations must view each other because of menacing challenges to human survival. With a focus on the interrelated variables of population, nonrenewable resources, industrial production, pollution, social justice, and the quality of life, there have already been some 25 years of restiveness about the Earth's fragility, its finite carrying capacity, and the like-it-or-not interdependence of its nations.

At no time in recent years was ecological interdependence more poignantly demonstrated than in the unprecedented nuclear accident at Chernobyl on April 26, 1986. Coinciding as it did with the Kremlin's debate over official information policy in the name of greater *glasnost* or openness, the accident revealed a great deal: the Soviet Union could not remain aloof from foreign medical help and the outrage of world public opinion; national frontiers were useless in containing the explosion's deadly radiation and information about it.

Sensing the enormous, sinister threat of nuclear energy that escaped control, Gorbachev responded to an appeal by major West European leaders to provide speedier information about nuclear emergencies. Pledging early warnings of future accidents, he called upon the International Atomic Energy Agency (IAEA) to help create "a system of prompt warning and supply of information in the event of faults at nuclear power stations, specifically when accompanied by the escape of radioactivity."[7]

Proposals for more rigorous international regulation of nuclear energy and an agreement to monitor Chernobyl accident victims for life must also be considered auspicious outcomes of the tragedy. Dr. Robert Gale, a U.S. specialist on bone marrow transplants, reached a private agreement with Soviet physicians to undertake a long-term study of radiation exposure and the risks of cancer.[8] Medical treatment in future incidents is bound to benefit.

Although reliable information was too long in coming, Western specialists were impressed by the frank and informative account provided by the Soviets at the Vienna conference of the International Atomic Energy Agency in August 1986. Hans Blix, the IAEA's director general, concluded that much had been learned about the management and containment of nuclear accidents and also about medical and decontamination measures. The United States and the Soviet Union pledged themselves to publicize incidents that spread radiation across frontiers, even from military installations. Additional benefits are likely from a nuclear safety and research agreement signed on August 22, 1986. Reciprocal on-site inspections of selected atomic research stations are included, as are exchange visits of nuclear safety specialists and expanded collaboration on the development of breeder and liquid-metal-moderated reactors.

One must not minimize the considerable anxiety and anguish caused the world community by what appeared to be callous negligence and sluggish initial reporting by the Soviet leadership. It was, after all, the Swedes who first informed the world that something was amiss and that the ecosystem was in jeopardy. Yet one can also detect in the uncharacteristic, if belated, Soviet forthrightness a new era in reporting accident information for the benefit of the world community. Superpower rivalry has thus been tempered by the recognition that in modern technology, there is a fragile boundary between progress and catastrophe, and that the rewards from cooperation on ecological issues clearly outweigh behavior that may render humankind's only planetary home uninhabitable.

Functionalist Benefits

As set forth in Chapter 8, functionalism, posited by David Mitrany in his classical work *A Working Peace System* (1943), argues that nation-states, increasingly unable to meet pressing needs, are forced to cooperate. Humankind must muster the ingenuity to accelerate interchange because habits of international cooperation can multiply rewarding relationships. The guiding thesis of modern functionalists is that a project succeeds, but with time becomes inadequate and no longer satisfies the parties completely; therefore it must be expanded or upgraded. Success thus serves as a foundation for confidence building and as a catalyst for fresh projects.

A most impressive achievement of superpower collaboration—indeed, a paragon of functionalism—has been the initiation and steady upgrading of the hotline, the direct communications link between the White House and the Kremlin. Originated as a simple teletype system employing a transatlantic cable, the direct hookup advanced to utilize sophisticated satellite technology of the 1970s, and was improved still further by a 1984 agreement to provide facsimile capability for the transmission of charts, maps, and graphs.

Mitrany probably never foresaw the inherent functionalist dynamic in engineering and technology that could play a positive role in U.S.-Soviet relations. Because today's electronic equipment is bound to become inadequate when outpaced by constant scientific discovery and innovation, it is natural that the prospect of more efficient, reliable, and speedy forms of joint emergency communication will entice the parties always to strive for the state of the art. Inevitable technological obsolescence is thus an important guarantee that the United States and the Soviet Union will have to work together to keep abreast of leaps in science.

Confirming a similar functionalist dynamic, exciting proposals for bilateral space projects have very likely exceeded even the most grandiose visions of participants in the Apollo-Soyuz joint space docking and circumnavigation of Earth in July 1975. Far more ambitious space ventures than Apollo-Soyuz have been proposed by Soviet cosmonauts and U.S. astronauts who met in an anniversary celebration ten years later to toast their historic success and propose a joint manned mission to Mars. Obvious benefits would include sharing costs and the glory of scientific achievement, plus reinforced habits of cooperation. A joint resolution by the U.S. Congress (October 30, 1984), signed by President Reagan, affirmed U.S. interest in precisely such a venture. Additional momentum was provided by the president in his 1985 Geneva summit proposal for increased space collaboration. Ever since, specialists from the two nations have maintained consultations on space medicine, extended space station missions, effects of weightlessness, and planetary research on Venus—all fields in which the Soviets have appreciable credibility.

The timing of a reinvigorated U.S.-Soviet space partnership could be particularly impressive. Some proposals for an International Space Year, beginning in 1992, would coincide with the five hundredth anniversary of Columbus's discovery of America and the seventy-fifth anniversary of the Russian Revolution. The year 1992 would also mark the thirty-fifth anniversary of the International Geophysical Year, whose programs preceded the Soviet Union's Sputnik and the U.S. Explorer and Vanguard satellites.

Physicist Carl Sagan has offered a thought-challenging plea for a joint U.S.-Soviet expedition beginning in 1992. Under the catchy title "Let's Go to Mars Together," he advanced an eloquent justification that such a mission is technologically feasible and would cost far less than the president's Strategic Defense Initiative.

Imagine these leaders deciding to do something not just for their nations but also for their species, something that would capture the imaginations of people everywhere and would lay the groundwork for a major advance in human history—the eventual settlement of another planet.

It can be done. It is technologically feasible. It requires no major "breakthroughs."[9]

Superpower cooperation thus bears striking examples of functionalism at work. Modest agreements that began with only a creative idea have been extended and upgraded. The hotline's success provided confidence and momentum for expanding and refining additional binational communications technology. Improvements in speed and reliability of transmission, and multiplying modes of emergency communication to include information about potentially dangerous activities of third parties, are easily separable from contentious political and ideological issues. There is in addition the possibility that agreements with carefully delimited objectives may spawn new, unrelated projects. Whether intentionally or not, problem-solving programs that also strengthen mutual confidence bear the exciting prospect of spilling over into political and military realms, although convincing evidence has long been wanting; and they even have heuristic values because of motivations and speculations about what else is achievable. Just by the compiling of wish lists of creative, even visionary, projects, to await the appropriate moment, cooperation can generate benign consequences, never foreseen, intended, or expected.

Cultural and Educational Benefits

A compelling case for benefits from cultural exchange has been made in Chapter 2 of this volume, based on a comprehensive summary of more than 20 years of experience with the Soviet Union and Eastern Europe. Its author's conclusion is:

The answer to the question, "Who wins, we or the Russians," is that we both win. In some exchanges there may be a ripoff, but in all of them there is a payoff.... Both sides find them mutually beneficial. Exchanges are now a well-established element in US-USSR bilateral relations, and the only question today is how we conduct them for maximum benefit to the United States.[10]

Debate over payoffs has persisted since the first bilateral program in 1955, just two years after Stalin's death. After many U.S. proposals, the musical *Porgy and Bess* traveled to Moscow and Leningrad; and the Boston Symphony Orchestra performed in 1956. The pianist Emil Gilels became the first Soviet artist to appear in the United States in the postwar period, followed by violinist David Oistrakh. Then came the first formal accord, the Lacy-Zarubin agreement (January 1958), formalizing exchanges in science, technology, agriculture, medicine, public health, radio, television, motion pictures, exhibitions, publications, government, youth, athletics, scholarly research, culture, tourism, and an understanding to establish direct air service.

The considerable improvement in superpower relations in the détente years, marked by Nixon-Brezhnev summits in 1972, 1973, and 1974, was paralleled by an expansive network of cooperative agreements. Fundamental to the Nixon-Kissinger strategy was the political idea that broadening and intensifying bilateral projects would encourage joint obligations and incentives for a more peaceful world. Shared work habits and understandings, it was thought, would motivate the Soviets to moderate their isolation and insecurity in international affairs.

Although cultural exchanges received a stunning setback by the deployment of Soviet forces in Afghanistan in 1979, President Reagan and General Secretary Gorbachev at their 1985 Geneva summit pledged to revive and intensify them. After an absence of 61 years, the incomparable pianist Vladimir Horowitz journeyed in the spring of 1986 to Moscow and Leningrad to perform in packed concert halls; and the famed Moiseyev, Kirov, and Bolshoi companies danced before rapt audiences in the United States as they had in previous years. A U.S. theater troup performed the children's play *Raggedy Ann Doll* in Moscow, and the Moscow Children's Musical Theater reciprocated with a ballet and concert rendition of Prokofiev's *Peter and the Wolf* in the United States. Art exhibitions included paintings from Leningrad's Hermitage and from Moscow's Pushkin Museum of Fine Arts and the Tretyakov Gallery. U.S. shows focused on three generations of art by the Wyeth family, an impressionist collection from the National Gallery, and nineteenth-century works, especially those of Thomas Eakins, from the Philadelphia Art Museum.

Cross-cultural enjoyment was given yet another boost when, in August 1986, symphonic concerts were conducted in Moscow by a Soviet (from the Moscow Philharmonic) and an American (from the Louisville Orchestra), including works by Mussorgsky, Gershwin, Shostakovich, Piston, Glazunov, Glinka, and Griffes. As conductors alternated on the podium, the musical union was being compared with the 1975 Apollo-Soyuz venture, history's only joint space mission.[11]

What can be surmised from the record of bilateral cultural agreements? Concert pianists, ballet troupes, children's theaters, and art exhibitions obviously cannot effect rapid transformations in political and military hostilities that have distinct origins and dynamics of their own. However, visual and performing arts *are* ecumenical. They have intellectual appeal and entertainment values that are unencumbered by national boundaries and ideologies.

If one focuses on less-heralded academic exchanges of teachers, undergraduate students, young faculty, senior professors, and researchers, there are impressive benefits from cross-cultural educational experiences. International Research and Exchanges Board (IREX) alumni can be found at almost every major U.S. college or university with a Soviet studies program, helping a new generation of students to unravel the complexities of the Soviet Union. According to IREX Executive Director Allen H. Kassof, the Commerce and State Departments, the CIA, and congressional staffs are peppered with alumni of the IREX exchanges. People with on-the-ground experience have brought back to the United States more refined sensitivities about what the Soviet Union is like.[12]

As for the impact of U.S. visits on Soviets:

An inevitable by-product of the exchanges, [is] exposing Soviet scholars and students to more explicitly open and plural contexts, alternative approaches, techniques and values—to experiences that would make better and more objective scholars of them (and incidentally may also lead them to rethink some of their beliefs).[13]

The boundary between perceptual benefits set forth earlier in this chapter, and personal cultural and educational enrichment emphasized here, may be easily blurred. Yet the distinction is significant. Once again, Kassof:

... In the rarefied atmosphere of things Soviet-American, [scholarly] exchanges have an impact quite out of proportion to their size. . . .

... The overwhelming majority not only manage to accomplish significant, even prodigious, research feats, but become profoundly involved in academic and personal relationships with their Soviet counterparts and hosts that, by their own testimony, count among the most memorable personal and intellectual experiences of their lives.... No wonder that they return home with exquisitely heightened sensitivities to the contours of their own culture that few can experience who have not shared their journey.[14]

Heightened sensitivities to one's own culture, plus those values inevitably deriving from experiences abroad, quite apparently motivated the Reagan White House. The president's October 13, 1986, address, following the Reykjavik summit, reiterated commitments to citizen exchanges, as if to elevate them to one of several major thrusts in U.S.-Soviet diplomacy.

Turning finally to a highly sophisticated aspect of culture and education, we should remind ourselves of benefits that have accrued from scientific cooperation. In principle, of course, science, like art, is international; its laws and processes are said to have universal characteristics. The record indicates, however, that all science takes place in national environments and is dependent on national financing. Earlier chapters in this volume, focusing on Antarctica, environmental protection, space, and medicine, recounted the ups and downs imposed by political considerations.

Yet despite intense Cold War hostilities and periodic crises, the record in science is remarkable for its achievements. Laboratories abound, whether in the vast ice cap and circumpolar waters of Antarctica, the earthquake-prone Pacific rim, the smog-ridden municipalities of the United States and the Soviet Union, an Earth-orbiting space capsule, or a hospital operating room ready for cardiological surgery. Naturalists, ecologists, geologists, astronauts, cosmonauts, engineers, technicians, physicians—they and others like them can pursue their craft with maximum benefits to humankind especially if Washington and Moscow will it. And they can be safe in assuming that contemporary challenges to the quality of life the world over would be eased (and even alleviated considerably) by collaborative research—work that unreservedly shares existing knowledge, technology, labor, costs, and recognition.

Commercial Benefits

U.S. conventional wisdom has been that in U.S.-Soviet trade, the Soviets have little of value, and when they sell, their gain is markedly greater. In addition to U.S. fears of technology transfer, bilateral trade has been dominated by the desire to punish the Soviets or to pressure them into social and political reforms at home and less intervention

in Third World areas. As Chapter 4 recounts, extending back to the
Cold War, when the U.S. economy was a mightier force, trade was
manipulated as a lever and political weapon against the Kremlin. The
critical reality is, however, that the U.S. ability to affect Soviet thought
and actions through commerce has been very small: less than 2 percent
of Soviet trade is conducted with the United States, clearly minuscule
for any genuine leverage, although the notion of U.S. omnipotence
persists.[15]

So much of the U.S.-Soviet economic relationship has been distorted
by one myth and then another: that the Soviets sit atop a gigantic,
enticing market just waiting to be tapped; that their inefficient, center-
heavy, Rube Goldberg-style economic system will cause them eventually to fold their tents; that the lure of foreign trade will stimulate
fundamental political transformations; that their perennial shortages
will make them prone to making diplomatic concessions; and that U.S.
trade policies, however erratic, will eventually turn out to make sound
political sense.

One must avoid exaggerating the value of bilateral trade and at the
same time recognize that worthwhile opportunities exist. Both nations
have immense military power alongside economies that are in trouble.
The Gorbachev leadership is seized with the need to vitalize technology
and heighten domestic efficiency in order to deliver on long-standing
commitments to Soviet consumers. Compared with its gargantuan military capabilities, Communist economic performance is frustrated and
dwarfish. U.S. leaders, for their part, have appeared confused over the
most efficacious ways of exporting in order to stimulate economic productivity and create a more favorable balance of payments and greater
financial stability. There is, moreover, the lingering myth that U.S.
commodities are a favor to the other side, a gift to be bestowed for
exemplary deportment. (Actually, the balance of U.S.-Soviet trade has
consistently been in favor of the United States.)

For the world's two largest grain and food producers, there are obvious interdependence and benefits: gigantic U.S. agrobusinesses suffer
from chronic overproduction; the Soviet Union's collectivized agriculture, from historic underproduction. For example, although there was
an avalanche of criticism, on both economic and foreign policy grounds,
President Reagan's 1983 rescission of the Carter grain embargo made
eminent sense. The decision to increase grain sales to the Soviets by
50 percent (from 6 million metric tons a year to 9 million) spoke elo-
quently about his savvy instinct for domestic politics. Both elections
in midwestern farm states and U.S. economic interests played a role.

It should not be assumed that the Soviets would be the only bene-
ficiaries from stepped-up trade. Soviet strategic minerals, essential to
U.S. technology and military industries, have for many years been

traded for hard currencies. Since the United States is dependent on a number of rare metals and minerals—in many cases the country imports over 50 percent of its needs for certain resources—increasing imports from the Soviet Union could be an attractive proposition. The Soviets, for their part, have repeatedly attempted to obtain easier terms for purchases of high-grade oil and gas drilling equipment, pipeline-laying machines, tractors, and sophisticated information systems for entering the computerized microchip and robotics world.

Although U.S. companies do not ordinarily look to the Soviet Union for advanced technologies, some have; and many more could if it were not for leeriness about quality. Surprisingly, outstanding Soviet technologies have been sold to the United States. These have included electro-slag casting (used to achieve high purity in composite metals), magnetic impact bonding (with applications for sealing nuclear fuel rods and making bullets), flash butt welding (for joining large-diameter pipe), and surgical stapling, used in suturing. The Soviets are reportedly pioneers in electro impulse deicing, detonation ultrathin spray coating, technology for welding thick titanium plate, intraocular lenses (silicone replacements for damaged human eye lenses), biodegradable bone-setting implants, and the use of ultrasound surgery. In recent years, the total value of some 2,000–3,000 commodity license sales—only about 30 to U.S. firms—has not amounted to much: only $75–100 million.[16]

Much more could be accomplished profitably by the adoption of a new agenda for bilateral trade set forth later in this chapter. It will not be easy; for aside from the life-or-death issues of arms control, no area of superpower relations with potential and mutually valuable gains has been fraught with more contentiousness and skepticism.

Security Benefits

That the superpowers consider security against each other the greatest challenge in contemporary global politics heightens the value of joint ventures to contain and manage tensions. From this perspective, all the cooperative enterprises described in these pages offer encouragement in the direction of greater conciliation and the recognition that threats and conflict are at the least unproductive, and at the worst very dangerous.

Years ago, Winston Churchill addressed the nuclear age and the Cold War in a characteristically eloquent farsighted prediction. "It may well be," he said, "that we shall by a process of sublime irony have reached a stage in this story where safety will be the sturdy child of terror, and survival the twin brother of annihilation" (House of Commons, March 1, 1955). According to this formulation, the awesomeness of nuclear war would serve to discourage the superpowers from military gambles against each other.

Today, a bold rethinking of the global threat to human survival must take account of much more than the threat of intentional nuclear war. International order is under siege because of terrorism (including that condoned by national governments), the proliferation of military flash points throughout the world, and the escalation of regional conflicts. Also compelling is the need to constrain crises that may grow out of control because of miscalculation, miscommunication, or accident.

Response to these challenges has come through impressive break-throughs in emergency communications, information exchange, and treaty verification that were unimaginable a decade ago. Vital messages can be transmitted speedily and accurately between the White House and the Kremlin. For the first time in East-West relations, the 1986 Stockholm Agreement provides that there shall be on-site inspection of major NATO and Warsaw Pact activities from the North Atlantic to the Ural Mountains. The Intermediate Nuclear Force Treaty not only scraps an entire category of nuclear weapons but also mandates long-term monitoring of each country's defense plants: Americans will inspect munitions production at Votkinsk in the Urals; the Soviets, at Magna, Utah. U.S. and Soviet scientific teams have exchanged visits to each other's nuclear test sites in order to calibrate more accurately instruments for detecting and measuring underground test explosions. The agreement on risk reduction centers in Washington and Moscow, finalized in 1987, multiplies the channels for treaty verification and the exchange of reliable information on the world's hot spots.

To recapitulate, the foregoing typology of mutual benefits can serve to ease the muddle and irritants of U.S.-Soviet rivalry, and also can make public comprehension of collaborative projects easier. Six distinct types of payoffs are possible:

1. No one can deny that heightened mutual understanding, reality testing, and more realistic perceptions are preferable to outmoded, irrelevant stereotypes on both sides.

2. No one can justify rendering the Earth uninhabitable because of runaway ecological abuse. (Safeguarding humanity's only foreseeable home has become an urgent collective responsibility.)

3. No one can ignore the upgrading of hotline capabilities, which illustrates the functionalist precept that success can beget success, or ignore the U.S.-Soviet COSPAS/SARSAT satellite-aided search-and-rescue program, which confirms that a pilot project in one area can encourage experimentation in another—for instance, from joint space docking in 1975 to joint space rescue in 1982. (The obverse of Murphy's Law comes to mind: If anything unintended can go right, it might.)

4. No one should forget that cultural and scientific agreements have created more permeable borders and a rich yield of intellectual experience, pleasure, education, and breakthroughs in knowledge.

5. No one should overlook the genuine payoffs in cash, technology, and products that stepped-up binational commerce could provide.

6. No one should underestimate the critical importance of dependable communications for greater transparency of superpower arsenals and clarity in military intentions.

WHY COOPERATE?

Six benefit models are not likely to change the minds of those who are forever convinced that superpower agreements are a ruse for Soviet strategic advance and world domination. At the very least, however, performance records confirm that competitors and antagonists can cooperate out of self-interest: thus the puzzling mix of intense hostility and meaningful cooperation that has characterized U.S.-Soviet relations.

Trust is not the issue; were it present, nothing would have to be done. Indeed, exaggerated *distrust* and hostility have made explicit verifiable agreements more imperative as guidelines for interactions and incremental advances in confidence building. Notwithstanding tense incidents and excoriation from both sides over respective political sins, shootdowns, spy feuds, loading embassy walls with bugging devices, and reciprocal expulsions, serious negotiations and agreements have edged forward as commitments to issues of transcendent importance. With full awareness that each side's strategic perceptions and armaments drive the other side, sometimes one senses an eerie paradox that the superpowers believe they must generate a modicum of tensions while striving with greater momentum to solve problems.

A key to an understanding of this momentum has been supplied by Robert Axelrod in his neofunctionalist studies. Under what conditions, he asks, will cooperation emerge in a world of egoists without central authority? Drawing upon classical game theory, he concludes that a player seeking to maximize success seeks to avoid unnecessary conflict by cooperating as long as other players do. Citing experience from World War I and what he calls a "live and let live" system, he argues that friendship is unnecessary for the evolution of cooperation. Appropriate conditions can produce it on the basis of reciprocity, even between antagonists. Trust need not be assumed, because the values of reciprocity can be sufficient to render defection unproductive. Altruism is unnecessary because successful projects can, in and of themselves, attract even egoists. Central authority is not needed because collaborative enterprises based on reciprocity can be self-reinforcing and self-policing. In Axelrod's view, the possibility of mutual rewards is a powerful incentive:

Once the U.S. and the USSR know that they will be dealing with each other indefinitely, the necessary preconditions for cooperation will exist....

The foundation of cooperation is not really trust, but the durability of the relationship. When the conditions are right, the players can come to cooperate with each other through trial-and-error learning about possibilities for mutual rewards, through imitation of other successful players, or even through a blind process of selection of the more successful strategies with a weeding out of the less successful ones.[17]

A NEW POLICY AGENDA

By inviting us to rethink the most dangerous adversarial relationship of our time, the preceding ideas constitute a new foundation, based not on amity, trust, or forbearance but on commitments to an elevated quality of social and economic life in the domestic realm, and a more promising future for human survival on Earth. Since the mid-1980s, both nations' leaders have offered fresh ideas pointing the way.

A bold transformation in the Kremlin's view of international relations has been taking place. General Secretary Gorbachev has been grappling with the complexities of how to make Communism work more than seven decades after its initial revolutionary impulses. At the same time, he is describing a world quite different from the one we are accustomed to hearing about from official Communist platforms, one that is truly interdependent, including new thinking about capitalism, war, economic and social policy, and the carrying capacity of the planet.[18]

Ever since the Bolshevik Revolution, Marxist-Leninist ideologues have predicted that capitalism would consume itself in an orgy of financial crises and wars, and that international turmoil would persist until Communism's inevitable triumph. Today, Kremlin leaders prefer a world in which security is served by stability and order, a world in which their interests in cooperative projects have more than tactical significance.

In his unprecedented interview with *Time* magazine (September 8, 1985), Gorbachev speculated about the important connections between domestic reforms and international relations:

...I don't remember who, but somebody said that foreign policy is a continuation of domestic policy. If that is so, then I ask you to ponder one thing: If we in the Soviet Union are setting for ourselves such truly grandiose plans in the domestic sphere, then what are the external conditions that we need to be able to fulfill those domestic plans? I leave the answer to that question with you.

It has always been agreed by scholars of international politics that domestic factors work to shape a nation's security policy. Gorbachev has said two things more profound: world affairs shape what the Soviets can be expected to achieve in their domestic life; and not just their foreign policy, but their domestic accomplishments as well, will be affected by what the United States does. Superpower one-upmanship thus calls for reassessment and more meticulous measurement of military needs, thereby posing a challenge to Washington: How best to draw the Soviets into agreements with mutual benefits in the interest of a more stable and productive world—un-Communist though this may be—that they themselves appear to be seeking?

In a remarkable turnaround from conventional understandings about the utility of foreign threats and wars, Robert C. Tucker has suggested a clue to the Soviet Union's new stance. When a great power is compelled toward a thoroughgoing reform of economic, social, cultural, and political life, its government loses the need to conjure up an external environment of threatening enemies. The ardor for risk taking in foreign policy is dampened. There is consequently less of an imperative constantly to expand military strength. Says Tucker:

When a government is willing to openly confront the existence of profound internal problems, it becomes free to take a less combative and more cooperative stance in external relations. In the years during which Gorbachev has been Soviet Russia's foremost leader, there have been many signs of a shift in the regime's outlook.[19]

U.S. leaders, too, have shown a willingness to see things in a fresher, more contemporary perspective. During much of the early period after World War II, productive relations were kept at a minimum. Notwithstanding occasional flashes of new thinking, such as John F. Kennedy's American University speech in 1963 and the functionalist principles underpinning much of the Nixon-Kissinger program of détente, genuine collaboration on global problems was undercut by Darth Vader images and illusions of absolute military security. Early in his first administration (1981), President Reagan's denunciation of the Soviets as liars, cheats, and an evil empire—even if correct—only exacerbated the diplomatic atmosphere, making accommodation on matters of transcendent importance too difficult.

During the latter part of Reagan's first term and the beginning of the second, more promising trends appeared. Speaking on June 27, 1984, at a conference on U.S.-Soviet exchanges, the president pledged to revive many of the agreements covered in this book, including those on environmental protection, housing, health, and agriculture. Emphasis was also placed on economic, industrial, technical, and commercial cooperation. Wide-ranging projects were given new life. Included were avoiding incidents at sea; the World Oceans Agreement and joint oceanographic research; a resolution of differences over the maritime boundary off Alaska; a joint simulated space rescue mission; search-and-rescue procedures to assist citizens of any country lost at sea; upgrading the hotline; discussions on potential nuclear terrorist incidents; a joint military communications line; and improving embassy communications in both countries.[20]

Further bilateral measures were advanced by the president in his fall 1984 address to the United Nations General Assembly. Pressing for greater openness and mutual understanding, he advocated regular cabinet-level meetings on U.S.-Soviet issues. Also proposed were expanded exchanges to include data on five-year plans for weapons procurement and development, observers at military exercises, and experts for on-site measurement of nuclear test yields.

In his speech before a joint session of Congress, following the November 1985 Geneva summit, the president again expounded on an extraordinary array of mutual interests: 50 percent cuts in strategic arsenals; the elimination of intermediate nuclear forces in Europe, along with tough verification; safeguards against nuclear weapons proliferation; a ban on chemical weapons; lessening the chances of surprise attack in Europe; risk-reduction centers in the superpower capitals; and a reciprocal program of open laboratories for Strategic Defense Initiative research. Focusing prominently on building a more stable relationship, the president chose to accentuate people-to-people initiatives extending beyond political leaders to include more students, teachers, and youth exchanges. All of this, he emphasized, could serve to erode stereotypes, build friendships, and supply alternatives to propaganda. The president was unequivocal in his belief (and about his agreement with General Secretary Gorbachev) that mistrust and suspicions must be reduced as a prerequisite to winding down the arms spiral.[21]

Deputy Secretary of State John C. Whitehead echoed many of these themes during the third annual U.S.-Soviet conference in Chautauqua, New York, in August 1987. With a keen eye toward the future, he speculated about *glasnost* and new thinking. Preoccupying much of his vision of a more promising future were hopes for positive outcomes from four major agendas: arms control, conflicting interests in Third World countries, human rights, and bilateral cooperation stressing trade, investment, travel, the elimination of childhood diseases, countering ozone depletion, a joint space flight to Mars, and the multinational development of fusion power. Once again, the most vivid comments were reserved for cultural and citizen exchanges as a sound foundation for peace. Whitehead reminded his audience that in 1988, the two powers would celebrate the thirtieth anniversary of the first U.S.-Soviet cultural exchange agreement. He then quoted the president's assessment of progress in the making:

It may seem an impossible dream to think there could be a time when Americans and Soviet citizens of all walks of life travel freely back and forth, visit each other's homes, look up friends and professional colleagues, work together on all sorts of problems, and, if they feel like it, sit up all night talking about the meaning of life and the different ways to look at the world.

In most countries... people take these contacts for granted. We should never accept the idea that American and Soviet citizens cannot enjoy the same contacts and communication. I don't believe it's an impossible dream....[22]

The deputy secretary challenged both sides to double the number of high school and college students exchanged and to multiply the number of conferences:

...conferences where our everyday citizens can meet, share their homes and their tables with each other, and get to know one another's family and home town, whether in the United States or in the Soviet Union.

These are small steps, but they are reachable. We challenge the Soviet Union to join with us in this goal, to create a future that holds so much promise for our children and for our grandchildren.[23]

The failed opportunities of the past for more stable relations teach a lesson. It is not likely that the small steps Deputy Secretary Whitehead advocated alone can generate significant transformations in U.S.-Soviet relations, pervaded by both nightmares and dreams for more than 70 years. Citizen participation, though fundamental and very valuable, cannot produce the quantum jumps that are the conventional responsibility of government. What is called for is *a new public policy agenda*, comprehensive and long-range, with vision, courage, and coherence.

For the United States, deriving greater benefits from bilateral cooperation necessitates major policy revisions and new directions, many stated in the research and published papers of the Atlantic Council in March 1987.[24] Urging the improvement of relations within a peaceful framework, and stressing the most pressing global challenges of our time, several of the Council's recommendations can be strongly supported by the detailed findings of this volume. Three agendas highlight what has yet to be achieved.

Political/Administrative Agenda

At the more general level, U.S. willingness to engage in dialogue with the Soviet Union must be unwavering. Success requires that dialogue be undertaken with consistency and regularity, all the while steadfastly resisting Soviet military expansion. Joint efforts must continue to reduce the risks of war; to build down and stabilize weapons in all categories through verifiable agreements; to preclude the militarization of space; to achieve substantial savings through select cuts in military spending; and to collaborate in moderating and resolving volatile regional conflicts. In every case, the finest, most effective tools of diplomacy must be marshaled steadily to convince the Soviet Union that it, too, has a stake in the benefits that ensue from cooperative, as opposed to conflictual, relations. Conspicuous for their appeal as areas of obvious mutual interest are the prevention (not merely the avoidance) of nuclear war, collaboration to thwart international state-supported terrorism, and joint steps toward more enlightened planetary preservation. So much of a new, more productive future will, of course, depend upon Moscow's willingness to convert words into deeds and the skill with which the United States encourages the Soviet Union to do so.

Skill cannot be divorced from personnel. The United States cannot continue to elect governments devoid of experts on the Soviet Union in top policymaking positions. Personal friendships with the president, though important for smooth policy formulation and administration, must not be substitutes for foreign policy expertise.

General Secretary Gorbachev's closest advisers on world affairs include specialists who have accumulated years of valuable experience and insights about U.S. life, eccentricities and all. Included in the inner Kremlin circle are Aleksandr Yakovlev (a Politburo member) and Georgi Arbatov (director of the Institute for USA and Canadian Studies).

U.S. political leaders will need to muster greater shrewdness in dealing with the new generation of Soviets. It is a generation that has in such uncommon fashion captivated the imagination of respected observers worldwide and has exhibited deftness in manipulating media and public relations, in addition to its tough bargaining and perseverance, long hallmarks of Soviet diplomacy. Where will these U.S. experts come from, and how will they be trained? How will they enter government? And how expeditiously will their expertise be joined with policymaking at the highest levels?

Also urgent on the list of measures for more effective policy is greater government support for increased scholarships, fellowships, and academic research, with high priority for congressional funding. The inauguration of the United States Institute of Peace in 1984 and the diversification of its grant programs have proved to be valuable initiatives. But funds more commensurate with the importance of peace studies—particularly nonmilitary cooperation—in addition to studies on conflict and crises, are required.

Nothing in this policy agenda is meant to disparage the importance of coping. Real policy breakthroughs and quantum jumps, however, require major intellectual investments, something more creative, more cerebral than day-to-day crisis management.[25] Further empirical research and analysis are essential to a fuller understanding of cooperation. Many questions merit continuous exploration: Which types of U.S.-Soviet interactions are more durable, which are more vulnerable to retaliation, and under what circumstances? How can collaborative projects be infused with enough cogency and incentives to render defection unproductive? What is the role of international agreements for domestic constituencies in which the bureaucratic positions of some actors can be bolstered at the expense of others? What hard evidence is there that the Gorbachev administration's reformist bent is connected to research by influential Soviet scholars in foreign policy and international affairs, especially concerning superpower responsibilities? How extensively is Soviet scholarship departing from the traditional Marxist-Leninist mind-set on world issues? Certainly more explicit data on Soviet perceptions of interdependence and benefits from joint projects would enlighten the relationship. Finally, what can be learned from the negotiating behaviors and styles of major participants whose labors have produced accords that have helped to keep the peace? While many are still living, their memoirs and verbal recollections should be searched systematically for expertise and guidance in future negotiations.

Trade Agenda

Deriving greater benefits from bilateral commerce necessitates several caveats and policy changes.

First, the need to restrict exotic technology for national security reasons is unequivocal. But the COCOM (Coordinating Committee for Export Controls) list of restricted items has usually been out of date and overly broad by some 30–40 percent.[26] It should be regularly overhauled through close consultations between Washington and its European allies to include only those technologies that are strategic and critical. Beyond strategic items with obvious military applications lie numerous products that the Soviets desire for economic modernization.

Second, the Jackson-Vanik amendment and the Stevenson amendment to the 1974 Trade Act should be repealed. It is, of course, arguable that their effects on such a low volume of exchange would be minimal and, even without the amendments, trade would be only a trickle unless there is a resolution of other issues, such as price, quality, reliability of supply, and fears about technology transfer. Recall, however, that the Jackson-Vanik and Stevenson stipulations sought to deny most-favored-nation treatment in trade and vital Export-Import Bank credits in order to free up the emigration of Soviet Jews and other minorities from the Soviet Union. Jewish emigration, roughly 8,000 in 1987, has yet to approximate the highs of 30,000–50,000 per year before the 1974 amendments, thus confirming warnings all along that U.S. congressional steps to legislate reforms in Soviet public policy can backfire and create more irritants than success.

Third, experience shows that using trade as a political weapon has severe limitations. In a world of widely available goods, erratic, politically motivated controls have served mainly to hurt the U.S. economy and cost its workers their jobs. Fitful sanctions and embargoes that deprive the Soviets of nothing and open up commercial advantages to third parties have turned out to be exercises in atmospherics and ineptitude.

The grain trade provides an especially glaring case of Moscow's inclination toward strict economic interests, diversified buying, and a reluctance to be pressured or taken for granted. President Reagan's August 1986 offer of heavily subsidized midwestern grain was met by silence and then a surprising activation of a five-year Soviet agreement to purchase 25 million metric tons of Canadian wheat and feed grains with a value of $8–10 billion.[27]

Structural and institutional eccentricities in the U.S. political system, especially abrupt policy shifts between presidential administrations, show a need in foreign trade to see things more steadily and consistently. Particularly urgent is the reality that U.S. trade leverage is weakening due to a steady imbalance in international payments and a somewhat alarming new status as a debtor nation. Primary guidance must come from economic self-interest rather than from the illusion that commercial pressures will tame Soviet interventions in Eastern Europe and the Third World. Much more can be invested profitably in normalized trade that would stimulate sales of a wide variety of U.S. goods for Soviet civilian use. To be resisted are illusory short-term gambles that punitive trade can effect a quick fix in superpower relations.

Last, the policy of thwarting Soviet participation in major international economic organizations should be dropped. By engineering roadblocks against Soviet moves to become members of the General Agreement on Tariffs and Trade, the International Monetary Fund, and the World Bank, the United States is only making it more difficult for the Soviet Union to become a full and responsible participant in the world's economy. U.S. policy is better served by motivating the Soviets to increase their stake in more predictable and profitable international commerce.

Drawing upon some 30 years of trading experience, and that of other U.S. businessmen, Donald M. Kendall of Pepsico, Inc., outlined a straightforward four-point approach to a realistic trade policy. The United States should

1. Differentiate trade policy from foreign policy
2. End sanctions against nonstrategic trade
3. Make economic and trade advantage the sole basis for conferring tariff parity or most-favored-nation status on the Soviet Union
4. Grant customary export credits to the Soviet Union through the Export-Import Bank for the purchase of U.S. products, strictly on the basis of economic risk.[28]

Cultural/Educational Agenda

Improvements in exchanges at all levels offer excellent opportunities to effect more positive images and understanding through ideas and people. President Reagan's often-stated respect for the value of contacts at all levels, between both governments and private citizens, should be translated more vigorously into concrete policies to sustain and enhance the momentum illuminated in the foregoing seven case studies. There should be more regular dialogue between U.S. and Soviet military leaders; expansion of U.S.-Soviet scientific and technical cooperation, with, of course, realistic sensitivities for national security; stepped-up programs for collaborative disaster control, medical assistance, and planetary conservation, the necessity for which was underscored by the Chernobyl accident in April 1986[29]; and, most fundamentally, there needs to be more educational and cultural exchanges, with extensive development of language studies and academic programs stressing each nation's history and contemporary culture.

This latter recommendation merits special emphasis. Years ago in a farsighted study, Harvard Professor Edwin O. Reischauer warned of the pressing need to reshape education if humankind is to survive the sort of world that is fast evolving.[30] Stressing that the speed of change and increasingly complex international relationships dictate interdependency among the world's small and powerful alike, he predicted grave difficulties that would be solvable only on a global scale. Educational systems unable to keep up would saddle us all with outmoded perceptions and methods; yesterday's intellectual equipment would prove inadequate for tomorrow's challenges. The dilemma, he believed, would allow no relaxed inattention because the twenty-first century and its problems are already here.

New, more productive relations will in the long run depend upon a willingness on both sides to reshape education about each other. Great masses of students must no longer be ignorant about the most elementary geographical and political facts concerning international relations and the identities and roles of the superpowers. U.S. higher education, long preoccupied with deficiencies and a redefinition of curriculum, must weigh seriously the benefits of expanding Russian language programs and requiring—yes requiring—basic courses on the Soviet Union. The Soviets for their part should initiate genuine studies of parliamentary democracy, including U.S. politics and society. Successful U.S.-Soviet collaboration on textbooks for teaching English and Russian could provide a model for a cooperative project to develop jointly authored monographs on history, the social sciences, and the humanities.

It is not unduly self-serving to venture that if this book were translated into Russian and made readily available to Soviet readers, its potential value would at least double, and probably more; for while the American public's awareness of joint problem solving is notoriously distorted by Cold War images, the record of cooperation is, from available indicators, even more murky in the Soviet Union. Nothing in these pages by U.S. authors implies that public myopia is an exclusively U.S. malady. Much more can be done to entice Soviet proponents of *glasnost* into a freer, more unfettered official information policy, including publication of foreign works, basic to elevating public consciousness. Just as the vital issues are unquestionably bilateral, so, too, must information, awareness, and public discourse be.

Reshaping education about each other can have its most immediate effects at high levels of political, social, and economic leadership. Going beyond demanding official responsibilties, U.S. and Soviet leaders ought to schedule more varied international travel that exposes them to the hopes, fears, and aspirations of average citizens in their own historical and cultural settings. Special exchange programs and travel seminars for ambitious young politicians—budding leaders in both countries—could bear very valuable returns: intensive cross-cultural experiences could pay off in more realistic and reasoned assessments when their participants become powerful and influential decision makers.

Enlightenment about each other would also gain substantially if Soviet officials would streamline procedures. Historic complexities in arranging bilateral research and study projects would profit from hefty doses of both *glasnost* and *perestroika*. Scholars who have been frustrated by unexplainable silence and interminable delays in correspondence would be relieved by more forthright, dependable, and prompt communications. Certainly the Soviet government, perennially urging greater reciprocity in political and economic matters, could well lead the way toward loosening the proverbial bureaucratic logjams that so often frustrate collaboration with U.S. scholars.

Finally, public education on the importance of exchanges and cooperative agreements would be enhanced by better reporting and public information. During the summer of 1987, this author's inquiries at the major centers of U.S. foreign policy formulation revealed that official government appraisals of expectations, compliance, utility, and benefits of superpower agreements, if they exist, are not readily available to the public. No one at the National Security Council was able to provide unclassified assessments of how risk-reduction and confidence-building measures have been working. The same was true at the Pentagon, whose glossy annual studies of comparative U.S. and Soviet arsenals have entered public dialogue unaccompanied by comparable studies on joint projects in the vital areas of security communications and accident prevention. A similar story at the State Department and Arms Control and Disarmament Agency should alert us all to an important public information gap in a nation straining to orchestrate more effective foreign policy toward the Soviet Union.

A widely respected scholar of public policy, Aaron Wildavsky, fixes the responsibility squarely on the public's shoulders. Speaking truth to power, he says, requires at a minimum that one endeavor to know the truth and to make sense out of public affairs:

Citizens can act as analysts by becoming part of public policies through which they can determine what they are getting for what they give, by learning to perfect their preferences, and by exercising their autonomy so as to enhance reciprocity by taking others into account. Above all, policy analysis is about improvement, about improving citizen preferences for the policies they—the people—ought to prefer.[31]

Improving citizen preferences cannot be achieved without marshaling publics and governments on both sides. U.S. citizens and their Soviet counterparts stand to gain from a far more nuanced, comprehensive, and balanced picture of their bilateral relations—both the adversarial and the collaborative dimensions. Even brief, periodic summaries would help to produce a fuller picture of complex understandings that have served to moderate and protect the relationship, at least since the 1960s and even more since the mid–1980s. Public perceptions, awareness, and sensitivities would profit; the two sides might not appear quite so sinister to each other; and there could be a salutary impact on official commitments to confidence building as well.

A NEW FUTURE

There is no escape from one of the dominant verities of our time. Our world has experienced a revolutionary change in the competence of nation-states to protect single-handedly the quality of life for their citizens. Invented to sustain and elevate human survival, the nation-state today finds itself besieged and inadequate. International cooperation, once deemed ethically proper and driven by respectable ideals, now is more accurately seen as quintessential to survival. In this new and infinitely challenging environment, the relevance of the United States and the Soviet Union, vastly empowered and enriched by victory in World War II, will be measured by how effectively they tame their adversarial relationships in favor of concerted efforts to solve many of humankind's most threatening problems.

Leaders of both nations have already signaled extensively that the time has come for a new era in relations. The 1987 seventieth anniversary of the Bolshevik Revolution seemed to concede that the Soviet Union cannot achieve strategic superiority over the United States and conduct a foreign policy that makes enemies of all its neighbors. The economic and financial omnipotence of the United States has been shaken by a 1987 stock market crash and a slump in its status as a world trader. A well-received 1988 study by Yale historian Paul Kennedy, *The Rise and Fall of the Great Powers*, sounded a warning—not to small, underdeveloped nations that are traditionally poor but to the great and powerful ones whose overextension and quest for military superiority can lead to impoverishment and decline.

Most of all, leaders of both nations must be imbued with the realization that the survivability of our planet in our time is not a foregone conclusion and that enterprises with tangible benefits for both sides can have a leavening effect on destructive nationalistic impulses. Seen from this perspective, the joint programs highlighted in this book are major achievements serving *both* national and global purposes.

The dominant message of these pages is that joint problem solving was not fortuitous, miraculous, or a sterile Sisyphean struggle. It resulted from exceedingly complex, arduous, patient diplomacy. Life-threatening challenges were moderated and life-elevating projects undertaken, despite the persistence of ideological incompatibilities. Both real and potential benefits injected rationality into a relationship that in the popular mind is dominated by military antagonism and an arms race. Compared with a world staggering under the deadly threat and costs of nuclear armaments, invigorated problem-solving projects have been welcome episodes of stability and world order; they are examples for other nations.

The record says that the future we seek will not be given to us.

Understandings, mechanisms, procedures, and habits of cooperation can have no meaning apart from the forthright motives and diligence of the people who created them and the successors who are obligated to implement them. Political leaders, negotiators, and publics on both sides cannot expect to get more out of collaboration than they put in. A new future requires that U.S.-Soviet relations be managed ever so carefully, to nurture irresistible incentives that sustain and raise the values of cooperation. Each success must be seen as generator of the next. So compelling must the incentives be that neither partner would be willing to risk war if it means sacrificing the benefits of peace. Thus, from the perspectives of simple self-interest and anticipated utility, superpower governments will negotiate and observe agreements for their expected desirable outcomes. Benefits can in turn contribute to military deterrence by so raising the values of the status quo that conflict is rendered dysfunctional and unattractive.

Problems are bound to continue. Mutual accusations about treaty compliance and foot dragging on agreements will go on. A massive, inscrutable Soviet bureaucracy, traditionally obsessed with fear and secrecy, can be expected on occasion to frustrate joint programs. U.S. policy, blowing hot and cold, sometimes with overtones of democratic evangelism, may again produce sporadic starts and stops, to entice or to discipline the Soviets and elevate them in human rights and international deportment. Especially in contrast with collaborative medical research, space rescue, and security communications, initiatives in trade and technology with foreseeable military applications can always be accused of favoring the other side. For this reason, they are especially susceptible to the hurly-burly of dramatic high politics with frequent intrusions of theology and theater. Cooperative programs between rivals are unusually influenced by the ups and downs of a supportive political environment. With scant notice, *any* of them can be relegated to the fate of hostage, liable to be terminated, suspended, or slackened. Thus, as confirmed in all seven case studies, organizational structures born of cooperation during good times are particularly useful when relations falter over some transient political imbroglio.

Nothing, it seems, is simple in U.S.-Soviet relations. And even with the apparent ascendancy of Soviet Americanists in the Kremlin's hierarchy, it is not likely that Gorbachev has as easy a time assessing Washington's intentions and negotiating positions as Americans would like to believe. Although U.S. scholarship has achieved feats in unraveling the legendary mysteries of Soviet politics, threatening visions persist, in part because of the Kremlin's historically grim predisposition toward a closed society.

Because the potential benefits of collaboration are joint, all that this book portrays and recommends is addressed to the Soviet side as well as the American. So much of its proposed policy agenda depends on the vision, courage, and skill with which the Gorbachev leadership conducts its part of thge bilateral relationship—and with sound reason. Authoritarian characteristics of the Soviet political system allow for greater continuity and steadiness than its U.S. counterpart. Notwithstanding the glowing record of U.S. initiatives for cooperative projects, the Soviets, too, have an indispensable role. Today, they are exceptionally well positioned to assume their share of the lead. That Gorbachev could be in power for many years accentuates his enormous importance and the responsibilities of the Soviet people in facilitating a new, more promising future.

What is unarguable is that for the first time in the human story, two powers understand that they are the key to whether the planet survives as a life-support system. Their perceptions of self-interest and an intricate network of bilateral agreements militate toward the avoidance of war; yet the dependable peace they seek, and the maximization of reciprocal benefits, depend on translating all they know about each other's interests into long-range policy. What is contentious and disputed—and likely to persist—is the dilemma of how much each believes it can safely concede toward general survival without endangering its own survival.

Could it be that excessive optimism may generate illusive ideals and even some disappointments? Might the temptation to oversell create some false hopes? Probably so. One of the twentieth century's greatest political scientists, Karl Deutsch, is fond of saying that humans have rapidly growing aspirations; capabilities follow more slowly; and attainments even slower yet. The next 50 years are likely to be very dangerous for human survival. But they also provide boundless opportunities for controlling international crises by Americans and Soviets as leaders in search of a productive modus vivendi.

Every collaborative enterprise in this volume energizes the environment in which the new future in U.S.-Soviet relations must grow; but only if governments and publics alike strive harder to make it happen. Such a future would seem utopian and unimaginable, were it not for patent evidence that its solid foundations have already been laid.

NOTES

1. Marshall D. Shulman, "Tell Me, Daddy, Who's the Baddy?" in Erik P. Hoffman (ed.), *The Soviet Union in the 1980s* (New York: The Academy of Political Science, 1984), p. 177.

2. For the last point, see Arkady N. Shevchenko, *Breaking with Moscow* (New York: Knopf, 1985), p. 281.

3. Shulman, "Tell Me, Daddy," p. 183. For a persuasive explanation of why

Americans find it difficult to perceive and acknowledge improvements in the Soviet system, see Stephen F. Cohen, "America's Russia," *U.S.-Soviet Outlook*, 10, no. 2 (March 1987): 6–8.

4. Morton Deutsch, "Undoing Nuclear Insanity: A Psychological Perspective," paper presented at the 26th convention of the International Studies Association, Washington, D.C., March 8, 1985.

5. George D. Moffett III, "Superpower Cultural Exchanges," *Christian Science Monitor*, April 7, 1986, pp. 3–4.

6. Everett C. Ladd, "How Americans View the USSR," *Christian Science Monitor*, December 4, 1987.

7. Erik P. Hoffman, "Nuclear Deception: Soviet Information Policy," *Bulletin of the Atomic Scientists*, August/September, 1986, p. 25, quoted from a May 14, 1986 TV speech.

8. William J. Eaton, "100,000 Victims of Chernobyl Face Monitoring," *Los Angeles Times*, June 7, 1986.

9. Carl Sagan, "Let's Go to Mars Together," *Parade* magazine, February 2, 1986, p. 5. For an equally hopeful Soviet view, including a plan to put an American and a Soviet on Mars by 2001, see Roald Z. Sagdeyev, director of Moscow's Space Research Institute, "To Mars Together—A Soviet Proposal," *Washington Post*, December 13, 1987, pp. M1–2.

10. Yale Richmond, *Soviet-American Cultural Exchanges: Ripoff or Payoff?* (Washington, D.C.: Kennan Institute for Advanced Russian Studies, 1984), p. 77.

11. Thom Shanker, "U.S., Soviet Conductors Lead Music of Each Other's Nations," *Chicago Tribune*, August 31, 1986.

12. "Kennan Institute Holds Conferences on U.S.-Soviet Exchanges," *Wilson Center Reports*, September 1984, p. 2. See also Kennan Institute for Advanced Russian Studies, *U.S.-Soviet Exchanges* (Washington, D.C.: Woodrow Wilson International Center for Scholars, 1985).

13. "Kennan Institute Holds Conference," *Wilson Center Reports*, p. 2.

14. Allen Kassof, "The Status of Scholarly Exchanges with the USSR," *East/West Outlook* (American Committee on East-West Accord), January 1985, p. 6.

15. Hodding Carter III, "Trade as an Element of U.S.-Soviet Political Relations," *East/West Outlook* (American Committee on East-West Accord), September 1986, p. 6.

16. John Kiser, "How Good Is Our Knowledge of Soviet Technology?" presentation at the Kennan Institute for Advanced Russian Studies, November 13, 1985. See also John Kiser, "How the Arms Race Really Helps Moscow," *Foreign Policy* no. 60 (Fall 1985): 46.

17. Robert Axelrod, "The Evolution of Cooperation," in Anatoly Gromyko and Martin Hellman (eds.), *Breakthrough* (New York: Walker and Co., 1988), pp. 189–190.

18. Mikhail Gorbachev, *Perestroika: New Thinking for Our Country and the World* (New York: Harper & Row, 1987), pp. 135–157 and passim. For historical background on these ideas, see Walter C. Clemens, Jr., *The USSR and Global Interdependence* (Washington, D.C.: American Enterprise Institute for Public Policy Research, 1978). For an analysis of Soviet motivations and difficulties,

see Timothy J. Colton, *The Dilemma of Reform in the Soviet Union*, rev. ed. (New York: Council on Foreign Relations, 1986).

19. Robert C. Tucker, "Gorbachev and the Fight for Soviet Reform," *World Policy Journal*, Spring 1987, p. 204.

20. "Remarks of the President at Meeting with Participants in the Conference on U.S.-Soviet Exchanges," press release from Office of the Press Secretary, the White House, June 27, 1984.

21. "The Geneva Summit: A Fresh Start," press release, Bureau of Public Affairs, U.S. Department of State, November 21, 1985, pp. 2–3.

22. "Some Thoughts on the Future of U.S.-Soviet Relations," press release, Bureau of Public Affairs, U.S. Department of State, August 28, 1987, pp. 3–4.

23. Ibid.

24. *U.S. Policy Toward the Soviet Union: A Long-Term Western Perspective, 1987–2000* (Washington, D.C.: The Atlantic Council of the United States, 1987), pp. 39–42.

25. Robert O. Keohane, of the Center for Advanced Study in the Behavioral Sciences at Harvard, has posed challenging questions about how both rationalistic and reflective theory—encompassing both empirical analysis and normative values—can facilitate our understanding of international institutions and cooperation. See his "International Institutions: Two Research Programs," unpublished presidential address, International Studies Association, St. Louis, March 31, 1988.

26. Secretary of Commerce Malcolm Baldridge, "Forum on U.S.-Soviet Trade Relations: A Summary Report," *U.S.-Soviet Outlook* 10, no. 6 (November 1987): 9.

27. "5-Year Grain Deal Signed with Canada by Soviets," *Christian Science Monitor*, October 2, 1986.

28. Baldridge, "Forum on U.S.-Soviet Relations," p. 9.

29. *U.S. Policy Toward the Soviet Union*, p. 42.

30. Edwin O. Reischauer, *Toward the 21st Century: Education for a Changing World* (New York: Vintage Books, 1974), pp. 3–13.

31. Aaron Wildavsky, *Speaking Truth to Power* (Boston: Little, Brown, 1979), p. 19.

SELECTED BIBLIOGRAPHY

Allison, Graham T., Albert Carnesale, and Joseph S. Nye, Jr. (eds.). *Hawks, Doves, and Owls: An Agenda for Avoiding Nuclear War.* New York: W. W. Norton, 1985.

Auburn, F. M. *Antarctic Law and Politics.* Bloomington: Indiana University Press, 1981.

Beck, Peter J. *The International Politics of Antarctica.* Cambridge: Cambridge University Press, 1985.

Bertrand, Kenneth J. *Americans in Antarctica, 1775–1948.* New York: American Geographical Society, 1971.

Bialer, Seweryn, and Michael Mandelbaum (eds.). *Gorbachev's Russia and American Foreign Policy.* Boulder, Colo.: Westview Press, 1988.

Blacker, Coit D. *Reluctant Warriors: The United States, the Soviet Union, and Arms Control.* New York: W. H. Freeman, 1987.

Borawski, John (ed.). *Avoiding War in the Nuclear Age.* Boulder, Colo.: Westview Press, 1986.

Caldwell, Dan (ed.). *Soviet International Behavior and U.S. Policy Options.* Lexington, Mass.: D. C. Heath, 1985.

Caldwell, Lawrence T., and William Diebold, Jr. *Soviet-American Relations in the 1980s.* New York: McGraw-Hill, 1981.

Carnesale, Albert, et al. *Living with Nuclear Weapons.* New York: Bantam Books, 1983.

Chapman, Walter. *The Loneliest Continent.* Greenwich, Conn.: New York Geographical Society, 1964.

Clemens, Walter C., Jr. *The USSR and Global Interdependence.* Washington, D.C.: American Enterprise Institute for Public Policy Research, 1978.

Cohen, Stephen F. *Sovieticus: American Perceptions and Soviet Realities*. New York: Norton, 1986.

Colton, Timothy J. *The Dilemma of Reform in the Soviet Union*. Rev. ed. New York: Council on Foreign Relations, 1986.

Congressional Research Service. *Soviet Space Programs, 1976–80*. Washington, D.C.: U.S. Government Printing Office, 1982.

Eisenhower, Dwight D. *Waging Peace, 1956–1961, the White House Years*. New York: Doubleday, 1965.

Ezell, Edward, and Linda Ezell. *The Partnership: A History of the Apollo-Soyuz Test Project*. NASA-SP 4209. Washington, D.C.: NASA, 1978.

George, Alexander L. *Managing U.S.-Soviet Rivalry: Problems of Crisis Prevention*. Boulder, Colo.: Westview Press, 1983.

George, Alexander L., Philip J. Farley, and Alexander Dallin (eds.). *U.S.-Soviet Security Cooperation: Achievements, Failures, Lessons*. New York: Oxford University Press, 1988.

Global Commission for the Certification of Small Pox Eradication. *Final Report. The Global Eradication of Small Pox*. Geneva: World Health Organization, 1980.

Gorbachev, Mikhail. *Perestroika: New Thinking for Our Country and the World*. Harper & Row, 1987.

Gromyko, Anatoly, and Martin Hellman (eds.). *Breakthrough*. New York: Walker and Co., 1988.

Hammer, Armand, and Neil Hyndon. *Hammer*. New York: G. P. Putnam's Sons, 1987.

Hoffman, Erik P. (ed.). *The Soviet Union in the 1980s*. New York: The Academy of Political Science, 1984.

Horelick, Arnold L. (ed.). *U.S.-Soviet Relations: The Next Phase*. Ithaca, N.Y.: Cornell University Press, 1986.

Huber, Bruce A., and Sarah E. Rennie (eds.). *Reports of the U.S.-USSR Weddell Polynya Expedition, October–November 1981*. Vol. 1. New York: Columbia University Press, 1983.

Jamgotch, Nish, Jr. (ed.). *Sectors of Mutual Benefit in U.S.-Soviet Relations*. Durham, N.C.: Duke University Press, 1985.

Joyner, Christopher C., and Sudhir Chopra (eds.). *The Antarctic Legal Regime*. The Hague: Martinus Nijhoff, 1988.

Kelley, Donald R., Kenneth R. Stunkel, and Richard R. Wescott. *The Economic Superpowers and the Environment: The United States, the Soviet Union, and Japan*. San Francisco: W. H. Freeman, 1976.

Kennan, George F. *The Nuclear Delusion: Soviet-American Relations in the Atomic Age*. New York: Pantheon, 1982.

Kennan Institute for Advanced Russian Studies. *U.S.-Soviet Exchanges*. Washington, D.C.: Woodrow Wilson International Center for Scholars, 1985.

Kissinger, Henry. *The White House Years*. Boston: Little, Brown, 1979.

Knaus, William A. *Inside Russian Medicine: An American Doctor's Firsthand Report*. New York: Everest House, 1981.

Lewis, Richard S., and Philip M. Smith (eds.). *Frozen Future: A Prophetic Report from Antarctica*. New York: Quadrangle Books, 1973.

Mains, Richard C., and Edward W. Gomersall. *Final Reports of the U.S. Monkey* and Rat Experiments Flown on the Soviet Satellite Cosmos 1514. NASA TM–88223. Washington, D.C.: NASA, 1986.

Mandelbaum, Michael, and Strobe Talbott. *Reagan and Gorbachev*. New York: Vintage Books, 1987.

Marples, David R. *Chernobyl and Nuclear Power in the USSR*. New York: St. Martin's Press, 1986.

Nye, Joseph S., Jr. (ed.). *The Making of America's Soviet Policy*. New Haven: Yale University Press, 1984.

Open Doors: 1985/1986. Report on International Educational Exchange. New York: Institute of International Education, 1986.

Parks, J. D. *Culture, Conflict and Coexistence: American-Soviet Cultural Relations, 1917–1958*. Jefferson, N.C.: McFarland, 1983.

Parrott, Bruce (ed.). *Trade, Technology and Soviet-American Relations*. Bloomington: Indiana University Press, 1985.

Pravda, Alex. *Soviet Foreign Policy: Priorities Under Gorbachev*. New York: Routledge, 1988.

Reischauer, Edwin O. *Toward the 21st Century: Education for a Changing World*. New York: Vintage Books, 1974.

Report on International Activities: National Heart, Lung, and Blood Institute, October 1, 1985–September 30, 1986. Bethesda, Md.: National Institutes of Health, 1986.

Richmond, Yale. *Soviet-American Cultural Exchanges: Ripoff or Payoff?* Washington, D.C.: Kennan Institute for Advanced Russian Studies, 1984.

Sarukhanyan, E. I., and N. P. Smirnov (eds.). *Investigations of the POLEX South–78 Programs*. New Delhi: Oxonian Press, 1985.

Shulman, Marshall D. (ed.). *East-West Tensions in the Third World*. New York: Norton, 1986.

Sloss, Leon, and Scott M. Davis (eds.). *A Game for High Stakes: Lessons Learned in Negotiating with the Soviet Union*. Cambridge, Mass.: Ballinger, 1986.

Staar, Richard F. (ed.). *Public Diplomacy: USA Versus USSR*. Stanford, Calif.: Hoover Institution Press, 1986.

Stern, Paula. *Water's Edge: Domestic Policy and the Making of American Foreign Policy*. Westport, Conn.: Greenwood Press, 1979.

Sutton, Anthony C. *Western Technology and Soviet Economic Development*. Vol. 2. Stanford, Calif.: Hoover Institution Press, 1971.

Treshnikov, A. F. (ed.). *Investigations of the POLEX South–75 Program*. New Delhi: Oxonian Press, 1979.

Triska, J. F., and R. M. Slusser. *The Theory, Law, and Policy of Soviet Treaties*. Stanford, Calif.: Stanford University Press, 1962.

U.S. Policy Toward the Soviet Union: A Long-Term Western Perspective, 1987–2000. Washington, D.C.: The Atlantic Council of the United States, 1987.

U.S.-Soviet Cooperation in Space. Washington, D.C.: Office of Technology Assessment, 1985.

U.S.-Soviet Exchanges: A Conference Report. Washington, D.C.: Woodrow Wilson International Center for Scholars, 1984.

United States-Soviet Scientific Exchanges. Hearings Before the Committee on Foreign Affairs. Document no. 63–629 0. Washington, D.C.: U.S. Government Printing Office, 1986.

Ury, William, and Richard Smoke. *Beyond the Hotline: Controlling a Nuclear Crisis.* Cambridge, Mass.: Nuclear Negotiation Project, Harvard Law School, 1984.

Warner, Gale, and Michael Shuman. *Citizen Diplomats: Pathfinders in Soviet-American Relations—and How You Can Join Them.* New York: Continuum Press, 1987.

INDEX

ABOUT THE EDITOR AND CONTRIBUTORS

NISH JAMGOTCH, Jr. is professor of political science at the University of North Carolina at Charlotte. Published works include *Soviet-East European Dialogue: International Relations of a New Type?* (1968); "Alliance Management in Eastern Europe" (*World Politics*, 1975); *Thinking the Thinkable: Investment in Human Survival* (1978); *Soviet Security in Flux*, (1983); *Sectors of Mutual Benefit in U.S.-Soviet Relations* (1985); "Superpower Cooperation Often Overlooked" (*Bulletin of the Atomic Scientists*, 1986); and "Public Perceptions and Confidence Building in U.S.-Soviet Relations" (*United States-Soviet Scientific Exchanges*, 1986). Jamgotch chairs the American-Soviet Relations Section of the International Studies Association.

GARY K. BERTSCH is Sandy Beaver professor of political science and co-director of the Center for East-West Trade Policy at the University of Georgia. His academic specialization focuses on U.S. and Western trade policy toward the Soviet Union and other Communist states. His publications include *Controlling East-West Trade and Technology Transfer: Power, Politics and Policy* (1988); *East-West Strategic Trade, COCOM, and the Atlantic Alliance* (1983); and *National Security and Technology Transfer: The Strategic Dimensions of East-West Trade* (1983).

DAVID D. FINLEY is professor of political science and dean of the college at Colorado College in Colorado Springs. A long-time specialist in Soviet politics and comparative Communism, he is the coauthor of a text on Soviet foreign policy and has written chapters and articles that range over many dimensions of Soviet-U.S. relations. These include *Soviet Foreign Policy* (1968) and "Conventional Arms in Soviet Foreign Policy" (*World Politics*, Fall 1980). His recent scholarship has focused on the interplay of cooperative and conflictual elements in U.S.-Soviet relations.

CHRISTOPHER C. JOYNER is associate professor of political science and a member of the School of International Affairs at George Washington University. He has served as chairman of the International Law Section of the International Studies Association, and during 1986–1987 he was a senior research fellow with the Marine Policy Center at Woods Hole Oceanographic Institution. His publications include "The Antarctic Minerals Negotiating Process" (*American Journal of International Law*, October 1987) and *The Antarctic Legal Regime* (1988). He is currently completing a volume entitled *Antarctica and the Law of the Sea*.

DONALD R. KELLEY is professor of political science and senior research fellow of the Fulbright Institute of International Relations at the University of Arkansas, Fayetteville. His writings include *The Economic Superpowers and the Environment: The United States, the Soviet Union, and Japan* (with K. R. Stunkel and R. R. Wescott, 1975); *The Energy Crisis and the Environment: An International Perspective* (1977); *The Politics of Developed Socialism: The Soviet Union as a Post-Industrial State* (1986); and *Soviet Politics from Brezhnev to Gorbachev* (1987). His current work includes editing the 50-volume *Modern Encyclopedia of Russia and the Soviet Union*.

YALE RICHMOND is a retired foreign service officer who worked for more than 20 years on exchanges with the Soviet Union and the countries of Eastern Europe in culture, education, information, and science, including the negotiation of 16 intergovernmental agreements. He has served abroad in Germany, Laos, Poland, Austria, and the Soviet Union, and in Washington with the Department of State and the U.S. Information Agency. He is the author of *Soviet-American Cultural Exchanges: Ripoff or Payoff?* (1984) and *U.S.-Soviet Cultural Exchanges, 1958–1986: Who Wins?* (1987). Mr. Richmond is a writer and consultant on exchanges in Washington, D.C.

HAROLD SANDLER, M.D., is clinical professor of medicine at Stanford University School of Medicine and associate clinical professor of community medicine at Wright State Medical School, Dayton, Ohio. In 1973 he was appointed to the Joint Working Group in Space Medicine and Biology, established by President Nixon for interaction with the Soviet Union during détente. He is one of the founding members of Beyond War, a non-partisan educational movement, and a member of Physicians for Social Responsibility and International Physicians for the Prevention of Nuclear War. His published works include many articles and abstracts and seven books on cardiology and cardiovascular research.